George Hay

Works of the Right

George Hay
Works of the Right
ISBN/EAN: 9783743369177
Manufactured in Europe, USA, Canada, Australia, Japa
Cover: Foto ©Lupo / pixelio.de

Manufactured and distributed by brebook publishing software (www.brebook.com)

George Hay

Works of the Right

WORKS

OF THE

RIGHT REV. BISHOP HAY

OF EDINBURGH

VOL. VI.

ON MIRACLES: VOL. I.

A NEW EDITION

EDITED UNDER THE SUPERVISION OF

THE RIGHT REV. BISHOP STRAIN

WILLIAM BLACKWOOD AND SONS
EDINBURGH
1873

THE SCRIPTURE DOCTRINE

OF

MIRACLES

DISPLAYED

BY

THE RIGHT REV. DR GEORGE HAY

BISHOP OF DAULIS, VICAR APOSTOLIC OF THE
LOWLAND DISTRICT IN SCOTLAND

A NEW EDITION—IN TWO VOLUMES

VOL. I.

WILLIAM BLACKWOOD AND SONS
EDINBURGH
1873

AUTHOR'S PREFACE.

THE recent controversy between Dr Middleton and his opponents has produced so many elaborate treatises on Miracles that the public may well be weary of the subject, and of the various theories propounded. The line taken by Mr Hume and his free-thinking brethren is well known. They openly deny the existence of miracles, and their sophistry has called forth many zealous Christians to defend this highly-prized prerogative of revelation.

After the able arguments adduced by these gentlemen it may be thought that the subject is exhausted, and that a new work on Miracles must be superfluous. A little reflection, however, will show that this is not the case, and that much yet remains to be done. Indeed the chief point in dispute is still undecided; for, notwithstanding all that has appeared, learned writers themselves have not arrived at distinct and clearly-defined ideas upon various points, and therefore it is not wonderful that they have failed to impart settled convictions to their readers.

This may be traced chiefly to three causes. First, The several writers have conceived different ideas of a miracle, and these they have expressed by various definitions. Proceeding upon opposite principles, and treating different subjects under the same name, they have arrived at different and often contradictory conclusions, thus producing a still further confusion of ideas.

Secondly, In order to acquire a full knowledge of the subject of miracles, there are several preliminary points to be examined. Of these some are comparatively plain and simple, and ought to serve as guides in investigating others which are more abstruse and intricate. But none of the writers, so far as I have seen, have taken a full and comprehensive view of all the several heads. Generally confining their inquiries to one particular point, they assume that their readers are conversant with all the others from which their arguments are drawn. But, as this is rarely the case, their reasoning appears obscure and inconclusive, even when they have truth upon their side; and when they are defending error, it perplexes and bewilders their readers.

Thirdly, Even Christian writers, when treating of miracles, have paid too little attention to the teaching of the Holy Scriptures. This omission has not entirely escaped the observation of Dr Middleton and his opponents, for they mutually charge each other with the neglect of Scripture proof. Mr Hume and his followers not only discard the Holy Scriptures from their pages, but would ridicule any one who attempted to confute them from these sacred records. Thus the Word of God has been in a great measure excluded from this controversy, whereas, miracles being the work of the Omnipotent, it is chiefly, if not solely, from His sacred Word that we can be thoroughly instructed regarding them. Besides, the Word of God contains the most ample information upon every point relative to miracles, and therefore it is the more surprising that it has been overlooked and neglected by Christian authors.

Any attempt to supply this defect, and clearly to elucidate the Scripture Doctrine of Miracles, seems calculated to benefit the cause of religion, and may not be unacceptable to Christians generally. This has been the author's aim, but how far he has succeeded, the judgment of his readers must decide. Of his own deficiencies he is fully sensible. To elegance of style—a pleasing kind of argument, and skilfully used by the enemies of Christian miracles, he has no pretension. His entire reliance is upon the intrinsic goodness of his cause; and if he has failed to do it justice, he can only hope that his efforts may induce some abler hand to undertake and prosecute the work.

EDINBURGH, 1775.

CONTENTS OF VOL. I.

		PAGE
CHAP. I.	THE NATURE OF MIRACLES, ACCORDING TO THE CHRISTIAN IDEA, AND THEIR DIFFERENT KINDS,	1
" II.	THE AGENCY OF SPIRITUAL BEINGS IN THE MATERIAL CREATION,	20
" III.	THE POSSIBILITY OF MIRACLES,	53
" IV.	THE ENDS FOR WHICH MIRACLES MAY BE WROUGHT, AS DISCOVERED BY REASON,	65
" V.	THE GENERAL ENDS OF MIRACLES, AS DISCOVERED BY REVELATION,	82
" VI.	OTHER GENERAL ENDS OF MIRACLES, AS DISCOVERED BY REVELATION,	108
" VII.	THE PARTICULAR ENDS OF MIRACLES KNOWN FROM REVELATION,	137
" VIII.	THE INSTRUMENTS USED IN PERFORMING MIRACLES,	169
" IX.	THE AUTHORITY OF MIRACLES,	220
" X.	THE CRITERION OF MIRACLES,	259

THE SCRIPTURE DOCTRINE

OF

MIRACLES DISPLAYED.

CHAPTER I.

THE NATURE OF MIRACLES, ACCORDING TO THE CHRISTIAN IDEA, AND THEIR DIFFERENT KINDS.

I. OF the word *miracle* we find a great variety of definitions given by the learned. Some writers, looking only to the results, tell us that as "effects produced by the regular operation of the laws of nature are called *natural*, so effects contrary to this settled constitution and course of things are *miraculous*." Others include the producing cause, without which they think we cannot have a proper idea of what a miracle is. "A true miracle," says Le Moine, "is a sensible, unusual operation or effect above the natural ability or inherent power of natural agents—that is, of all created beings—and therefore performable by God alone."

Some confine their notion of the producing cause to God only, as in Le Moine's definition; others admit as true miracles what may be performed by created beings of a nature superior to man. Thus Mr Chub, defining what he understands by miracles, expresses himself as follows: "This term, I think, is used to express a sensible effect, which is above the natural ability or inherent power of man to cause or produce; which is likewise above, or besides, the ordinary course of nature; and which also is produced by the agency or co-operation of an invisible being." Dr Chandler, in his discourse on the nature and use of miracles, gives a very singular definition of them, and says that only is a miracle "where the action exceeds the utmost capacity of the agent."

We find another cause of this difference among these writers regarding the nature of a miracle arising from their different ideas of what is natural and what is supernatural. According to Le Moine, the words *nature* and *natural* are the same as *creation* and *created*; and consequently, in his opinion, nothing is supernatural but what immediately belongs to or is done by God alone. Others confine the words *nature* and *natural* to the material creation, and consequently give the term *supernatural* to the operations of spiritual created beings, as well as to those of the Creator, as we have seen in the definition of a miracle given by Mr Chub. Others, again, use these terms without explaining whether they take them in the one sense or the other. Thus the Bishop of St David's, in his vindication of the miracles of our Saviour, says: "A true miracle is properly a supernatural operation, disagreeing with and repugnant to the usual course of things and the known laws of nature, either as to the subject-matter or the manner of its performance."

Many of our latest writers on this subject give a still

more vague definition of miracles, calling them "effects unusual above human power, and manifesting the interposition of superior power." According to Mr Locke, no more is requisite to constitute a miracle than that it should appear such to the spectator; for he calls it "a sensible operation, which exceeds the capacity of the spectator, and which he believes to be contrary to the course of nature, and judges to be divine." Mr Hume, with his vaunted precision, says: "A miracle may be accurately defined a transgression of a law of nature by a particular volition of the Deity, or by the interposition of some invisible agent."—Ess. on Mir., p. 182. And in another place he calls it a violation of the usual course of nature. Finally, to cite one more, "Every sensible deviation from, or contradiction to, the known laws of nature, must be an evident and incontestable miracle," says Mr Farmer, p. 21.

II. Whoever attentively considers these several definitions will easily perceive the very different ideas which they convey. It is not my intention to examine their respective merits or demerits. Some of the above-named gentlemen have already endeavoured to expose the defects of those given by others, while their own have not escaped the censure of their opponents. This great difference, however, among writers, is one plain cause of the many different systems that have been formed regarding miracles; and it seems surprising that so many great men should disagree so widely on a subject which has now for ages been discussed among the learned. For this, however, various reasons may be assigned. Some seem to have been prejudiced in favour of a preconceived hypothesis, and to have adopted only such ideas of miracles as could be reconciled with it. Some have considered the subject only in a partial manner, and hence their explanations are defective. Others have not sufficiently cleared their own ideas, nor assigned a precise meaning to their terms, and hence they use the same words in various senses, thereby causing confusion and obscurity. In order, therefore, to avoid as much as possible these defects, I propose first to take a view of the things themselves which are the subject-matter of miracles, and also of the agents by whom miracles are performed; and, in doing this, to give a precise explanation of the terms proper to the subject, from which the definition of a miracle, according to the Christian sense of the word, will naturally flow.

III. (1.) The works of God, which fall more or less under our observation and experience, are comprised in the visible and material creation. Of these, some are more immediately subject to the examination of our senses, as the earth on which we dwell and the things upon it; others, as the heavenly bodies, being at a distance, we know only by observation, and argue about chiefly by calculation and analogy. To this material visible creation we give the name of *nature*.

(2.) To all those parts of nature which fall under our immediate observation we find that the Creator has given certain powers or forces, which, when applied in their proper circumstances, produce certain uniform results. Thus the power of gravitation causes bodies near the earth to tend towards its centre; the rays of the sun falling upon the earth produce light and heat; seeds sown in a proper soil produce plants and trees; food taken into animal bodies nourishes and strengthens them; the annual motion of the earth round the sun produces the different seasons of the year, and its diurnal motion round its own axis causes day and night.

Now, as all these powers of created nature are found

by observation to act in a constant uniform manner, and in certain circumstances always produce the same effects, if we inquire whence arises this uniform connection between natural created causes and their effects, we must at last attribute it to the will of the Creator. It is true that in many particular cases we may observe a mechanical fitness between the cause and its effect, as in the mechanism of a watch or clock; yet, if we carry our inquiry farther, and ask whence these mechanical powers come to act in such and such a manner, we must eventually end in the will of the supreme Author of nature. Thus, in examining the powers of gravitation and attraction, the sensations excited in our mind by the action of external bodies on the organs of our senses, and the production of light and heat by the rays of the sun, we can see no mechanical connection between the cause and its effects, and therefore must attribute this constant uniformity to the will of the Creator impressed as a law at the creation. Hence the learned world has justly given the general name *the laws of nature* to these constant uniform rules by which natural causes in certain circumstances never fail to produce certain effects.

(3.) When a being in this visible creation exerts its natural powers, it is called a *natural agent*. If it be necessarily applied to action, without any free-will to continue or suspend its operations at pleasure, it is called a *necessary agent*. If it is endowed with free-will, and can act or not act by its own choice, it is called *a free agent*. Fire, for example, is a *necessary agent*, because it has no free-will nor choice in its operations, but of necessity burns and consumes the fuel placed upon it. Man, on the contrary, is a *free agent*, because he is not necessitated to perform the operations that are proper to him, but may or may not perform them, as he pleases.

(4.) We learn from experience that among the several powers or forces observed in different creatures, some are stronger, others weaker; and when two unequal powers meet in opposition to each other, the weaker is overcome; and that law of nature, by which it would otherwise produce its proper effect, is suspended by the superior acting power. Thus, though by the laws of gravitation a stone is always drawn towards the centre of the earth, and if left to itself would immediately fall towards it, yet, if a force superior to that of gravity in the stone be applied—from the strength of a man's hand, for example, or of gunpowder—it may be made to fly upwards from the earth by a motion diametrically opposite to that which the laws of gravitation produce, which laws are in this case said to be *suspended* by a superior force applied in opposition to them. Numberless similar examples might be mentioned, from which it is evident that the powers or forces given by the Almighty to different creatures have in each only a certain degree of strength, and that they may be hindered from producing their proper effects; or that even quite opposite effects may be produced in them by stronger and opposite powers counteracting them; or that the laws of nature, by which these powers produce their effects, may be suspended for a time by contrary and stronger laws acting in opposition to them.

(5.) A "suspension of the laws of nature," or "to suspend the laws of nature," are expressions frequently used by writers on miracles; but perhaps the term "a suspension of the usual effects of these laws" would convey a clearer and more precise idea. These expressions may be understood in two ways; for they may either imply a temporary annihilation or destruction of the very power itself in the agent, or they may only mean the preventing the sensible effect of that power, while the power itself remains entire. It is in this latter sense only that it seems necessary to use these expressions for the purpose of miracles. In fact, the former signification is not always true, nor is it at all requisite to suppose it for understanding this matter. When, therefore, I say that the laws of gravitation are suspended if a stone is made to fly upwards, I do not mean that the power of gravity is annihilated in the stone. I know it still continues to exert its usual force, but that its sensible effect of making the stone move towards the centre of the earth is suspended for the time, and a contrary effect produced by the superior power which opposes and overcomes it.

(6.) The above remarks on the *laws of nature*, and on the different degrees of strength bestowed by Almighty God on creatures, hold universally true in all the parts of nature which fall immediately under our observation, and in those also which are distant, as far as we can discover from their motions. If, therefore, we argue from analogy, it is reasonable to conclude that all the other parts of nature, without exception, are governed in the same manner by certain uniform and fixed laws, by which their powers, operations, and effects are regulated and determined according to the views and ends of their sovereign Creator. And when we consider the powers impressed by Him on the different parts of the material creation, differing from one another in degrees of strength, we see that the natural effects of the weaker forces must be superseded and suspended when a greater power acts in opposition to them. If, therefore, we gradually ascend from the weaker to the stronger powers, or from the weaker to the stronger laws, by which the operations of these powers are regulated, we must at last arrive at powers and laws superior to all corporeal agents, and whose effects can be suspended only by beings of a nature superior to this material creation.

(7.) The belief that there are amongst the works of God spiritual beings of a nature superior to man is conformable to reason; and revelation not only assures us of their existence, but also discloses to us various particulars concerning them, to the knowledge of which unassisted reason never could attain. It teaches us that these spirits, at their first creation, were placed for a time in a state of trial; that some of them, persevering in their fidelity, were confirmed in happiness, are now in full enjoyment of the presence of God, and are employed by Him in executing His sacred commands throughout the universe; that others, revolting against their Creator, were immediately punished, degraded from their high station, banished from the face of God, and condemned to eternal torments. Revelation teaches us that both are endowed with many qualities and powers very superior to those of man, as to knowledge, strength, and agility; that they can produce effects in the inferior creation contrary to all ordinary laws; that they have a spiritual nature, and are governed by laws peculiar to themselves, and very different from those which regulate this material creation. It is evident, then, that to include both the spiritual and material creation under the name of *nature* would occasion a confusion of ideas, as their respective natures, and the laws by which they are governed, are extremely different. In order, therefore, to distinguish them, we confine the word nature to the material creation, of which we are a part, and with which we are acquainted. And as spiritual beings are superior to man in their qualities and powers, to them we give the name of *supernatural* beings. When we consider them as acting in this our lower world, we call them supernatural agents;

and the effects which they produce in nature we term supernatural effects. But as these spiritual beings have a nature peculiar to themselves, with special qualities and powers, when speaking of these we are obliged, from the poverty of language, to apply the word *natural* to them also, meaning those particular properties which are essential to them, or necessarily belong to their spiritual natures.

(8.) The effects produced by supernatural agents in this material creation may be conceived to be of two kinds,—they may be supernatural either as to the manner only, which must be always the case; or both as to the matter itself, or the thing done, and the manner of performing it. If the effect produced exceeds the power of natural agents, then it must be supernatural, both as to the matter and manner. For example, if a man should walk upon water without any visible support, but invisibly borne up by an angel, here the effect is supernatural, being contrary to the laws of gravity, by which the body of a man sinks in water; and the manner also is supernatural, the effect being produced by the ministry of a supernatural agent.

But if the effect could be procured by natural means, and is produced in the present case only in a way superior to the abilities of any natural agent, then it will be supernatural only in the manner. A man may naturally acquire the knowledge of what is passing in the most distant parts of the world, but time is necessary that proper information may be brought; so that this acquisition of knowledge is a natural effect, which may be procured by natural means. But if an angel, coming in an instant from some distant part, should communicate intelligence of what was occurring there, this acquisition of knowledge would be supernatural, not in the thing done, but only in the manner of doing it.

(9.) It is not necessary that every supernatural operation or effect should consist in or imply a suspension of any of the laws of nature. A suspension of any of these laws necessarily supposes the existence of some positive law, and of some real force or power, whose effects are superseded by such suspension. Now, many effects may be produced in nature by supernatural agents which do not suspend the effects of any positive law, but only require a power superior to that of a natural agent to perform them. Even man can perform many things in creatures, and produce many effects in them, without violating or suspending any positive law of nature: much more may we suppose supernatural beings capable of doing so.

In the case above mentioned of an angel communicating almost instantaneously the knowledge of events occurring in the most distant parts of the world, there is no positive law of nature suspended, but an effect produced which, as to its manner, no natural agent is capable of performing. In like manner, should Almighty God in a moment give to any man an infused knowledge of the sciences, or the power of speaking all languages, these effects would not be contrary to any positive law of nature, nor would they imply a suspension of any power in nature; but it is plain that they would be the effects of a power superior to that of any natural agent, as no power in nature can communicate the instantaneous knowledge of these things to man. Of the same nature also is the raising a person from the dead, in which there is no positive law of nature violated, no effect of any natural power suspended; but, as in the former cases, a new effect is produced out of the ordinary course of nature, and exceeding the power of all natural agents. Many other similar cases will occur to every intelligent reader, which we shall call effects produced out of, or besides, the usual course of nature, to distinguish them from those which imply a suspension of any of its laws.

(10.) However great may be the strength of created supernatural agents, it has its limits, beyond which it cannot reach. How far it can extend in affecting the material creation, we are unable to determine. It would seem probable that no created agent could suspend those higher laws of nature by which the general frame of this universe is preserved; for to what purpose would a power have been given to them which they will never have occasion to exercise as long as the world shall endure? And when the final dissolution comes, it seems altogether more befitting that the same Almighty Word which at first enacted these laws should Himself annul them. Besides these more universal laws there may even be many others the suspension of which exceeds the strength of any created agent; and as for effects which are out of the usual course of nature, there must be many such producible in the material creation, which can be performed only by the almighty hand of the Creator. As He made all creatures at the beginning, and gave them their respective natures, qualities, and powers, so He alone can dispose of them as He pleases—alter their natures, deprive them of their powers, change or annihilate them entirely, as He pleases. These effects are all supernatural with regard to us, and indeed are so in the most extensive signification of the word; but when we have occasion to speak of them as distinct from the operations of supernatural created agents, we shall call them *divine*.

IV. From these observations it will be easy to ascertain the proper meaning to be affixed to the word *miracle*. When we see any of the known laws of nature suspended by the power of a superior known law acting against it—for instance, when a stone is thrown upwards by a man's hand, or when we see any effect produced for which we know an adequate natural cause—we are not surprised. But were we to see any of the known laws of nature suspended without perceiving any cause capable of doing so—were we to see a stone rising from the earth and flying upwards—or, if never having seen nor heard of an eclipse, we should hear an astronomer foretell that at such an hour the sun would become dark, and if this prediction should be literally fulfilled at the time appointed,—we would be filled with wonder and astonishment. Now, as the word *miracle*, according to its etymology, signifies a wonderful thing, or a thing that causes wonder, in its most general sense it may be used to signify all cases of this kind, whether natural or supernatural; and in this more loose and general signification it is not unfrequently applied in common conversation; for, in relating or hearing anything extraordinary or unusual, we say, It is a miracle! it is miraculous! without considering whether it may arise from natural causes or not. But this is not the sense in which it is used when we speak with precision; and if we examine the idea which we have when we mean a miracle properly such, and which accords with the general sentiments of the Christian world, we shall find the following observations holding true:—

1. That it implies an operation, or an effect produced, in this material creation, consequently capable of being known to one or other of our senses; so that the material sensible creation, to which we give the name of nature, is the subject-matter in which miracles are performed.

2. That this effect must be extraordinary—that is,

either directly contrary to the known laws of nature, and to the natural powers of creatures, which are regulated and determined by those laws; or, that it be besides the usual course of nature, either as to the effect produced or the manner of producing it. For the moment we conceive that any event, however uncommon, may arise from natural causes, or is conformable to the usual course of nature, we immediately lose the idea of its being a miracle.

3. That this operation or effect be not only performed by a supernatural agent, but also that we be persuaded there is no natural agent capable of performing it, at least in the manner; for here also we find that our idea of the miraculous in any event immediately ceases the moment we suspect that it may be produced by natural agents.

4. That this supernatural agent be either God Himself, or His holy angels commissioned by Him. In Christian theology, there is no doubt but that the devil and his wicked spirits can, by the strength and abilities which are natural to them, perform many extraordinary things in the material creation; yet certain it is, as the same theology assures us, and as we shall afterwards see in its proper place,* that Almighty God will never permit them so to exercise this power as that their operations cannot be distinguished from those of God Himself, or of His good angels. One idea which the Christian world has constantly attached to miracles is, that they are the seal and language of God, by which He speaks to the heart of man; and it has always been convinced that God never will permit Satan so to usurp this seal, or so to speak in this language, as to be mistaken for God Himself; but

* See Chapter X. on the Criterion.

that all the extraordinary operations which he is ever permitted to perform in the material world, are either in the things done, the end proposed, in the manner of performing them, attended with such circumstances as evidently manifest the source from which they flow.

This firm persuasion is grounded upon the prediction of our Saviour, of the extraordinary signs and wonders that will be performed towards the end of the world by false Christs and false prophets, through the agency of Satan, whose ministers these are; and which signs, He tells us, will be so many and so great at that time, "as to lead (if it were possible) even the elect into error," Matt. xxiv.; which expression evidently shows that though those signs and wonders will be great, yet their delusion will not be undiscoverable, but that the elect will discover it, and escape being deceived by it. So strongly impressed are Christians with the idea that miracles are the work of God, or of His good angels only, that as soon as they suspect any extraordinary event to be the work of Satan, they immediately lose all thought of it being miraculous. They call it a prestige, an illusion, a prodigy, an enchantment, and the like; or, as such operations are emphatically termed in Holy Writ, lying signs and wonders: but their idea of a miracle is exclusively confined to such extraordinary effects as they believe to be the work of God, or of good angels commissioned by Him.

V. These observations being premised, the definition of a miracle, according to the Christian idea of the word, naturally follows—namely, that it is "an extraordinary effect produced in the material creation, either contrary to the known laws of nature, or besides the usual course of nature, above the abilities of natural agents, and performed either by God Himself, or by His holy angels."

VI. Words indeed are but arbitrary signs, and every

one is at liberty to attach what idea he pleases to any word he uses, provided he explains his meaning. I am therefore far from blaming any other writer who has given a definition of the word miracle different from mine. If he understood the word, according to his definition, he had a perfect right to do so. I have abstained, therefore, from examining the several definitions, and from pointing out what may be thought defective or praiseworthy in them. But as Christian miracles are realities which have actually existed in the world, they must have some peculiar properties by which a correct idea can be formed of them, and by which they can be distinguished from what they are not. These properties I have endeavoured to investigate, according to what seems the opinion most general in the Christian world, and the most comformable to the doctrine of Holy Scripture; and from these properties I have composed my definition of the word *miracle*.

If this definition be strictly accurate and fully expressive of what is meant by a miracle, according to the Christian revelation, then it follows that those writers who have assigned to that word different significations, have not had Christian miracles for the subject of their inquiries, but ideas of their own, to which perhaps there is no corresponding object in existence. Thus, when Mr Hume gives us his idea of a miracle, and tells us "that a miracle may be accurately defined a transgression of a law of nature by a particular volition of the Deity, or by the interposal of some invisible agent," it is evident that, in this sense of the word, there is no such thing as a miracle existing, or possibly can exist; for, as Dr Campbell justly observes, the word transgression invariably denotes a criminal opposition to authority; and of this God Almighty is here represented as guilty in working a miracle, which is an evident impossibility. Also, if the miracle be wrought by an invisible created agent, in performing it this agent is always guilty of a crime, of an opposition to the divine will. What monstrous absurdities must necessarily follow from such ideas as these! If, therefore, Mr Hume, or others, instead of miracles have substituted the creations of their own fancy, and have drawn from them conclusions which the Christian religion abhors and condemns, we need not be surprised. These conclusions may naturally flow from the principles which they lay down, but Christianity cannot be affected by them. For, though these writers insidiously employ the same word to signify their ideas, that Christians use to denote real miracles, it is plain that their reasonings and conclusions cannot in the least degree affect either Christian miracles or Christianity.

VII. Before leaving this subject, I must observe that some Christian authors of note define the word *miracle* in a more limited manner than I have done, excluding all created agents, and understanding by it only such extraordinary operations as require the arm of the Almighty to perform them.

Their reasons are two: First, that when an angel performs anything unusual to us in this material creation, it is no less conformable to nature than if it were done by man; nor is it in the least surprising or wonderful to those spiritual beings, who see and know the cause performing it—for the angel in this case only acts according to his natural power, and produces an effect naturally corresponding to it. Secondly, because the sacred Scripture expressly attributes miracles to God only. Thus, Ps. lxxii. 18: "Blessed be the Lord the God of Israel, who only doth wonderful things." Also Ps. lxxxvi. 10: "For Thou art great, and dost wondrous things; Thou art God alone." Again, Ps. cxxxvi. 4 : "To Him who alone doth great wonders : for His mercy endureth for ever." Add to these, Ecclus. xi. 4 : " The works of the Highest only are wonderful." Hence they conclude, that those operations only are to be admitted as miracles which are peculiar to Almighty power, and can be done by none but God. It does not appear, however, that this is the opinion of the Christian world, or that it is the true idea which the Scripture itself conveys. For, according to this limited sense of the word, several remarkable effects related in the Scripture as miraculous, and yet performed by angels, and many others evidently within the power of angels, which fully answer all the ends of miracles, would be entirely excluded.

It would certainly be thought a miracle were a man to stand in the fire and not be touched by it, as was the case with the three children in the fiery furnace; and yet the Scripture declares that this was done by the ministry of an angel. In like manner the deliverance of Daniel from the lions is justly esteemed miraculous, and yet that prophet himself declared that "God had sent His angel and shut up the lions' mouths that they had not power to hurt him." Now both these events produced the full effect intended of convincing two heathen princes that Almighty God alone was the supreme Lord and Master of all things, as much as if they had been the immediate operation of God Himself; yet they, as well as many others, cannot be recognised as miracles if the above limited sense of that word be adopted. However, as there is a great difference between any operation which can be performed by the ordinary power of a created agent, and such as can be done only by the almighty hand of the Creator, it is proper to make a distinction, and we shall see this more particularly when we come to consider the criterion of miracles.

To miraculous operations, therefore, which can be performed by created agents, we shall give the name of relative miracles; because, though to man they be real miracles, yet they are not so with relation to the angels, but are effects produced by an adequate cause, natural in that order of beings. Miracles which can be performed by none but God we shall call absolute miracles, because they are really miracles with relation to all creatures, and exceed the natural powers of every created being. This distinction will fully answer the argument from reason, that nothing is to be esteemed a miracle which does not require Almighty power. And to reconcile the Scripture with itself, in answer to those texts above cited, we must say, either that they speak only of absolute miracles, which are peculiar to God alone; or, if both kinds are to be understood, the meaning is, that God alone doth wonderful things, either immediately by His own hand, or by the ministry of His holy angels, who never perform such wonders but when commissioned and authorised by Him to act.

VIII. We shall now conclude this explanation by taking a view of the different kinds of miracles.

First, then, if we consider the nature of the miraculous effects performed, we find two kinds specifically different,— the one being a suspension of some known law of nature; and those of this kind we call miracles contrary to the laws of nature. Miraculous effects of the other kind not being contrary to these laws, but new or unusual operations performed in nature beyond the power of any natural agent, we call miracles out of, or besides, the ordinary course of nature.

Secondly, if we consider the character of the operations, this will give us two other kinds no less distinct than the former, such as are supernatural, both in the thing done and in the manner of doing it; and such as are miraculous and supernatural only in the manner of performing it, but where the thing itself is natural, and may be brought about by natural means.

Thirdly, if we consider the agents, we shall find another division into relative miracles, which can be performed by the natural ability of supernatural created agents, and absolute miracles, which exceed all created power, and can be done only by the great Creator.

CHAPTER II.

THE AGENCY OF SPIRITUAL BEINGS IN THE MATERIAL CREATION.

I. BEFORE we proceed to particulars concerning miracles, it may be proper to consider the idea which the Holy Scriptures give us of the power of supernatural created beings to act upon matter, and of their agency in this world. This will illustrate the explanation given of miracles, and will facilitate our understanding the doctrine of the sacred writings concerning them.

I observed above, that it is from revelation alone that we know with certainty of the existence of spiritual beings, and consequently it is only from the same source that we can draw information regarding their nature, qualities, powers, and operations. It is unjust, therefore, in the adversaries of Christianity, to deny the existence of such beings, or at least to assert that they have no communication with the affairs of men, and, from this groundless supposition, to ridicule, and argue against Christianity and its miracles. For if the existence and agency of spirits in nature be the manifest doctrine of the Holy Scriptures, it is unreasonable to deny this doctrine, while they cannot disprove the divine origin of those sacred writings which contain it. It is no less unjust in certain pretended friends of Christianity to allege that the teaching of the holy fathers and primitive Christians concerning the agency of spiritual beings in the material creation, was solely owing to their attachment to the heathen mythology, and was the remains of their belief in demons before their conversion; for we find not only that their teaching concerning spirits is strictly conformable to the Holy Scriptures, but that these very Scriptures are brought by them to prove this doctrine, and are the sources from which they profess to draw it. But still more unjustifiable is it in Christians themselves, who receive the sacred Scripture as divine truths, to call in question what they clearly express concerning spiritual beings and their agency in nature, and to pervert the plain and obvious meaning of the text on this subject, rather than surrender some favourite preconceived opinion on pretence of being superior to what they call the prejudices of vulgar minds. A plain view of what is contained in the Word of God, will at once show the folly of such conduct.

II. The belief in the agency of spiritual beings in the material world has passed through various phases within the last two centuries. At the period of the Reformation, when Catholics urged the invincible weight of miracles in their communion as a proof of the truth of what they taught, and consequently as the strongest refutation of the new tenets, the first reformers had not yet discovered Dr Middleton's ready answer to all pleas of this kind. They could not deny the reality of the facts, and therefore did not hesitate to attribute them to the agency of Satan, willingly allowing an unbounded power of this kind even to wicked spirits during what they called the "reign of Papacy."

Afterwards, when Deism and Freethinking became

more prevalent, gentlemen of that party found it extremely inconvenient to admit the existence of evil spirits; for devils, hell, eternity, and the like, were incompatible with the leading articles of their belief, and still more with their morality. They sought, therefore, to resolve all miracles into juggling tricks and human imposture. But this plea was soon abandoned as untenable by various serious inquirers, who saw on the one hand many miraculous effects which they could not attribute to the art of man; and on the other, being unable to find any show of reason for absolutely denying the possibility of supernatural agents, they gladly admitted this, and from it pretended to invalidate the authority of miracles in general, even those of Jesus Christ Himself and of His holy apostles. For how, say they, do we know but that all miracles without exception may be only the work of different genii or demons, of whom there be many different degrees? And if the things done be some more and some less wonderful, this may be owing only to the greater or less degree of strength in the assisting demon. Thus, if Moses performed greater miracles than the magicians of Pharaoh, it only shows that his invisible helper was of a higher order than theirs; and if the miracles of Jesus Christ were above all that had ever been seen in the world before, it was owing only to the superior abilities of His assisting genius. Now, say they, as this is possible, it may be true, and all miracles may be the work of demons; and if this be the case, in vain do we appeal to miracles as interpositions of the Deity, and as proofs of doctrines revealed by Him.

The futility of this line of argument will afterwards be seen, and is indeed a natural consequence of what shall be shown upon the authority and criterion of miracles. At present I shall only observe that these various theories concerning the existence and agency of spiritual beings in the material world, show clearly that their respective advocates have no solid ground on which to stand; that they adopt their opinions at random, as fancy prompts; or, at best, that they are forced to embrace them in support of the different systems in which they have been previously engaged, without consulting the only certain source from which they could be fully informed, and, indeed, without examining whether their opinions be conformable to what is there taught or not.

There is still another system regarding the agency of spiritual beings, differing from all the former, lately set forth with great pomp by Mr Farmer. In this it is pretended that though these beings be of a nature superior to man, and may possess many qualities and powers of a more excellent kind, yet the exercise of them is limited to their own peculiar spheres for which they are adapted; that naturally they have no power to act in the material creation; and that when Almighty God is pleased at any time to employ them as His agents in performing anything miraculous, it is not enough that He order or authorise them, but it is also necessary that He impart to them a particular power, extraordinary, and otherwise not competent to their nature, to enable them to perform what He so commands.

III. In refutation of these and other such hypotheses, it will be sufficient to display the doctrine of the Holy Scriptures in their own words, where we shall find the following truths clearly declared by the authority of God Himself: 1. That spiritual beings, whether good or bad angels, have in their own nature an inherent power to act in this material creation; that they can move, dispose of, and affect bodies in many different ways; and that their strength is great, far superior to anything we know or can conceive in this world; so that they can perform many things marvellous in our eyes, and far above the abilities of any natural agent. 2. That evil spirits have an implacable hatred both to God and man; and consequently are most desirous to exert this their natural strength for the injury and destruction of man, and to perform great signs and wonders in order more effectually to delude and deceive him. 3. That, however, in the present dispensation of Providence, their malice is much restrained by Almighty God, who never permits them to exert their natural power to the injury of mankind, but in such manner and degree as He pleases for His own wise ends—that is, either for the good of mankind, according to the views of His mercy, or for the punishment of their sins, according to the order of His justice. This restraint appears, as we shall afterwards see, both from the nature of the things they are permitted to do, and from other circumstances attending them. 4. That good angels on many occasions have had communication with men, and have often performed extraordinary things on their account, and at their desire, by divine appointment for the benefit and consolation of God's friends and servants. 5. That wicked spirits also, by God's permission, have had frequent communication with men, and have often done extraordinary things at their desire, and by their means, for most wicked ends on their part, although justly and wisely permitted by Almighty God for His own most righteous views and purposes. Each of these heads we shall now illustrate separately from the Holy Scriptures; and afterwards we shall make a short inquiry into the power of spiritual beings to perform things miraculous to us in the material world.

IV. As the first of these is the most important, I shall be more explicit upon it, and show that spiritual beings act not only upon matter, but upon all the different parts of it—upon things on the surface of the earth and in the air; the bodies of animals, their health and life; and upon the mind of man: that they can move bodies, change their parts and appearances, and in several other ways dispose of and affect them. The proofs of this from the Holy Scripture are of the most convincing kind, and free from all ambiguity, consisting of repeated facts related in these sacred oracles.

With regard to strength, the angels are represented as excelling in it: "Bless the Lord," says the royal prophet, "ye His angels that excel in strength"—or, as the Hebrew expresses it, "mighty in strength"—Ps. ciii. 20. St Peter assures us that the "angels are greater in power and might than men," 2 Pet., ii. 11; and on this account they are called in Scripture, Dominations, Virtues, Powers. This appears also from the strength which the devils sometimes communicate to those whom they possess. Thus we are told in the Gospel of a possessed person, who "had his dwelling among the tombs, and no man could bind him, no, not with chains; because he had been often bound with fetters and chains, and the chains had been plucked asunder by him, and the fetters broken in pieces," Mark, v.

That spiritual beings can exert this power by acting upon matter, is evident from the following instances. An angel wrestled with Jacob. The two angels that were sent to destroy Sodom "put forth their hand and pulled Lot into the house," to deliver him from the fury of the people; "and they shut the door, and smote the men that were at the door of the house with blindness, both great and small," Gen. xix. 10. The angel Gabriel several times touched Daniel, and set him upright, when he had fallen flat on the ground from fear, Dan. viii. ix. x. "An angel came down and rolled away the stone, for it was very great, from the door of the sepulchre." When the apostles were cast into prison, "the angel of the Lord, by night, opened the prison doors and brought them forth," Acts, v. 19. And the angel that delivered St Peter out of prison smote him on the side and awoke him.

These facts clearly prove that spiritual beings can act upon matter, touch it, move it, and dispose of it in different ways. This is still further evident from the following examples of the several parts of nature wherein their power has been exercised. 1. In things upon the earth, we find that the devil changed the rods of the magicians into serpents; turned water into blood, and brought up frogs. This is not the place to inquire how this was done; we only consider the fact, which proves to a demonstration the agency of wicked spirits upon material objects, even to a very high degree, in whatever manner the change, whether real or apparent, was effected. The same Scripture that relates these facts informs us that they were done by enchantment, and in opposition to God, consequently they were therefore the operations of wicked spirits.

2. With regard to their agency in the air, we are told that the devil sent a great wind, which threw down the house where Job's children were assembled and destroyed them; and that he sent fire and lightning from heaven, which consumed Job's sheep and their keepers. From the power which these wicked spirits have in the air, St Paul calls the devil "the prince of the power of the air," Eph. ii. 2. And again he says, that our spiritual enemies are "principalities and powers, the rulers of the darkness of this world," Eph. vi. 12.

3. We find they can inflict diseases upon the bodies of men. Thus, "Satan went forth from the presence of the

Lord, and smote Job with sore boils, from the sole of his foot unto his crown," Job, ii. 7. And our blessed Saviour Himself assures us, that the crooked woman whom He cured upon the Sabbath, and who for eighteen years had not been able to raise herself up, had been kept bound for so long a time in this miserable manner by the devil: "Ought not this woman," says He, "being a daughter of Abraham, whom Satan hath bound, lo, these eighteen years, be loosed from this bond on the Sabbath-day?" Luke, xiii. 16. Of those persons who were possessed by the devil, as related in the Gospel, some he made dumb, some deaf, and some he threw into fits, tormenting them miserably, and endeavouring even to destroy them by throwing them sometimes into fire and sometimes into water. We are also told that "an angel of the Lord smote Herod, because he gave not glory to God," and that he died in a few days of a most loathsome disease, "being consumed by worms," Acts, xii. 23.

4. It appears further, from the same sacred records, that spiritual beings can take away the life of man and of other animals. Satan destroyed Job's children and his cattle; a devil killed Sarah's seven husbands; the destroying angel, in one night's time, killed all the first-born of Egypt, both man and beast. "An angel of the Lord went forth and smote, in the camp of the Assyrians, an hundred and fourscore and five thousand," Isa. xxxvii. 36. The two angels entertained by Lot told him, "we will destroy this place, because the cry of them is waxen great before the face of the Lord, and the Lord hath sent us to destroy it," Gen. xix. 13. The devils that entered into the herd of swine drowned them in the sea; and the angel that withstood Balaam's journey declared to him that he would surely have killed him if the ass had not turned out of the way, Num. xxii.

5. That wicked spirits have power to tempt men to sin, both by external occasions and by exciting bad ideas, is, and always has been, a fundamental article of Christian faith clearly laid down in holy writ. As to external temptations, we find the devil, at the beginning, either taking upon himself the appearance of a serpent, or entering into that creature, and making use of its organs to converse with Eve, thereby tempting and seducing her to sin. In like manner, when our blessed Saviour was pleased for our instruction to submit to be tempted, the devil appeared visibly, spoke to Him, and carried Him up to a pinnacle of the temple, and to the top of a very high mountain; and St Paul, writing to the Thessalonians, says: "We could have come unto you (even I Paul) once and again, but Satan hindered us," 1 Thess. ii. 18. And on another occasion he tells us that "an angel of Satan was given to buffet him." With regard to his internal temptations, the Scripture tells us, "That he taketh away the word of God out of our hearts," Luke, viii. 12. "That he blinds the minds of them that believe not," 2 Cor. iv. 4. "That he transforms himself into an angel of light," 2 Cor. xi. 14, in order to deceive us. "That he goes about like a roaring lion, seeking to devour us," 1 Pet. v. 8. "That he is the old serpent, who is called the devil, and Satan who seduces the whole earth," Rev. xii. 9. These texts require no comment, as they clearly show how great is the strength of wicked spirits to act upon our organs, both external and internal, and even upon our whole persons.

6. As to the agency of good angels, the Scriptures are full of the most convincing examples. Besides what we have seen above, we are assured that these holy "angels are ministering spirits, sent for the ministry of those who are the heirs of salvation," Heb. i. 14. That "God has given them charge over us to

keep us in all our ways," and that "they carry us in their hands, lest we dash our foot against a stone," Ps. xci. That "they encamp round about those that fear God and deliver them," Ps. xxxiv. That "an angel delivered Jacob from all evil," Gen. xlviii. That "an angel brought bread and water to Elijah in the wilderness," 1 Kings, xix. That an angel deprived the fire of its power to burn or touch the three children who were thrown into the fiery furnace by the king of Babylon. That an angel shut up the mouths of the lions, that they might not hurt Daniel. That an angel delivered St Peter out of prison, before whom the iron gate opened of its own accord, as if sensible of the presence and power of that heavenly being.

Now, let any one consider these facts, so repeatedly occurring in the Word of God, and say if he thinks it possible to give more convincing proofs of the power which these spiritual beings have to act upon every part of the material world. For the question is not, how far human ingenuity may wrest the words of Scripture, but whether the plain and obvious teaching of all the above facts is not calculated to imprint upon the mind the strongest conviction of the agency of spiritual beings in the material creation.

I conclude, then—1. That it is a truth plainly and repeatedly revealed by God in His Holy Scriptures, that spiritual beings, both good and bad angels, have power to act upon bodies in this material world in many different ways, and that they frequently exercise it. 2. That this power is natural and inherent in them as spiritual beings; for this is the obvious idea conveyed by all the above testimonies of holy writ. There is not the slightest insinuation to the contrary—nay, in many of the above examples the evil spirits exert their power in opposition to God; and it would be impious to suppose that in these cases He gives them extraordinary powers, not competent to their natures, to enable them to act against Himself. 3. That it is shameful in any one who calls himself a Christian to assert that the doctrines taught by the holy fathers concerning the agency of spirits are only the remains of heathenism. How little can such pretended Christians be acquainted with the Scriptures! or what idea must they have of a Christian world, when they dare to impose such a manifest calumny upon it! 4. That as it is only from revelation we can learn anything certain of the existence of spirits, and their agency on material beings, and as revelation is so explicit on that head, it is in vain to pretend to argue from reason against it. Reason has no data to go upon, either for or against the existence of spirits or their agency—nay, the analogy from our own soul, and its agency upon the body, is evidently in favour of both. For as by interior consciousness we have the most feeling conviction that our soul, though a spirit, acts in many ways upon our body, it is evident that a spirit can act upon matter; and will any one dare to assert that the only way by which Almighty God can communicate this power to spirits, of acting upon bodies, is to unite them in one principle, as our souls and bodies are?

Seeing, then, the fact of spiritual beings acting in numberless ways on the material creation is so repeatedly affirmed by the Word of God, and that there is not in the whole Scripture the least insinuation to the contrary, with what colour of reason can it be called in question, at least by any one who believes the Scriptures? That spiritual beings do act on bodies, is evidently a revealed truth. How they do so we cannot comprehend, because God has not been pleased to reveal this to us; but our ignorance is no more a reason for denying the fact, than it would be a reason to deny the action of the soul upon the body, because how this is performed we do not comprehend.

That one particle of matter acts upon another, even at a distance, by the power of gravitation and attraction, is a point that will readily be admitted by all Newtonian philosophers; and, indeed, it is a fundamental principle of their system. But how this is effected we cannot conceive. Those who have attempted to explain this mechanically have only bewildered themselves to no purpose, and have been forced to end at last in the difficulty which they attempted to explain. The most judicious, both among divines and philosophers, have resolved this power of attraction, so universally diffused through every particle of matter, to an immediate act of the divine will impressed upon matter as a law, by which it is ordained that all particles of matter, when within certain distances, should act upon one another by attraction, and produce all the various effects which we perceive to follow. And is it not equally easy for the same Almighty will to make a similar law between spirits and bodies, that these latter should be subjected to the former?

The possibility of this cannot be called in question, even in sound philosophy; and since revelation assures us of the fact, it is most unphilosophical to pretend from reason to argue against it. We must conclude, then, that supernatural created agents have great and extensive powers inherent in their nature as spiritual beings to act upon matter throughout every part of nature; and that by these powers they can move bodies, change their parts, suspend their natural effects upon each other, and perform many operations in them superior to the abilities of any natural agent, which therefore, with respect to us, are real miracles.

V. Having thus proved the first of the five heads proposed, I now proceed to consider the others, which will be more easily disposed of. The second—that evil spirits, from their malice and hatred to God and man, are most desirous to exert their strength for the destruction of man—is declared in the plainest terms by the Word of God, and is indeed the foundation of some of the most important rules of morality in religion.

Besides what we have seen above of the devil's power to tempt man to sin, we are also assured, that "by the envy of the devil death entered into the world," Wis. ii.; and our blessed Saviour Himself declares, that "the devil was a murderer from the beginning," John viii. St Peter compares his rage and fury against us to that of a roaring lion seeking to devour us, continually going about, and always upon the watch to seize every opportunity of doing so. Our Saviour showed the same in the strongest light when he said to St Peter, "Simon, Simon, Satan hath desired to have you, that he may sift you as wheat, but I have prayed for thee," Luke xxii. 31; and it was only by this prayer that the desire of Satan was disappointed, and his design against the apostles frustrated. These expressions show, beyond reply, how eager is the desire of Satan to ruin and destroy mankind both soul and body; and consequently that he would do so, were not his power restrained and bounds set to his malice by Almighty God.

This restraint put upon the power of Satan, which was the third point above mentioned, is no less plainly delivered in holy writ than the two former. The Egyptian magicians, at whose desire the devil turned the rods into serpents, and water into blood, and even brought up frogs, could not by their enchantments bring up lice. Here the devil's power was restrained, and the magicians were forced to confess that this was the finger of God. Why the devil, by his natural abilities, might not have brought up lice as well as frogs, we see no reason—the one appears as easy as the other; but it now pleased God to show Himself master; and therefore, though He permitted Satan to imitate the former miracles of Moses, yet He thought proper now to restrain his power, and put an end to the contest, by securing the victory to Himself and His holy servant.

Notwithstanding the hatred of Satan against Job, yet, till he was permitted, he could not so much as touch a single thing that belonged to him. And it is to be observed, that when the Lord gave this permission to Satan, there is not the slightest hint of giving him any extraordinary strength to enable him to injure Job, but, on the contrary, a plain intimation of his having already strength sufficient for that purpose; and the authority conveyed to Satan by the expression used, is plainly nothing more than leave to exercise his natural strength, first upon Job's goods, and afterwards upon his person: "Behold," saith Almighty God, "all that he hath is in thy power, only upon himself put not forth thine hand," Job, i. 12; and afterwards, "Behold, he is in thine hand, but save his life," Job, ii. 6. In both these expressions, the restricting clause plainly shows the nature of the leave given to Satan, and what further he could have done by his own natural strength, had not that clause been added.

In like manner, though the devil killed the seven husbands of Sarah, yet he had no power to touch young Tobias; and when the angel Raphael explained this to him, he said, "Hear me, and I will show thee who they are over whom the devil can prevail: for they who in such manner receive matrimony as to shut out God from themselves and from their mind, and to give themselves to their lust, as the horse and the mule, which have not understanding; over them the devil hath power," Tob. vi. 16, 17—where we see that it is not any extraordinary increase of strength given to Satan which enables him to injure men, but our own sins, which, depriving us of the friendship of God, and rendering us slaves of the devil, give him power over us, and permission to exercise his natural strength against us.

What our Saviour told St Peter, that "Satan desired to have him, that he might sift him as wheat," not only shows the rage of that wicked spirit against God's servants, but proves at the same time how much his power is restrained by the divine providence. He eagerly desired to injure, but he was rendered powerless, the execution of his desire being prevented by the prayers of Jesus Christ; nay, what is still more remarkable is, that when our Saviour dispossessed the poor man in whom there was a legion of devils, they could not even enter into the herd of swine till they had asked and received permission.

Lastly, our blessed Saviour not only restrains the power of Satan, and sets bounds to his malice Himself, but He has also given a similar power to His apostles and disciples; for "He gave them power and authority over all devils," Luke, ix. 1. And in the following chapter, when they had exercised this power, and found the effects of it, they returned and said to their Master with joy, "Lord, even the devils are subject to us through Thy name;" upon which He renews the grant to them again, saying, "Behold I give you power to tread upon serpents and scorpions, and over all the power of the enemy, and nothing shall by any means hurt you." But to repress all emotions of pride or vanity which might arise in their minds on that account, he immediately adds, "Notwithstanding, in this rejoice not that the spirits are subject unto you, but rather rejoice because your names are written in heaven," Luke, x. 17, 19, 20. All this manifestly shows that in the present dispensation of providence the devil's power is much restrained, and such bounds are set to his malice against man as best suit the views and designs of the divine wisdom.

We come now to consider the fourth point above proposed—the agency of good angels, and their communication with men; but of this we have already seen several manifest examples, and therefore here I mention only one other—that of the angel Raphael with Tobias.

VI. In the Christian revelation it is a well-known truth that pride was the ruin of the fallen angels. Dazzled with their supereminent excellences, they forgot the hand from which they had received them, and arrogated to themselves that glory which belonged only to their great Creator. Banished from heaven, and condemned to eternal misery in punishment of their crime, they did not become wiser by their fall, but rather were confirmed in pride and hardened in ambition.

To see man, formed of the dust of the earth, and so much inferior to them in dignity of nature, created in such happiness, and destined by the Almighty to fill up the places which they had lost in heaven, was a humiliation to their pride and envy. They resolved, therefore, on his destruction, and unhappily accomplished it. Having brought man into subjection to themselves, and being continually urged on by pride to put themselves on a level with their Maker, they have, since the very beginning, used every effort to procure honour from deluded mortals, and to imitate, among their votaries, whatever Almighty God was pleased to ordain for His own glory among His servants. Hence we find, throughout the whole heathen world, that the devils had their temples, their altars, their priests, their sacrifices, their oracles, their prophets, and even their miracles also; thereby imitating the works of God, and procuring to themselves the vain homage of worship and adoration on earth, which they could never have obtained in heaven.

From this known disposition of these proud spirits, it is not surprising to a Christian that they should aim at having their sacraments also, and should form compacts with such unhappy mortals as they could delude, engaging to work certain uncommon effects in nature, or such as their votaries should require, whenever these should perform, on their part, such exterior signs or actions as should be agreed upon between them. This would serve to gratify several passions of the human heart, particularly pride, envy, and hatred, and therefore would be readily agreed to by such unhappy souls as either knew not God or had lost all sense and fear of Him, and were by their vices become slaves to the above or other violent passions. It would no less gratify the pride of these infernal spirits to be thus honoured by men in their having recourse to them for such things as they desired, instead of applying to the great God that made them.

Seeing, therefore, that spiritual beings, both good and bad, have frequently appeared to men, and have conversed with them, there is clearly no impossibility that such compacts should be entered into between wicked spirits and men. It is even natural to expect them, from the known dispositions of both. Now, if such a compact be supposed, in which the devil appoints certain outward actions to be done, and engages to perform such and such extraordinary effects in nature, it is plain that the knowledge of the connection between the outward sign and the effect to be produced may be communicated to others who had not themselves been parties to the compact, and be again by them communicated to others. It is also plain that this knowledge may be imparted to others merely as a secret or curiosity of nature, without any intimation that the effect so produced is the work of the devil; nay, as the exterior signs used may even be sacred things, and the words pronounced taken from the Holy Scriptures, ignorant persons may thus be so far deluded as to believe them lawful or even holy, and think they are serving God, while they are honouring the devil.

Compacts of this kind with wicked spirits, and the using and trusting to their infernal signs for procuring the effect intended, is what is meant in general by the terms *witchcraft, sorcery, enchantment, magic, charms,* and the like. But as there are different degrees of guilt in the thing done, so, strictly speaking, the idea connected with these terms is different accordingly; for witchcraft and sorcery seem properly to signify the very being in such compact with wicked spirits, and having a personal familiar intercourse with them; and those who have this are termed witches and sorcerers. Enchantment and art magic seem rather to imply the knowledge and use of these signs and their effects, knowing them to be from an evil principle, though the persons who use them did not themselves make the compact, nor had any personal intercourse with the devil, but had learned it from others. Even the Scripture speaks of magic as an art: "And the delusions of their art magic were put down, and their boasting of wisdom was rebuked reproachfully," speaking of the magicians of Egypt, Wis. xvii. 7. Now an art implies a thing taught by one person to another; and it would appear from other parts of Scripture that this art magic was professedly taught among the Egyptians and Chaldeans. See Daniel, in several places.

Charms, spells, and superstitious practices imply the use of these signs, with a confidence in them as curiosities or natural secrets, without knowing, or at least without fully adverting to the source from which they come. Besides these general names, there are also many particular appellations given to the different practices, and to those who use them, according to the effects produced and the various means employed—as diviners, augurs, soothsayers, pythonesses, necromancers, fortune-tellers, and the like.

VII. Deists and freethinkers ridicule all these things, regarding them as impossibilities, chimeras, and the result of weakness of mind and childish credulity. Nor is this surprising, as they do not admit the existence of the devil. Unbelievers, however, have never yet been able to bring the shadow of proof why spiritual beings may not exist; and if they do, why they may not act in the affairs of this material creation. All they can say on this subject is reduced to a witticism and a sneer. In Christianity, the possibility of these diabolical operations admits of no doubt. That they have often been done, and a communication kept up by their means between wicked spirits and men, is a truth most manifestly revealed in the Holy Scriptures; and if such intercourse be possible, and has actually existed in former times, who will be so bold as to say that it never can exist again? It would, indeed, be a weak credulity to believe every idle tale related; but it would be a no less blamable folly to deny the possibility of its existence, when we consider what the Word of God teaches. This we find contained under the following heads :—

1. All commerce of this kind, and all connection with those who practise such things, is severely prohibited by Almighty God, as a crime most detestable in His eyes. Thus, Exod. xxii. 18: "Thou shalt not suffer a witch to live." Levit. xix. 31: "Regard not them that have familiar spirits, neither seek after wizards, to be defiled by them." Levit. xx. 6: "And the soul that turneth after such as have familiar spirits, and after wizards, to go a-whoring after them, I will even set my face against that soul, and cut him off from among his people." *Ib.*, verse 27: "A man also or a woman that hath a familiar spirit, or that is a wizard, shall surely be put to death; they shall stone them with stones; their blood shall be upon them." And Deut. xviii. 10: "There shall not be found among you any one . . . that uses divination, or an observer of times, or an enchanter, or a witch, or a charmer, or a consulter with familiar spirits, or a wizard, or a necromancer: for all that do these things are an abomination to the Lord." And, in the new law, witchcraft is reckoned by St Paul among those works of the flesh of which those who are guilty, he assures us, "shall not inherit the kingdom of God," Gal. v. And, Rev. xxi. 8, it is declared, that "murderers, and whoremongers, and sorcerers, shall have their part in the lake which burneth with fire and brimstone." Now, can anything be more impious than to suppose, that God Almighty would have made such severe prohibitions of a crime, which not only had no existence in nature, but could not possibly exist? Can there be a more blasphemous arraignment of the divine wisdom than to suppose it capable of such folly? Besides, it is plain from all the above texts that they speak of the thing as real and certain, and as actually practised in the world.

2. Those who, contrary to this prohibition, were

guilty of this crime, are severely condemned by the Word of God, and their punishments proposed as monuments of the divine justice against it. Thus, 2 Kings xvii. 17, it is expressly declared that this was one of the principal causes of the ruin and dispersion of the ten tribes: "They caused their sons and daughters to pass through the fire; they used divinations and enchantments—therefore the Lord was very angry with Israel, and removed them out of His sight." This also is represented as one of the greatest crimes of Manasses, which provoked the wrath of God so highly against him; for "he observed times, and used enchantments, and dealt with familiar spirits and wizards; he wrought much wickedness in the sight of the Lord, to provoke him to anger," 2 Kings, xxi. 6. Here we find commerce with familiar spirits, and the existence of wizards and witches, expressly affirmed, and this commerce declared to be the crime of which this wicked prince was actually guilty, and for which he incurred the just displeasure of Almighty God. Now, can any one who believes the Scriptures deny the reality, much less the possibility, of these things?

3. Those good princes who, in obedience to the divine command, put away those who dealt in these impieties, and discouraged such wicked practices, are highly praised in the Holy Scriptures for so doing. Thus it is recorded in praise of Saul, who at the beginning was an excellent prince, that "he had put away those that had familiar spirits, and the wizards, out of the land," 1 Sam. xxviii. 3. Among the many good things that Josiah did, it is particularly observed of him, that "the workers with familiar spirits, and the wizards, and all the abominations that were spied in the land of Judah and in Jerusalem, did Josiah put away, that he

might perform the words of the law," 2 Kings, xxiii. 24. Now, how could they be put away if they had no existence? And how can their existence be called in question without denying the Scripture?

4. We find several examples in Scripture of particular persons who dealt in those practices to a very great degree, and which show to what length the power of Satan is sometimes permitted to go, in doing things extraordinary by means of those his agents. Thus the magicians of Egypt are expressly affirmed to have performed prodigies similar to the miracles of Moses by their enchantments. The witch of En-dor also is particularly taken notice of as a person who had such intercourse with wicked spirits; and in the New Testament, every one knows of Simon the magician, of whom we are told, Acts viii., that, for some time before Philip went to Samaria to preach the Gospel there, he had "in the same city used sorcery, and bewitched the people of Samaria, giving out that himself was some great one." So many and great were the wonders which he did among them, whether real or only apparent, that "to him they all gave heed, from the least to the greatest, saying, This man is the great power of God; and to him they had regard, because that for a long time he had bewitched them with his sorceries."

Here we not only see an example of one guilty of this diabolical commerce, but we also find that such persons are sometimes permitted to hurt others, to bewitch and delude them by their sorceries. We also read of Elymas, another magician, who opposed the preaching of the Gospel by St Paul, and whom that great apostle struck blind for his impiety: "O full of all subtilty and all mischief, and child of the devil and enemy of all righteousness, wilt thou not cease to pervert the right ways of the

Lord?" Acts, xiii. 10. In these words the apostle gives us the true character of all such persons, and the light in which they appear in the eyes of God. We must not here omit the young woman "possessed with a spirit of divination, which brought her masters much gain by soothsaying," who was dispossessed by St Paul, as we read, Acts, xvi. 16.

5. Now let any Christian attentively consider these repeated testimonies of the Word of God on the agency of evil spirits, and say if it is possible to express the actual existence of these diabolical operations, and of the interposition of wicked spirits with the affairs of men, in clearer or stronger terms; and consequently, if it would not be the height of impiety to deny a truth so repeatedly affirmed in these sacred oracles. It is therefore undeniable, according to the Christian revelation, that wicked spirits have often had communication with men; that they have great power and strength, natural to them as spirits, for performing many extraordinary things in the material creation; and that they have often exercised this power at the desire and by means of those who had intercourse and communication with them.

VIII. Here perhaps a question may be proposed, Are there at present any persons in the world who are guilty of these practices? In answer to this, I may observe, that it is unimportant to my argument whether there be or be not. It is enough to show that the agency of these infernal beings, as well as of good angels, in this lower world, is a truth revealed by God in the Holy Scriptures. However, as the above question is curious, and it may be agreeable to my readers to have a solution of it, what seems to be the real case is as follows:—

1. That there have been such persons in the world who have had compacts and familiar personal com-

merce with wicked spirits is undoubted. The Word of God affirms it, gives several examples of those who have practised these crimes, and makes severe laws against them.

2. That there may still be such persons in the world cannot be denied. What has been may be again; and the prohibition of these crimes which we find in the New Testament, where they are condemned as grievous sins, evidently supposes that they may be found even among Christians.

3. That such persons are as common among Christians as is frequently imagined is evidently a mistake; for it is certain that the devil's power is much restrained wherever the Gospel is planted: and among the many glorious promises made by Almighty God to the Church, and foretold by the prophets, this is one,—" I will take away sorceries out of the land, and there shall be no divinations in thee," Micah, v. 11. These words imply, at least, that such things will be less common under the Gospel; that the devil will not be permitted to delude the people to such a degree as in former times; and that men will not be so much given to these abominations.

4. That there are, or may be, many who attempt to have commerce with wicked spirits, is very possible; because it is natural to suppose that the passions of men will urge them on to such extremes; and because those who are conversant with the care of souls know it from experience, as this case sometimes does actually come before them.

5. As to those who have no personal intercourse with spiritual beings, but who use charms and superstitious practices in order to procure some desired end, whether they know and reflect that these are diabolical inventions, or have no idea that they are such, it is incredible how

many are to be found, especially among the lower classes, in all countries.

IX. It is evident, then, that nothing is more certain, according to the Christian revelation, than the existence of spiritual beings, both good and bad, and their agency in nature; that they are endowed with great power and many qualities superior to man, and of course can perform things in the material creation which will appear miraculous to us, and above the abilities of all natural agents. We shall now briefly inquire in what manner they effect these miraculous operations; at least, what light our reason, and the knowledge we have of their nature and qualities from revelation, can afford us.

The Scriptures everywhere represent these beings as exceedingly strong ("mighty in strength," as the Psalmist expresses it), and therefore they must be able to perform many things in moving bodies and altering their parts, in suspending the usual effects of the laws of nature, and the like, far superior to anything that can be performed by any natural agent. Again, the agility of angelic beings is doubtless great, so that they can transport themselves from one place to another with an amazing velocity, far superior to anything we can conceive in bodies. Of this we may form some idea by considering that the light of the sun, though a material substance, has such immense velocity as to reach the earth in less than ten minutes of time. If, therefore, spirits can move with much greater velocity than bodies, with what inconceivable quickness must these beings be able to transport themselves from one part to another! They will also be able to do many things truly wonderful, both by communicating intelligence of what is passing at a distance almost instantaneously, and also by transporting bodies to distant places with the greatest velocity. Of this last we have a remarkable instance in Daniel, where we are told that when that holy prophet was for the second time cast into the den of lions, and had had no food for a considerable time, the prophet Habakkuk in Judea, some hundreds of miles distant, going out one morning to the field with a mess of pottage to the reapers, was caught up by an angel of God, and in an instant carried to Daniel; and when Daniel had eaten the pottage, he was brought back in the same manner, Dan. xiv.

This chapter of Daniel, it is true, is not found in the Hebrew, and on that account is thrown into the Apocrypha by Protestants; but it has, from the earliest ages, been received by the Catholic Church as divine Scripture, and its authority as an ancient history is not called in question.

Tertullian, speaking of the velocity with which spirits transport themselves from one place to another, says: "*Every* spirit is winged; both angels and demons are so; on that account they are everywhere in a moment: the whole world is one place to them; they know where anything is doing as easily as they can declare it."*

X. Great knowledge is another prerogative of spiritual beings, which enables them to do many things above the abilities of natural agents. Experimental philosophy has of late been making daily improvements, and discovering more and more of the wonderful powers of nature, particularly in magnetism and electricity; and it cannot be doubted but that there are many more secrets in nature of which mankind are still totally ignorant. Spiritual beings have doubtless a much greater knowledge of these

---

* Omnis spiritus ales; hoc et angeli et dæmones. Igitur momento ubique sunt. Totus orbis locus illis unus est, quid ubi geratur, tam facile sciunt quam enuntiant.—Tert., Apol., circa medium.

things than men, and consequently are capable of producing many extraordinary effects in the material creation, which, from our ignorance of these powers of nature, would appear to us astonishing. But, as all they can perform is only by exerting these natural powers, which require time to produce their effects, such extraordinary things cannot be instantaneous, even with all the strength of spiritual beings. Hence miraculous operations, which are merely the effect of strength or agility, or which are done by the application of natural means, are known by these circumstances to be within the range of the natural abilities of spirits, and therefore cannot of themselves alone afford proof of divine interposition.

From this more intimate knowledge possessed by spiritual beings of the powers and properties of material agents, which are concealed from us, they will, no doubt, foresee many natural effects which will result from these powers when exerted, and from their necessary or occasional combinations; and this they may know a considerable time before these effects are actually produced. If now they should communicate this their foreknowledge of these necessary events to any man, and he should foretell them to the world, this prediction and its subsequent verification would appear miraculous to those who know nothing of the natural causes producing the effect foretold; just as the prediction of an eclipse, and its verification when the eclipse happens, will be miraculous to those who are ignorant of astronomy.

As spiritual beings have also a much more thorough knowledge of the human frame than we have, they may in like manner, with great probability, conjecture what particular persons, with whose temper and disposition they are well acquainted, will do on such and such occasions; and hence they may, with considerable certainty, foretell even future contingent events, and their prediction may afterwards be verified. Even human sagacity, from a thorough knowledge of the subject, frequently arrives at a considerable degree of foreknowledge of this kind. By these two kinds of foreknowledge, soothsayers, false prophets, and those who had familiar spirits, mentioned in the Scriptures, might sometimes foretell things which actually come to pass; and the same is the explanation of the predictions of the heathen oracles, which were afterwards verified by the event. St Augustin, speaking on the divination of evil spirits, says: "First, we must know that for the most part they foretell only such things as they themselves are going to do; for they often receive power to cause diseases, and by vitiating the air to render it morbific; sometimes also they foretell not those things which they do themselves, but which, from natural signs, they foresee are to happen; which signs cannot fall under the knowledge of man."*

XI. Another way by which spiritual beings may appear to do things miraculous in our eyes, is by what is called fascination or bewitching, which may be conceived possible in two different ways, either by making such impressions upon the organs of our senses, as if the real material object that naturally could make them were present and acting on them, or by taking upon themselves the outward appearances of the things which they wish to represent. That spiritual beings, both good and bad,

---

* Primum sciendum est, quoniam de divinatione dæmonum questio est, illos ea plerumque prenuntiare quæ ipsi facturi sunt: accipiunt enim sæpe potestatem et morbos immittere, e tipsum aerem vitiando morbidum reddere; aliquando autem non quæ ipsi facient, sed quæ, naturalibus signis, futura prænoscunt; quæ signa in hominum sensus venire non possunt. — Aug. de Divin. Dæmon. C. V.

have a very great power in acting upon our internal senses, by altering and moving the humours of the body, so as to raise many ideas in our imagination, and affections in our appetite, will not be called in question by any who profess the Christian religion.

With regard to wicked spirits, those texts of Scripture which we have seen above concerning internal temptations, manifestly show this; and, indeed, how else can we account for those violent temptations to blasphemy, despair, scruples, involuntary doubts against faith, and the like, which often bear in upon the mind with the utmost violence, to the unspeakable torment of the sufferer, and in spite of his earnest efforts to expel them? How can this be accounted for, but from the action of those wicked spirits violently disturbing the imagination?

As to good angels, the Christian religion assures us that they inspire us with pious thoughts, calm our fears, assuage our passions, and that they also represent things to our imagination in sleep, so as to manifest to the servants of God what the divine will requires of them. Thus the angel of God appeared to Joseph in a dream, and told him to fly into Egypt from the fury of Herod; and Almighty God Himself, speaking to His people on this subject, says: "Behold I send an angel before thee: . . . beware of him and obey his voice, provoke him not; for he will not pardon your transgressions. . . . If thou shalt indeed obey his voice, and do all that I speak, then I will be an enemy to thine enemies," Exod. xxiii.

Now, if spiritual beings have such power to act upon our internal senses, there can be no doubt that they may do the same upon our external organs also. In the Holy Scriptures we have many examples of angels appearing to men and conversing with them. The common way of explaining these apparitions, is by saying that these spiritual beings assumed an aerial body, or some other matter, by which the same natural impressions were made upon the senses of the beholders as by the natural body of a man. But this opinion is subject to several difficulties.

There is not the least necessity for supposing this. If these spiritual beings can make such strong impressions as they sometimes do upon our internal senses, for which they certainly stand in no need of help of aerial bodies, why should they stand in need of such help to make what impressions they please upon our external senses? If an angel could deprive the fire of its power to hurt the three holy children that were thrown into the furnace without taking any material body to assist him, could he not with equal ease communicate any motion he pleased to the air, and excite the sound of words in the ears of those present, or reflect the rays of light to their eyes, so as to excite in their minds the idea of any colour or figure he might think proper? If the angels can at all act upon bodies, why not upon the air and light as well as on any other body, without taking a material body to assist them? Nay, if an angel could make to himself a body of air, or any other matter, in order thereby to move the air or light so as to affect the senses of those present, why could he not as well directly move the air or light itself, without the intervention of any material instrument?

Several of the apparitions related in Scripture plainly show that the impressions were made immediately by the spiritual agent upon the senses of those present. Had a material body been taken by the angels who appeared to men, this must have reflected the light, and moved the air equally on all sides as other bodies do, and consequently all present must have been equally sensible of the angel's presence, and must equally have heard his words. But we find that frequently this was not the case. The angel that appeared to Balaam was seen by the ass for some time before he appeared to the master. The angel who appeared to Daniel by the great river was seen by him alone; and Daniel says, "I alone saw the vision; for the men that were with me saw not the vision, but a great quaking fell upon them," Dan. x. 7. At the conversion of St Paul, though our Saviour spoke to him in an audible manner, and conversed with him, yet he himself tells us, that "they that were with him saw indeed the light and were afraid, but they heard not the voice of Him that spoke to him," Acts, xxii. 9.

It is evident, then, that these apparitions were exhibited by an impression made upon the organs of some particular persons, and not of others who were equally present, which could not have been the case without another miracle, had they been performed by means of any assumed aerial body; and therefore it is most reasonable to conclude that they were immediate impressions made by those who appeared upon the organs of those who saw them.

This is further confirmed by the words of Scripture mentioning the appearance of any spiritual being to those who, though present, saw him not before; for the expression used on these occasions plainly implies an impression made immediately on the organs of those to whom the apparition is exhibited. Thus, though the angel had appeared for some time to Balaam's ass, yet he had never been seen by himself. At last "the Lord opened the eyes of Balaam, and he saw the angel," Num. xxii. 31. So also, when Elisha's servant expressed great fear on seeing the army of the Syrians, his master said, "Fear not; for they that be with us are more than they that be with them. And Elisha prayed, and said, Lord, I pray Thee, open his eyes that he may see. And the Lord opened the eyes of the young man, and he saw; and, behold, the mountain was full of horses and chariots of fire round about Elisha," 2 Kings, vi. 16, 17. Shall we say here that all these angels took in an instant material bodies to appear to the young man, and not rather that the impression was made immediately on his eyes without the use of any material means? This is certainly the more natural meaning of the expression, "the Lord opened his eyes."

It seems most reasonable, then, to conclude, that spiritual beings can themselves make immediate impressions upon our outward senses, exciting in our minds the same ideas that bodily objects would, and can make objects appear to us which really have no existence. They can also, by acting on our internal senses, excite strong ideas in our imagination. When this is done by evil spirits for their wicked ends, it is called fascination; when by good angels, to communicate the will of God to His servants, it is a species of revelation. At the same time, these spiritual agents may occasionally make use of bodily instruments, as was probably the case with the angel that attended the people of God in the appearance of a pillar of fire and of a cloud, which was visibly seen by the people. From their strength and agility, also, they can doubtless present and take away bodily objects almost instantaneously, so as to render them imperceptible to those present, and by all these different operations perform things far above the abilities of natural agents. It is in one or other of these ways that several of the holy fathers and other learned men account for what the magicians of Egypt did by their enchantments.

XII. In these different ways spiritual beings act upon matter and exhibit various effects, real or apparent, to our eyes. How far they can go in such operations we know not; but certain we are, as we shall afterwards see when explaining the criterion, that Almighty God will never allow wicked spirits to use this power so as invincibly to deceive us; and that whatever good angels do is only by authority from God for our benefit.

CHAPTER III.

THE POSSIBILITY OF MIRACLES.

I. TO call in question the possibility of miracles seems strange to a true Christian, and ought, according to right reason, to appear absurd to any one who, believing the existence of the Deity, acknowledges the universe to be the work of His almighty power. Still, we know that in this enlightened age this is actually done; nay, not only is the possibility of miracles called in question, but plainly denied by many who, whilst they glory in the discoveries made in the works of nature, and boast of the improvement of the human intellect, show that their light is mere darkness, and that their pretended intellectual improvement serves only to make them more learnedly fools. This charge might seem severe, and justly expose me to the ridicule of the accused, did I pretend to support it only by the authority of revelation, which they deny. But this is not my intention, nor is there here any need of the aid of revelation. The possibility of miracles is so natural a consequence of their definition itself, and of the idea which we have given of them, that those who pretend to deny it must be determined to lay aside reason, and to act in direct opposition to its clearest light. Their case, however, is so far to be pitied, as it is necessity that drives them to these extremes—

the authority of miracles carrying with it invincible argument against their tenets. It is impossible to evade the weight of this authority if miracles be admitted to exist, and therefore to deny their possibility is the easiest method of escaping from a difficulty. But it is one thing to deny and another to prove. Those who deny the possibility of miracles do indeed offer something by way of justification of their denial, but a little attention will show how unreasonable are all their arguments.

II. We have seen above that miracles, considered in themselves, are of two kinds: first, such as consist in a suspension of the effects of some of the known laws of nature; and, secondly, such as are not contrary to any of these laws, but out of the ordinary course of nature, and require a power superior to that of any natural agent to perform them. Of the first kind are the following: if a stone should fly upwards; if the waters of a river should be divided, those below running down, and those above standing still or being gathered up; if the sun should stop in his course; if a man should walk on water, and the like: which are all contrary to the known laws of nature, and imply a suspension of their usual effects. It would be of the second kind were a man to cure diseases in an instant by only willing, by commanding, or by a simple touch; should a person know and foretell contingent future events; were a man to be raised from the dead, and suchlike. These two kinds of facts must be considered separately, in order to show, in the most distinct and convincing manner, that miracles are possible.

III. With regard to those of the first kind, or such as consist in a suspension of any of the laws of nature, it is evident that if miracles of this class be impossible, the impossibility must arise from one of three causes—either that these laws are in themselves absolutely immutable and incapable of suspension, so that their effects cannot be superseded by any power whatever, or that there exists no agent whose abilities are capable of suspending them, or that it would argue inconstancy and mutability in the divine Author of those laws, if, having once established them for the regulation of the universe, He should either Himself at any time suspend their effects, or allow them to be suspended by others. But none of these can be affirmed, and therefore we justly conclude that miracles of this kind are not impossible.

That the laws of nature are not in themselves immutable is evident from experience. Many of those with which we are acquainted, not only may be, but actually are, suspended and hindered by other stronger laws acting against them; nay, effects directly opposed to them are not unfrequently produced. Hence we may justly argue, that those other laws of nature which do not fall under our observation, though we see no natural created cause capable of suspending their effects, yet in themselves are not unsusceptible of suspension, but would undoubtedly be suspended were any agent, with sufficient power, to act against them. We see no impossibility in this conclusion, no reason why some laws should be immutable in their effects and others not; and if analogy have any weight, we must acknowledge this conclusion to be just and reasonable; therefore the laws of nature are not in themselves incapable of being suspended, and consequently miracles are not impossible.

IV. Experience shows that man by his own natural strength, still more if he calls in the help of art, and employs the power of other creatures, is able to produce many effects quite contrary to some of the known laws of nature. From this we justly argue that beings of a superior nature—who are endowed with much greater strength, possess far superior abilities, and at the same time know better all the powers of creatures—must be able to suspend many more of the laws of nature, to prevent their ordinary effects, and to produce others contrary to them.

Let us suppose, for instance, the strength of man to be as one, with which he can raise a weight of ten stone. If we suppose an angel to have a degree of strength as ten thousand, he will be able to raise a weight of one hundred thousand stone. Let us again suppose that this angel, invisible to us, should, by compact with man, immediately at his desire raise into the air a body weighing a hundred thousand stone, this would be an evident miracle to all beholders. Now, can the possibility of such a miracle be denied, either from the thing done, or the agent that is supposed to do it? Not from the thing done, which is not in itself impossible if there be an agent endowed with strength sufficient to perform it. Shall we then deny that an angel can exist endowed with such strength? Where is the impossibility? Upon what grounds shall we deny it? And even if this be not allowed, it will not surely be denied that God Himself has strength sufficient to produce the effect supposed; and therefore its possibility cannot be called in question, though the thing be evidently in opposition to all the laws of gravitation.

The same reasoning will equally hold in every imaginable case; and therefore we must justly conclude in general that whatever laws of nature there may be superior to the powers of beings of an inferior order, there are supernatural agents of a higher order capable of suspending them. And if there be any of those laws superior to the powers of all created agents, they can never exceed the almighty power of God. Consequently there can never be wanting an agent, either among creatures or in the Creator Himself, capable of suspending any law of nature, since these laws are in themselves capable of suspension; and therefore miracles of this class are not impossible from want of a proper agent.

V. The last resort of infidelity is to say that it would argue inconstancy and mutability in God, the divine Author of the laws of nature, either Himself to suspend their effects in particular instances, or to permit any other to suspend them. But here, again, I must appeal to experience, by which we know that several of the laws of nature, even the most general, as those of gravity and attraction, are in many cases suspended without any prejudice to the immutability of God. If, therefore, some laws of nature may be suspended, and yet God remain immutable, why not others? why not all, when an adequate power is exerted against them? Does it argue mutability in God that an angel, for instance, should stop the course of water in a river, supposing him capable by his own natural strength to do so, contrary to the known laws of gravitation, whilst yet it argues no such mutability that man, by his natural strength, or by the help of gunpowder, should make a ball of iron fly upwards from the earth in direct opposition to these same laws?

If neither of these cases can prejudice the immutability of God, why should it be thought to do so if He Himself should be pleased to stop for a time the diurnal motion of the earth, and thereby lengthen the day, and make the sun appear to stand still in the heavens? Does it argue mutability in God to suspend any of those laws by the sole act of His will, while it argues no such mutability when he does it by using secondary causes?

Were this the case, an absurd consequence would follow—namely, that God could perform any miraculous effect which He pleased, in suspending the laws of nature by the ministry of angels, giving them strength for this purpose, but could do no such thing Himself without destroying His own immutability, and becoming changeable.

We may conclude, therefore, that as those laws of nature which fall under our observation are often suspended by other natural causes acting against them without any prejudice to the immutability of God, so it never can affect that divine prerogative when He Himself, by the sole act of His will, shall be pleased to suspend any law without employing created secondary causes; and consequently, that such miracles as consist in a suspension of any of the laws of nature are possible, without the least prejudice to the immutability of the Deity. In a word, the whole creation, and all the laws by which it is maintained, proceed from the free will and good pleasure of Almighty God. He made choice of the present system of nature with a view to those wise moral ends which He proposed to Himself. He freely made all things in nature as they are; He can with equal ease change them as He pleases. As He freely enacted those laws by which all nature is governed for the best of ends, so He can dispense with them when He sees proper—that is, when the end proposed can better be accomplished by such dispensation; and though this good end happens in time, both it, and the dispensing with any law of nature in order to procure it, were always present with God from all eternity; and therefore, when it is actually accomplished in time, it can argue no change in Him. He forms no new decrees, He makes no new laws, He acquires no new knowledge.

What He wills in time He willed from all eternity; and, as St Augustin justly observes, "opera mutat, consilia non mutat;" "He changes His works, but His counsels and views remain the same." This the Holy Scripture beautifully expresses in the books of Wisdom: "Nothing is hidden from His eyes; He sees from eternity to eternity, and nothing is wonderful to Him," Ecclus. xxxix. Consequently to Him there is nothing new, nothing that in Him can cause change.

Seeing, therefore, that the laws of nature in themselves are not incapable of being suspended, provided an adequate force acts against them; that there can be found, either in created agents or in God, power and strength fully capable of this; and that they may be suspended by any of these causes without prejudice to the divine immutability,—it evidently follows, therefore, that miracles of this kind are not impossible.

VI. We come now to consider the possibility of those miracles which are *beside* the ordinary course of nature. And here there seems to be little difficulty; for can any one doubt that the same almighty power which created all things, and gave to each its being, powers, and properties, is still able to perform numberless effects which far exceed the powers bestowed on these His creatures? Will any one deny that Almighty God is able in a moment to do by a single act of His own will what He does in a certain space of time by the ordinary powers of created agents? It is not contrary to any law of nature to cure diseases in the human body, to cause plants to grow from seed. These effects are daily produced by natural causes, but they require time for their production. Almighty God gave to natural causes the power of producing these effects; and will any one deny that He Himself can produce them in an instant by the sole act of His will, without making use of created powers? Or will it be said that Almighty God, in giving such powers to creatures, has divested Himself of the right to act without their agency? Has He bound Himself by an immutable law never to produce the above effects without them? The bare statement exhibits its absurdity; and it is evident that all such miraculous effects as exceed the power of created agents are possible to Almighty God whenever He pleases to perform them.

Miracles of this second class are the most excellent of all, and the most proper for securing the ends intended to be gained by miracles, as they are the most incontestable proof of divine interposition. Besides, the argument of freethinkers, drawn from the immutability of God, has no place here, where these laws are neither changed nor suspended, but a new effect produced by the almighty hand of God out of the ordinary course of these laws, and superior to the strength of creatures.

VII. There is still another argument advanced against the possibility of miracles, drawn from the wisdom of God, as if it would argue a defect of wisdom in the Deity were the laws established by Him for the regulation of the universe insufficient for this purpose, and should require at any time to be suspended in order to obtain the ends which He had in view. What I have said above concerning the immutability of God is equally applicable to His wisdom, and equally shows the weakness of this objection. Besides, we may further add, what Mr Farmer justly observes—"Whoever reflects on the boundless extent and duration of the divine government, will easily perceive that nothing can be more absurd, as well as arrogant, than for man, a creature whose faculties are so limited, and who is but of yesterday, to presume to determine that no fit occasion for extraordinary interposals can ever occur in that administration, the plan of which transcends his comprehension. By what principles of reason can it be demonstrated that He who reigns from eternity to eternity never formed any designs, except such as may be accomplished by the present establishment and structure of the universe?"

Now, if Almighty God has from eternity formed designs to be executed at various times among His creatures, the exhibition of miracles at these times, in order to the more perfect execution of these designs, so far from being an arraignment of His wisdom, shows it forth in a still more striking light. Again, had the universe been composed only of necessary agents, devoid of liberty or free-will, extraordinary interpositions of the Deity by miracles would have been less required. But the rational creatures, whom Almighty God governs by moral laws, are endowed with free-will and liberty to obey or disobey His commands; and experience too clearly shows how apt they are to neglect their duty, and even to forget their obligations. The many proofs of His providence and perfections displayed in the regular course of the universe, by use and custom, cease to move our hearts; and nothing can more display the infinite wisdom and goodness of the Creator, than that He should at certain times give extraordinary proofs of His power, by controlling the usual course of nature, thereby to awaken intelligent beings from their lethargy, to rouse them to a sense of their duty and dependence, and to give them a deep impression of the power and presence of their sovereign Master.

"It would be difficult to prove" (says Mr Farmer) "that God may not, in certain circumstances, have greater reasons for varying from His stated rules of acting than for adhering to them; and whenever this is the case, and the end proposed is proportionable to the means for accomplishing it, the miracles are worthy of a divine interposition. Nor does this imply any inconsistency in the divine conduct, or any defect or disturbance of the laws of nature. When the Deity occasionally controls or supersedes them, He does not hereby contradict or defeat His intention in their first establishment; He proposes a design different from it, but not inconsistent with it. The laws of nature being the laws of God, are certainly perfect—that is, perfectly adapted to answer all the uses for which they are designed; but miracles derogate not from this perfection, because they aim at an end which the laws of nature were not intended to answer."

To this just remark we must add, that both the ends proposed and the miracles wrought to obtain them, were from eternity known and present to the wisdom of God, and comprehended in the general plan of His operations, to be put in execution at the time appointed. This again shows that miracles, instead of derogating from this wisdom, still further display its immensity, which comprehends all things, foresees all things, and wonderfully adapts the means to the ends and designs proposed. I shall conclude this subject by inserting another passage from Mr Farmer, wherein he very judiciously sets forth the possibility of miracles with regard to the power of God.

"Infinite power, though it does not extend to contradictions, performs with ease whatever is possible in its nature. And so far are miraculous works from being impossible, that they are similar to what we see actually effected in the common course of divine providence. I will endeavour to illustrate this by the following example: To cause water to be both water and wine at the same time, is a manifest absurdity and contradiction, and therefore cannot be the object of any power; but to turn water into wine, or to change one liquid into another specifically different, is certainly within the reach of divine omnipotence, inasmuch as there is nothing contradictory in the idea of such transformation, and we observe continual changes of a like kind in many parts of the creation. Thus the moisture of the earth, by a common, but admirable operation in the natural world, is converted into the juice of the grape, and numberless other juices differing in kind from each other, according to the different nature of the plant or tree which imbibes it. This observation might be extended farther, and applied to other instances. Revelation itself is a miracle; but wherefore should it be thought impossible with God? To His inspiration we owe our understandings, with all their powers; from Him we derive the noble faculty of speech, by which we communicate our ideas to each other; and has the Father of our spirits no access to them, no ability of imparting immediately and directly the knowledge of His will, and of affording sufficient evidence of His own extraordinary presence and operation? Is there anything in this more inexplicable than in the common action of mind on body, and body on mind? Will any assert that the Almighty Author of our frame is unable to repair the disorders of it?—that He who, with such exquisite skill, formed the seeing eye and hearing ear, cannot restore sight to the blind, and hearing to the deaf? or that it is impossible for Him to raise the dead, who every year renews the face of nature, and revives the seed sown in the earth, and every day awakens mankind from the death of sleep to new life, in a manner as incomprehensible by us as the greatest miracle? He gave being to every living thing; to innumerable kinds of animals, and to a great diversity of rational creatures; continually does He call into existence ten thousand new individuals; and is the second gift of life more difficult than the first? The analogy between miracles and the common operations of God in the settled course of nature, is a convincing demonstration of the possibility of the former."

This passage is a specimen of the excellent abilities of Mr Farmer in solid reasoning, when he advocates a good cause. It excites our regret that, in his 'Dissertation upon Miracles,' he has employed his talents in advancing several statements, and in giving such explanations of the sacred Scriptures, as will not stand the test of sound theology.

CHAPTER IV.

THE ENDS FOR WHICH MIRACLES MAY BE WROUGHT, AS DISCOVERED BY REASON.

I. TO pretend to investigate all the various ends and particular designs which the divine wisdom has ever had, or may have, in performing miracles, would be presumptuous; for "who has known the sense of the Lord, or who hath been His counsellor?" Rom. xi. 14. Still it is important to examine what can be known with certainty on this head, not only because the enemies of Christianity assert that no good end can be attained by miracles, but also because some Christians seem to think this argument sufficient to disprove the continuation and existence of them in these later ages of the Church. They allege that, as the Gospel is now sufficiently confirmed and widely propagated, it seems unnecessary that God should any more interpose by miracles, and therefore they conclude that in fact He does not.

This argument assumes that the propagation and confirmation of the Gospel is the only end worthy of God's interposition; but even were this the case, the conclusion would not follow, seeing that the planting the Gospel among heathen nations, who have not yet received it, must require the assistance of miracles, as well as the first planting it did in those nations who have long since embraced it. The difficulties in this great work are no less now among heathen nations than they were at the beginning of Christianity; and the majority of men are still as incapable of understanding the rational arguments and proofs in favour of the Christian religion as our ancestors were at the time of their conversion : nor can it be thought that the present heathen world would give either the time or application necessary for examining these proofs, even though it had sufficient capacity for doing so.

But miracles are a language suited to all. They require no time nor application of study to comprehend them; they conquer at once, and convince at sight. They are the most certain means of gaining the ends intended, and of subduing the obstinacy of the heart of man. Even were it true, then, that the propagation of the Gospel was the only end worthy of God's interposing by miracles, still we might reasonably expect from a God of infinite goodness that He would continue from time to time to perform them, at least for the propagation of His Gospel among those heathen nations who as yet do not know Him. But if we reflect, we shall see that the propagation of the Gospel, though doubtless a very principal end of miracles, is by no means the only one, and that there are others which have been actually judged by God Himself worthy of such interposition.

II. First, from the very nature of miracles, as above explained, it is evident that no operation whatever, no possible effect produced in the creation, can be miraculous with regard to God, or wonderful in His sight. He thoroughly knows all that can be known concerning every possible effect or operation in His creatures, and also He possesses in Himself a power not only adequate, but infinitely superior, to every possible effect producible in them; so that nothing is either hard or difficult to Him. With the same ease that He maintains the present order in the universe, He can in a moment alter or destroy it. With the same ease that He created all things at the beginning, He can, if He pleases, reduce them again to nothing; and consequently, with respect to the almighty power of God, the most stupendous work in the creation is as easy as the smallest, and infinitely more so to Him than the throwing a stone upwards, contrary to the laws of gravity, is to man. It is enough that He wills anything to be done; and be it what it may, great or small, His all-powerful will is instantly obeyed.

Secondly, No change, alteration, or unusual effect produced in the material insensible part of the universe—merely as such, that is, when considered only in itself, without relation to sensible or intelligent creatures—can properly be called either good or evil. Our idea of evil seems always to include a relation to sensible or intelligent beings, and consists either in making them unhappy by suffering, or in bringing upon them moral guilt and turpitude, which is disgraceful to their nature, and renders them odious in the eyes of their Creator. The evil of guilt and the evil of suffering, therefore, are the only things we mean by the word evil, in the strict and proper acceptation of the term. Now these, it is plain, can have place only in intelligent creatures, and not in the mere material parts of the creation — the former only being capable of suffering or guilt, but not the latter. Whatever change or alteration can be produced in material beings, may alter their form, motion, or the configuration of their parts; but nothing of this enters into the proper idea of evil.

Thirdly, As the very essence of evil consists in rendering intelligent creatures guilty or miserable; so good, being the contrary of evil, is, properly speaking, whatever renders these creatures innocent, virtuous, or happy; and the more anything contributes to this, the greater and more excellent it is. Mr Hutchison, in his admirable treatise of moral philosophy, speaking on this subject, very justly observes, "that our moral sense or conscience is implanted in us by the Author of our being as the proper judge of what is good and evil, and that the several objects which this judge approves as good are only such as have these two qualities—a tendency to the happiness of others, and a tendency to the moral perfection of the mind possessing them; and that the objects which this judge condemns as evil, are such as have the contrary tendencies." From this we justly infer that no change or effect produced in the inanimate creation, which is incapable of moral perfection or of happiness, can properly be called either good or evil, and that these can have place only in sensible or intelligent creatures.

Fourthly, Our idea of God as a Being infinitely perfect, convinces us that He must essentially approve and desire the moral excellence and virtuous perfection of His creatures; and that the procuring this is an object worthy of His divine goodness and sanctity. On the contrary, we feel that He must detest and abhor moral turpitude in His creatures, and that to prohibit and prevent this is highly becoming His divine goodness and sanctity. In fact, what is this moral sense or conscience implanted in us by the Creator but the promulgation of His law in our hearts—the manifestation of His will, declaring in the most touching manner what He requires from us—the most intimate and convincing proof that He wills our moral excellence and perfection, and severely prohibits our moral turpitude? The whole exterior manifestation of His will to man by revelation, both in the old and new law, proves this truth, as the uniform tendency of revelation is to exhort, persuade, encourage, and assist us to advance and improve our souls in virtue and perfection, and to prohibit and deter us from the contrary.

Fifthly, Our idea of God, as a Being of infinite goodness, convinces us that He can never directly will the misery of His creatures in itself. In our sufferings, merely as such, He cannot possibly have pleasure. He must essentially desire and will the happiness of His creatures as an object most becoming the supreme mind, and most worthy His infinite goodness: and if at any time He inflicts sufferings upon His creatures, and renders them for a time unhappy, we cannot conceive that He rests in this as the ultimate object of His complacency, but must have in view some other end more congenial to His infinite perfections; and the light of reason points out two such ends, either in goodness procuring the moral perfection of His creatures, their greatest good, or punishing them in justice for having voluntarily, and therefore culpably, incurred the guilt of moral turpitude. Revelation also confirms this in the strongest terms; for through the whole series of the sacred Scriptures we find Almighty God everywhere represented as having the most tender love and concern for His creatures, earnestly desiring their happiness, and doing all on His part, without infringing the freedom of their will, to procure it. It is true that these same sacred writings do also sometimes represent Him in the most awful colours, as threatening or inflicting the most dreadful sufferings upon His creatures; but then we are assured that He does so against His inclinations, forced to it by their crimes, and that even then His chief design is their greater good, to reclaim them from their evil ways, and to secure their eternal happiness. To procure the good of His creatures, then, both by rendering them happy and by promoting their moral excellence and perfection, is an object worthy of God. This is our very idea of God, and it is confirmed by His own express declaration in holy writ.

Sixthly, With regard to the material insensible creation, however, the case is very different. We have seen above that the present order established in the universe, and the laws of nature by which that order is maintained, are not in themselves essentially necessary, but depend entirely upon the free choice of Almighty God. It is true that God did not make this choice without the most consummate wisdom, according to the wise ends which He had in view; neither can we suppose that He will capriciously alter the laws and order which He has once established; but then, as they are not self-necessary, but depend entirely upon His will, it cannot be denied that He may alter, change, or even annihilate them, if and when He pleases.

The material world, as far as our reason can discover, is in itself perfectly indifferent to exist in its present form or in any other, to be guided by its present laws or by any other; nor can we imagine of good or evil accruing to material or insensible creatures, whatever change or alteration may happen in their forms, or in those laws of nature by which they are at present regulated. It is indifferent to a particle of matter whether it be employed to compose the sun or the meanest object, whether it shines in the form of gold or is trampled under foot in the form of dust. It is neither more or less happy, more or less virtuous, in the one case than in the other; because it is incapable either of happiness or misery, vice or virtue. Neither can we possibly imagine that any change in matter, or its laws, should in the least degree affect the happiness of God, to whom, considering it only with regard to His own happiness, and independently of any particular design He may have in view, it must be perfectly indifferent whether the material world be of this form or of that, be guided by its present laws or by any other, or, indeed, whether it has an existence or not.

From this it follows that the whole material creation, and its present order and laws, are not in themselves the immediate and ultimate objects of the divine will, intended by Almighty God; they are only the means for procuring those ends which the divine wisdom had in view to be obtained by them. They are therefore neither good nor evil in themselves, but only in so far as they conduce to promote or to impede the ends for which they exist.

III. The preservation or suspension, then, of the laws of nature, is neither good nor evil in itself, but only in so far as it conduces to or hinders some good end. On the other hand, as the happiness or moral perfection of intelligent creatures is a real good, and their misery or moral turpitude a real evil, the suspending the laws of nature, in order to procure these ends, is truly worthy of the divine wisdom and goodness. And if it be worthy of Almighty God even to suspend the general laws of the creation in order to obtain those ends, it is no less so to exert His almighty power in producing other effects in the material world superior to the power of all created agents when such are necessary; that is, to procure the happiness or moral perfection of intelligent creatures, and to prevent their misery and moral turpitude, are ends truly worthy of the divine interposition, even by *miracle*.

IV. But to place this in a still clearer light, let us consider what are the ends of the divine wisdom in creating this universe, and in establishing its present laws and order. For if at any time a suspension of these laws, or an alteration of the present order, might be required for more easily procuring these ends, it would then not only be becoming and worthy the divine goodness and wisdom so to suspend the laws, or alter the present order of things, but to do so would even be in some degree incumbent upon Him. If in this inquiry we find that the procuring the happiness and perfection of intelligent creatures was certainly one of the principal, if not the ultimate end of the creation, the above conclusion will appear still more evident.

V. Now, whether we examine this subject by the light of reason only, taking a view of those beneficent purposes which manifestly appear throughout the whole creation, or by the light of revelation, we shall see that this is actually the case—namely, that the happiness of intelligent creatures is one of the principal, if not the ultimate end of the creation. For, first, let us suppose that there were no rational or intelligent creatures upon earth—nothing but inanimate matter and the brute creation—what idea can we form of such a work from the hand of an all-wise and an all-powerful Being! Can we regard it in any way becoming such a Being to create such a world? What satisfaction can we imagine it could give Him to see inanimate matter formed and moved in such and such a manner, and a number of irrational creatures, without judgment or reflection, existing on the face of the earth? Could the actual existence of such a world make the smallest difference to Him in point of happiness? For my own part, I cannot imagine that it should; and to me it would seem altogether unbecoming a Being of infinite perfection to create such a world.

But suppose rational and intelligent creatures placed in this world, and immediately everything is changed. These are capable of knowing the God who made them, of understanding the wise and beneficent purposes which shine forth in His works, of rising up thence to a sense of His amiable perfections, of admiring, loving, serving, praising, and adoring their great Creator, and of enjoying a sublime happiness, almost a divine pleasure, in so doing. The feelings of our heart tell us that to receive such voluntary and just service from intelligent and free creatures must be agreeable to the Creator, and a source of joy and happiness to Him, and consequently worthy of Him to procure for Himself; also that to make such creatures happy, and to provide for them all the means necessary for being so, is no less worthy the infinite goodness of this sovereign mind, and must afford new joy and pleasure to Himself, and therefore is an object becoming Him to procure.

From this we justly conclude, "that rational and intelligent creatures are the chief, the most excellent part of the creation; that without them all the rest would be to little or no purpose; that they are the principal objects of the care and attention of the Creator; that all inferior beings are made only to be, either mediately or immediately, subservient to their happiness and perfection, and can have no end but for this purpose; and consequently, that the happiness and perfection of intelligent creatures is one of the greatest, if not the ultimate end of the creation."

VI. If, again, we take a view of that portion of the works of God which falls under our observation, how strongly will not this lead us to the same conclusion? For what do we find in all the creatures that surround us but the most manifest and convincing proofs that the grand intention of Almighty God in their creation was, that they might all concur and co-operate to the happiness and moral excellence of man? With what admirable design, with what consummate wisdom, are they formed to promote our comfort, by supplying our wants, relieving our necessities, and contributing to our pleasure and contentment; to our moral excellence and perfection, by displaying to our understanding the infinite power, wisdom, and goodness of their Creator, and by engaging our hearts from the most powerful motives of duty and gratitude to love, serve, praise, and adore the kind, the beneficent Author of our happiness! It is true, indeed, that the malice of the heart of man too often perverts creatures from those great ends for which they were created, prostituting them, in the most ungrateful manner, to the very worst of purposes; but this does not in the least degree alter our view of the original design of Almighty God in creating them. That design still shines forth in the midst of all the bad uses to which the wickedness of man perverts them; and the rational and impartial inquirer must still confess, "that the happiness and moral excellence of man is one of the greatest, if not the ultimate end for which they have their being."

VII. I say, *if not the ultimate end*, because reason alone, unassisted by revelation, though it clearly discerns that the happiness and perfection of man must be one of the chief ends for which the material world was created, not being able to penetrate farther with certainty, finds many difficulties in concluding it to be the ultimate or only end. These difficulties arise from that deluge of moral turpitude which overspreads the earth, and the numberless miseries to which human nature is exposed; and the solution of them can only be obtained from revelation. But if we have recourse to its light, we shall find that it dispels the difficulties of natural reason, confirms the conclusion which reason makes, improves her light, and sets the subject in the clearest point of view.

According to revelation, the design of Almighty God in creating the universe is as follows. That the first, the principal, the ultimate end which He had in view in giving existence to creatures was His own pleasure, His own honour and glory—to display the magnificence of His divine perfections and excellences to beings capable of knowing them, and to receive from them that homage of service and praise which their essential dependence upon Him, and His divine perfections, justly demand from them. Thus we are expressly taught in holy writ that " the Lord hath made all things for Himself," Prov. xvi. 4. Again, that His primary and chief design was to procure this ultimate end of the creation, His own glory, by the moral excellence and happiness of His rational creatures and their voluntary service. For this purpose He endows them with free-will, instructs them both by the light of reason placed within their breasts, and also by the external revelation of His will wherein this their perfection consists. He gives them every help necessary for acquiring it. He engages them to apply themselves earnestly to the pursuit of it by the most sacred promises of making them eternally and perfectly happy. He deters them from the contrary by threatening them with the most dreadful of all conceivable miseries; declares to them in the most amiable manner His infinite goodness and love. He assures them that He wills not their death nor misery, but, on the contrary, that He most ardently desires their eternal life and happiness, and has given them the strongest proofs of the sincerity of this desire in what He has done and suffered for them. Having, however, made them free agents, He will not force them, but leaves them to their own choice to comply or not with this great end of their creation, the promoting His honour and glory by means of their own perfection and happiness.

But if they refuse to comply with what their great Creator thus bounteously demands from them—if, abusing their liberty, they refuse to promote His honour and glory by their own perfection and happiness—will His views be disappointed? will His intentions be frustrated? will He be deprived of that glory which He proposed to Himself by creating them? No, this is impossible. God created them for His own glory, which He absolutely wills to procure by His creatures; and to this grand, to this ultimate end, they must all co-operate. His primary intention, His first desire is, that they should do so by means of their own perfection and happiness; but if, abusing their free-will, they refuse to comply with this, He then has recourse to a secondary intention, which is to inflict sufferings and misery upon them as the just punishment of their ingratitude and infidelity; and thus, whilst they refuse to glorify His goodness and mercy, He obliges them to exalt and set forth the glory of His justice.

VIII. To cite here the numberless testimonies of holy writ wherein Almighty God has made known to us these His views and ends in creating this universe, would carry us to too great a length; nor, indeed, is it necessary, seeing that they are interwoven with the whole history of revealed truth. But, from what is said, we see a clear and full solution of those difficulties, which reason alone could not penetrate. We see the cause of that deluge of vice and immorality which has overspread the world through the abuse of that liberty which God has bestowed upon us as free agents; and we see also whence all those miseries flow under which we daily groan—namely, not from any want of goodness in God, who takes no pleasure in our sufferings as such, but from the malice of our own hearts in abusing our liberty, which forces Almighty God, contrary to His primary intention, to inflict these sufferings upon us as the just punishment of our crimes.

From these principles it follows: "That rational and intelligent creatures are the chief and most excellent part of the creation; that without them all the rest are of little or no importance; that they are the principal object of the care and attention of the Creator; that all inferior beings are made only to be, either mediately or immediately, subservient to their happiness and perfection, and can have no end but for this purpose. Consequently, since all inferior creatures, and of course the whole present order and laws of nature, are established only as subservient to the above great ends, it is not only reasonable, but highly becoming and worthy of the infinite wisdom and goodness of God, to suspend any of these laws, to alter the present order of things, or to perform any other miraculous effects which He pleases, when the promotion of His own honour and glory, either by procuring the happiness and perfection of His rational creatures, or by averting their misery and moral turpitude, or even by inflicting just punishments upon them, may require Him to do so. Nay, should the case happen wherein these ends could not so properly nor so perfectly be acquired by ordinary means, it would then be not only becoming Almighty God, but even in some manner incumbent upon Him, to work a miracle in order to procure them."

IX. But perhaps it will be asked, May not the divine wisdom procure these ends sufficiently by natural and ordinary means, without having recourse to miracles?

In answer to this we must observe, that all I have affirmed in the former part of the above conclusion is, that the procuring moral good, and preventing moral evil, are objects truly worthy of the divine interposition, even by miracles. God may procure them indeed by natural means, if and when He pleases; but they are in themselves so valuable as to be an immediate object of the divine will; whereas the preserving or suspending the laws of nature is by no means a primary object of God's desire, nor does it contain either good or evil in itself, irrespective of the end to be obtained by it. If, then, the former good ends can be better or more easily attained by a temporary suspension of these laws, or by any other supernatural operation, it would be highly reasonable, and most becoming the divine wisdom, so to suspend these laws, or perform that operation in order to procure them. And should it at any time happen that these ends could not be obtained by ordinary natural means, it would in some manner be incumbent on Almighty God, if He willed the ends, to perform the miracle in order to obtain them.

To us, however, it does not belong to judge what are the most proper means to be employed, whether natural or miraculous. To God they are both equally easy; and the Christian religion assures us that sometimes He uses one and sometimes the other—sometimes He procures the sanctity and perfection of His servants by ordinary and natural means, and sometimes He employs miraculous and supernatural means for this purpose, as He in His wisdom judges proper. But it cannot be denied that it is most becoming the divine goodness and wisdom to use the means for attaining His views which are most proper and conducive thereto. Now it is certain that miraculous interpositions of the divine power are much more efficacious for procuring moral good, and preventing moral evil, in intelligent creatures, than all the natural means by the agency of secondary causes. The reason of this is plain; because, though surrounding objects present us with numberless proofs of the divine perfections, and call upon us to love and serve their great Creator, yet by custom they become familiar, and the mind being habituated to them, ceases to attend to the great instructions they convey. But a miracle rouses our attention, awakens us from our lethargy, makes the divine presence more sensible to us, and excites in our minds pious sentiments and affections of respect, fear, veneration, love, and gratitude, which the wonderful things around us would also do, did they not by custom lose their power and efficacy.

It is a most incomprehensible effect of the divine power and goodness to multiply a few grains when sown in the earth to such an amazing quantity of corn as to afford food for thousands; but being used to see this every day we think nothing of it, and seldom or never take occasion from it to conceive in our hearts suitable affections to the great Author of so stupendous a benefit. But were these natural and ordinary means to fail, as in time of famine, and should God then, by his almighty power, multiply a handful of meal in our granaries so as amply to supply our wants till plenty should return to the land, what sentiments would this excite in our hearts! what admiration, what thanks, what gratitude, love, confidence, and the like! And why? Not because this latter is more difficult to Almighty God than the former, or a greater effort of His power—not because it is more wonderful in itself—but because it is uncommon, more strikingly shows the hand of God, and makes us more sensible both of His divine presence and power, and of His infinite goodness towards us.

X. The learned authors of the 'Christian Magazine,' in their dissertations entitled "The Truth of the Christian Religion Vindicated," p. 159, speak on this subject as follows: "Without doubt the general order of nature perfectly displays the greatness of the Supreme Being; but this order, thus perpetual and constant, shouts to the deafest ears, and speaks aloud to the most obdurate hearts. This is a continual miracle, and one that comprehends a multitude of miracles; but yet in vain does it seek to call back mortals to the knowledge of their Maker.

"We are accustomed to every object in nature; the great wonders of the world are fallen into a kind of disparagement and disregard, and no longer strike our attention, because they are ever present. It is the same God who every day works all those miracles wherewith nature is replete, and those which are less common and more remarkable. But because custom induces forgetfulness of the grandeur of the former; because mankind, diverted by many objects, no longer attend to ordinary events, or take occasion from them to elevate their minds to their Almighty Dispenser, and to render Him that worship which therefore is so justly His due; on these accounts, and in amazing condescension to our weakness, He hath graciously reserved certain extraordinary events, which He assiduously takes care from time to time to produce, with a view to arouse mankind from their lethargy of negligence. If these less usual miracles have a more striking effect upon us than others, it is not that they are more excellent than those of which we are daily spectators, but that, being less frequent, they render us more sensible of the presence of their Author."

Seeing, therefore, that miracles are thus a much more powerful means to procure the moral perfection of intelligent beings than the ordinary means from secondary causes, it follows not only that Almighty God may procure these good ends by such miraculous operations, but that it is most worthy of His divine goodness, and highly becoming His infinite power and wisdom from time to time to do so.

CHAPTER V.

THE ENDS OF MIRACLES AS DISCLOSED BY REVELATION.

I. HAVING seen by the light of reason the ends which appear worthy to be procured by miracles, we now proceed to examine what revelation points out on this subject. Several of the principles which we have made use of are not only evident to reason, but also conformable to revelation. This gives them a double value, and will put the conclusion we have drawn beyond contradiction, if, upon further inquiry, we shall find that it is the very same which revelation itself discloses to us. That this is really the case may, I think, be easily proved by an argument the most convincing; I mean the consideration of facts related and attested by God Himself in the Holy Scriptures.

There cannot be a more certain way of knowing what is becoming Almighty God to do than to consider what He has already done; and as He has performed among His people numbers of miracles in different ages, which He has carefully recorded in His Holy Scriptures for our instruction, if we attentively consider the ends for which these miracles were wrought, and which were actually attained by them, we must conclude that they were most worthy of the divine interposition, because expressly judged by almighty wisdom itself to be so. And if we farther see that these ends are the very same which, by the light of reason, we have found worthy of such interposition, this will illustrate the above conclusion of reason in the most convincing manner, and place it beyond all doubt, at least to those who believe the Holy Scriptures. But before we proceed to the facts themselves, it will be proper to premise a few observations on the moral perfection of intelligent creatures.

II. First, then, as Almighty God is a Being of infinite perfection, and cannot possibly contradict Himself by willing anything contrary to His own divine perfection, it follows that the divine will is the sovereign rule and standard of all perfection and righteousness. Consequently our perfection as rational and intelligent creatures must consist in our resemblance to God—that is, in our thinking and acting conformably to His will, in entertaining such sentiments, and in pursuing such a tenor of conduct as He requires of us; and the more we resemble God in this respect, the more holy, the more righteous, the more perfect we become. That is what our blessed Saviour so earnestly recommends to us when He says, "Be ye perfect, as your heavenly Father is perfect;" and which He explains and confirms by His own example when He assures us, that "His meat was to do the will of Him that sent Him;" and that this was the very ultimate end of His incarnation,—" I came down from heaven not to do my own will, but to do the will of Him that sent me."

Secondly, When we consider the divine perfections, we immediately perceive certain corresponding dispositions and affections in our own heart, and the necessity of a corresponding mode of action naturally resulting from them. These dispositions appear to us natural consequences of the divine perfections from which they flow, and justly due to that sovereign Being in whom these perfections reside. Thus the infinite power of God demands from us respect and veneration; His infinite justice inspires a dread and fear of offending Him; His infinite veracity, a firm and unshaken belief in His word; His infinite sanctity, pious veneration; His infinite wisdom, perfect submission to the orders and dispositions of His providence; His infinite goodness and the innumerable benefits bestowed upon us, demand our most ardent love, gratitude, and confidence in Him; His sovereign dominion our most profound subjection and entire obedience;—and all these His divine perfections together essentially require, on our part, the most perfect resignation to His holy will, and an absolute and entire dependence upon Him in everything.

The connection between these divine perfections and their corresponding dispositions in ourselves, is evident at first sight to all who understand the terms, and the light by which we perceive it is a constitutional part of human nature. This stands in no need of arguments to prove it. It convinces as much as any first principle whatever the moment it is proposed and understood. This connection, then, is real. The divine perfections do actually require these corresponding duties and affections from us. This is the proper worship due to God from His creatures; it is therefore His will that we render it to Him, and our perfection consists in doing so.

The same observations hold good with regard to our feelings of the nature and obligation of our other moral duties, of which Mr Beattie, in his 'Essay on Truth,' very justly says: "The performance of certain actions, and the indulgence of certain affections, is attended with an agreeable feeling of a peculiar kind, which I call moral approbation; different actions and affections excite the opposite feeling of moral disapprobation. To relieve distress I find to be meritorious and praiseworthy; to pick a pocket I know to be blamable, and worthy of punishment. I am conscious that some actions are in my power, that others are not; that when I neglect to do what I ought to do, and can do, I deserve to be punished; and that when I act necessarily, or upon unavoidable and irresistible compulsion, I deserve neither punishment nor blame.

"Of all these sentiments I am as conscious and as certain as I am of my own existence. I cannot prove that I feel them, neither to myself nor to others; but that I do really feel them, is as evident to me as demonstration could make it. I ought to be grateful for a favour received. Why? Because my conscience tells me so. How do you know you ought to do that of which your conscience enjoins the performance? I can give no further reason for it, but that I feel that such is my duty. And here the investigation must stop; or, if carried a little further, it must return to this point—I know that I ought to do what my conscience enjoins, because God is the Author of my constitution, and I obey His will when I act according to the principles of my constitution. Why do you obey the will of God? Because it is my duty. How do you know that? Because my conscience tells me so," &c.—Part I. § 3.

To these just reflections we must further add, that we not only feel within us this sense of moral duty, this *something* which impels us to do or to avoid certain actions, and to cherish or repress certain affections; but, when we are conscious to ourselves of possessing these affections, and of acting conformably to them, we immediately feel the approbation of this internal monitor attended with a peaceful joy of mind; and when we possess them not, or act against them, we are instantly punished by self-condemnation and remorse for having acted in a manner contrary to our duty, and unworthy of the dignity of our nature. The result of all these observations is, that the perfection of our nature consists in entertaining such dispositions, and in following such a line of conduct, as are agreeable to the will of our Creator, and such as He, our Sovereign Master, manifests to us by this light which He has placed within us.

Thirdly, If we examine what Almighty God has declared to us by revelation, we shall find that it perfectly coincides with this. "Let us hear," says He by the mouth of the wise man, "the conclusion of the whole matter: fear God and keep His commandments, for this is the whole of man," Eccles. xii.—that is, his whole duty, his whole happiness, his whole perfection; in a word, his *all*. And, indeed, throughout the whole Scriptures, what do we find required of mankind by the great Author of our being but to believe in Him, to fear Him, to hope in Him, to thank and praise Him, to obey and serve Him, and, which comprises all other duties in one word, to love and prefer Him above all things, and to be ready to leave all things rather than, by sin, to offend and lose Him? In the practice of these holy virtues consists the perfection of our duty, and consequently in the same consists the perfection of our souls.

Fourthly, Had we no other feelings or inclinations in our hearts than these, it would be easy to comply with duty, and to render that just tribute of obedience and love which is so strictly due to our Creator. But this is far from being the case; for we feel within ourselves another principle—a violent propensity to things which our moral sense condemns. This strongly tends to turn our affections from God and to attach them to creatures. It induces us to seek happiness in sensual gratifications, opposed to the duties dictated by conscience. This inclination of the heart, which is called the sensual appetite, and our moral sense or conscience being contrary to each other, are at perpetual variance, and excite within us that war which is so afflicting to pious souls, and which St Paul so pathetically describes from his own experience: "I know," says he, "that in me (that is, in my flesh) dwelleth no good thing: for to will is present with me, but how to perform that which is good, I find not: for the good that I would I do not, but the evil which I would not, that I do. ... I delight in the law of God after the inward man: but I see another law in my members, warring against the law of my mind, and bringing me into captivity to the law of sin which is in my members. O wretched man that I am! who shall deliver me from the body of this death?" Rom. vii.

As these two principles are thus so opposed, we cannot satisfy both; and the more we encourage and gratify the one, the more we depress and weaken the other. Hence it is impossible that our Creator should have implanted both in our nature with the intention that they should both be fully indulged and gratified. The question then is, Which of the two ought we to hear, and which ought we to reject? A little reflection will easily enable us to answer these questions.

1st, The moral sense is always attended with the feeling that it is our duty to obey its call; whereas the sensual appetite has no such conviction connected with it, but consists in a blind impetuous inclination of the heart towards its sensual objects.

2dly, Compliance with the dictates of conscience is always followed by internal approbation, and a sense of having done well; and this approbation is the greater the more violent have been the solicitations of sensuality against our doing so. But when we indulge the inclinations of the sensual appetite, we experience no such self-approbation; on the contrary, we are tormented by self-condemnation and remorse, which is always the more severe the greater the length we have gone in sensual gratification.

Lastly, The most noble and exalted idea which we can form of human nature is that of a person guided solely by the dictates of conscience, and never influenced by selfish and sensual motives in his conduct; and on the other hand, the most despicable idea which we can conceive of man is to suppose a person enslaved to his passions, and totally lost to every sense of duty or moral virtue. It is plain, therefore, that our moral sense is placed within us as the delegate of God Himself, to be our guide, and that it ought to be our constant care to follow its dictates, and to subdue all risings of the sensual appetite opposed to its voice.

Fifthly, This the light of revelation confirms; for by it we are assured that at the beginning man was not created with such contrary principles within him, but that the opposition to duty which we now experience from sensuality, is owing to the fall of our nature from its original rectitude by sin; that the rebellion of sensuality is a defect within us which it ought to be our daily study to correct; that our perfection consists in opposing and subduing its corrupt desires, and thus asserting the liberty of our souls, that we may with greater ease and ardour be united to our Creator, and render Him that worship and homage which He requires. But to accomplish this is as difficult as it is important.

Our blessed Saviour calls it doing violence to ourselves. St Paul, with all the saints, complains of the pain which this spiritual warfare cost him; and experience daily shows, from the small number of those who have courage in earnest to undertake and persevere in it, and from the many rude assaults sustained by those who do, how arduous is the task to overcome this our corrupt nature. But how glorious the victory!

On the other hand, Almighty God ardently desires that we should gain this victory, because it alone can entitle us to the incorruptible crown of glory, for none shall be crowned but he who has lawfully fought. On His part, He leaves nothing undone to encourage and enable us to make this sacred conquest. He excites us to it by commands; by the most affectionate solicitation; by threatening the worst of evils if we neglect it; by promising us the greatest happiness if we obtain it; by assuring us that he is ever at hand to aid us, and "will never suffer us to be tempted above what we are able to bear," but, if we be not wanting on our part, "will always give us strength to come off with victory," 1 Cor. x. Besides, He declares in His own sacred Word, that in order more effectually to engage his people in this warfare, and to enable them to resist their sensuality, and promote the perfection of their souls, He has at various times been pleased to perform the most stupendous and amazing miracles. From this our conclusion necessarily follows, that to procure the moral perfection of our souls is an object worthy of the divine interposition, and which Almighty God Himself judges to be such, having actually wrought many miracles for that end.

Sixthly, When we consider the incomprehensible and endless bliss prepared for the good, and the eternal punishment which awaits the wicked in the next life, it will readily be admitted that all we can enjoy or suffer in this world is a mere nothing; and consequently, that it is a matter of the smallest moment what may be our state in this our mortal pilgrimage provided we only escape hell and obtain heaven at the end of life. What did all the wealth and enjoyments of the rich man avail him when at death he was buried in hell, where he could not command a single drop of water to cool his parched tongue? On the contrary, what worse was Lazarus for all his sufferings in this life, when at death his soul was carried to a place of rest and peace, and put in possession of the fulness of celestial joy and happiness?

As we are placed in this world, therefore, for no other end than to work out and secure our salvation, and as all the goods and evils of this life are so disposed by divine providence that they may serve as means for acquiring this end, it is a certain truth, that in no other respect do they deserve to be valued or esteemed than as they conduce to our avoiding eternal misery, and acquiring eternal happiness. If, therefore, the abundance of the goods of this life should prove to us, as to the rich man, a hindrance to that great end, we ought doubtless to regard them as the greatest evils. But if, on the contrary, the sufferings of this life should prove the means of more effectually securing our salvation, as was the case with Lazarus, we ought to esteem them as the greatest and most valuable blessings.

It is true, indeed, that a great degree of Christian perfection is required to have an experimental conviction of this truth; and it must be owned that the majority of mankind are chiefly affected by present goods and evils. We are naturally bent on procuring and enjoying present goods, as if we were capable of no other happiness; and we shrink from present sufferings, as if they were the only real evils. In consequence of this natural disposition of our hearts, nothing makes a greater impression upon us than to be plentifully supplied with the goods of this world, and to be delivered from its sufferings; and when this disposition does not prove a hindrance to our eternal happiness, but is regulated by reason and religion, it is far from being blamable, and may be made subservient to the best of purposes.

This constitution of the human mind Almighty God well knows, and, condescending with amazing goodness to our weakness, He employs it as a means to engage us to His service by promising to bestow upon us all the necessary things of this life, and to preserve us from its evils, so far as is consistent with our eternal happiness, if we continue faithful and obedient to Him. And in order to impress us more effectually by this promise, He has been pleased, on many occasions, so to order miracles wrought in favour of His servants, for the advancement of their souls in virtue, that they should at the same time procure them temporal blessings, or deliver them from temporal sufferings and dangers. Thus miracles make a deeper impression on the mind, and excite those pious sentiments of gratitude and love which God requires from us. On the other hand, He not only threatens obdurate sinners with temporal evils, to deter them from their wicked ways, but He has even judged it worthy of Himself to work surprising miracles in punishment of sinners, both with a view to their conversion, and from their example to excite a salutary fear in the hearts of others. This I shall now proceed to show from the facts themselves.

III. In the beginning, when God created man, He gave him a full and sufficient knowledge of his Maker, and of the service which he owed to Him. But when man, in process of time, from the corruption of his heart by sin, forgot his God and revolted from His service, the

Supreme Being was pleased to make choice of one nation, which by a particular dispensation of His providence He would preserve from the general corruption, and always maintain constant in the knowledge and service of the true God. This chosen people had been long oppressed in a cruel manner by the Egyptians, who kept them in slavery, till at last the time arrived when the God of their fathers was resolved not only to deliver them from their bondage, but also to give them an ample external revelation of His will, and of the worship and service which He required of them—that is, to plant among them His true religion, and to teach them the way to true happiness here and hereafter.

For this several things were necessary. First, to convince them that it was He Himself, the God of heaven and earth, who declared His will to them; secondly, to induce them to receive and obey His will so manifested to them; and, thirdly, to do this in a manner adapted to the constitution of the human heart, by interesting the affections, especially those of love, hope, and fear, in the performance of what he required of them. Now, to gain these ends, we find that Almighty God was pleased to employ miracles, and such a profusion of them, as plainly shows how much He esteems the moral perfection of the soul of man, though it should require the subversion of the most general laws of nature to procure it. For this purpose He makes choice of His servant Moses; appears to him in the wilderness in a miraculous manner in a burning bush; tells him who He is, what He is about to do for His people, and His intention to employ him as His instrument for that end.

Had Moses at once consented, had he been pleased with the charge conferred upon him, it might have been alleged that this was a delusion, and that he was only the dupe of his own imagination. But so far is this from being the case, that Moses, on hearing the intention of God, is alarmed, objects to the proposal, refuses to undertake the charge, and makes excuses from the difficulty of the enterprise, his own unfitness, and lastly, from the dispositions of the people, who would give no credit to him, a person who had long been absent from them, and of course was little known, except perhaps by name, to the greater number.

To obviate these difficulties, to convince Moses himself that this was the work of God, and at the same time to give him credentials to the people, what does the Almighty do? He makes use of miracles as the proper means for this purpose. He turns the rod of Moses into a serpent, and then into a rod again. He in an instant makes his hand white with leprosy, and immediately restores it to its former soundness. And these miracles He not only performs before Moses for his own satisfaction, but He also gives him the power of performing them before the people for their conviction. For thus He speaks to him after turning his rod into a serpent, "That they may believe that the Lord God of their fathers, the God of Abraham, the God of Isaac, the God of Jacob, hath appeared unto thee," Exod. iv. 5. A little after He tells him, that if the people should not give credit to these first signs, then he should turn the water of the river, when poured out upon the dry land, into red blood in their presence.

By these miracles Moses is convinced, he undertakes the charge, goes to the people, delivers his commission, and performs the miracles as his credentials. These had immediately the desired effect; for when the people were called together, and " Aaron spoke all these words which the Lord had spoken unto Moses, and *did the signs* in the sight of the people, the people believed, and bowed down their heads and worshipped," Exod. iv. 30, 31.

IV. Here, then, one main point was gained by means of miracles. The people of Israel were convinced that Moses was sent by the God of their fathers to deliver them from their present misery, and to carry them to the promised land. This, it is true, was the easiest part of the commission given to Moses. The affliction under which the people groaned, their ardent desire to be delivered, the expectation which they had that their deliverance would certainly come, and that they should be freed from that Egyptian slavery, and brought to the possession of that land which had been so often promised to their fathers, would dispose their minds readily to embrace every proposal, and to give credit to every appearance of the approach of that happiness which they expected and desired.

But it was not equally easy to convince Pharaoh. He had no favourable opinion of Moses or his commission. On the contrary, he had the strongest bias against it, both from his religious principles and from his worldly interest. Accordingly, though Almighty God commanded the same miracles to be wrought in his presence which had convinced the Israelites (see Exod. vii.), they made no impression upon him; nay, he looked upon them all as impostures, and called in his own magicians, who by their enchantments performed the same things that Moses did.

Observe here the admirable conduct of divine providence. God permits this opposition of Pharaoh. He permits the magicians to exert their utmost power, and to imitate the miracles wrought in His name, in order to show their determined will to oppose what He required, and their aversion to any design of favouring Moses, which might have been suspected had they at once acknowledged the divinity of his commission and his miracles. But after permitting this contest for a time, God at last asserts His own honour, works by the hand of His servant miracles, which far exceeded all the power of the magicians, and forced from the mouth of these His declared enemies an express acknowledgment, "that the finger of God was there."

Nothing could be more honourable to the cause of God than this confession, nothing more convincing to His people that Moses was sent by Him, and consequently nothing could more powerfully prepare their minds and hearts for receiving the religion which He was about to reveal to them by the hands of this His holy servant. But Almighty God was pleased to do still more. Pharaoh, by permission of God's unsearchable judgments, still hardens his heart, and God immediately works other wonders. Pharaoh's hardness of heart proceeded chiefly from his worldly interest, which rendered him unwilling to comply with what God required in letting the people go, lest they might not return, and he be deprived of their service; therefore does God work such miracles as served both to prove the divine commission of Moses, and at the same time to punish Pharaoh in those things in which he had sinned, by destroying his country, his cattle, his goods, and his people, in order the more readily to move his stubborn heart, and extort his consent to what God required of him.

In these miracles we observe, first, that generally they were above all the power of the magicians; secondly, that frequently they were foretold before they happened; thirdly, that they were taken away at the exact time appointed, and this appointment was sometimes left to Pharaoh's own choice; fourthly, that they were commonly performed at the word of Moses; fifthly, that a distinction was made between the Egyptians and the people of God, who were freed from the plagues with which the former were afflicted; sixthly, that this last circumstance was foretold and accomplished, as Almighty God Himself says to Pharaoh, "that thou mayest know that I am the Lord in the midst of the earth," Exod. viii. 22.

These circumstances clearly proved by whom these miracles were wrought, and evidently tended to imprint in the minds of Pharaoh and his servants, as well as of God's people, the most thorough conviction that the Lord was the only true God, and that Moses was His servant commissioned and sent by Him. And God Himself assures us that for this very purpose He wrought these miracles, attended with all their circumstances; for thus He says to Pharaoh, "I will at this time send all my plagues upon thy heart, and upon thy servants, and upon thy people, that thou mayest know there is none like me on all the earth," Exod. ix. 14. And to His own people He says, that He showed all these signs before Pharaoh, "that thou mayest tell in the ears of thy son, and of thy son's son, what things I have wrought in Egypt, and my signs which I have done amongst them, that ye may know that I am the Lord," Exod. x. 1, 2.

V. In this manner does Almighty God show how He esteems the sanctification of His rational creatures an end worthy of His interposition; and here we see also how admirably His infinite wisdom adapts His miracles to the end proposed. He knew the hardness of Pharaoh's heart, and the source whence it arose. It was necessary, therefore, that the miracles wrought, besides convincing him that Moses was sent from God, should strike at the root of the evil, and bend his heart to a compliance with the divine will. He knew also the rudeness of his own people, their obstinacy, their proneness to the superstitions of the Egyptians, and how ready they would be, upon all occasions, to forsake His service. It was necessary, therefore, that the miracles wrought to prove that the commission of Moses was from God Himself, should not barely be sufficient for this purpose, as was the turning the rod into a serpent, making his hand leprous, and changing water into blood; but also that they should be calculated to impress the minds of the people—to convince them that it was their only true interest to serve their God—to inspire them with confidence in Him, and with a salutary dread and fear of offending Him.

How admirably calculated for this were the wonders wrought! The particular protection shown to His people, the visible line drawn between them and the Egyptians, the design of their deliverance intended by all these wonders, and the actual accomplishment of it at last, were doubtless the most convincing proofs how much they were the favourites of heaven, and what happiness they might expect by faithfully serving that God Who had done such great things for them. On the other hand, the severe and dreadful punishments inflicted on Pharaoh for his disobedience, could not fail to imprint in their hearts the deepest sentiments of fear and dread of offending, by showing them what they might expect if they should follow his example. And as Moses was the person by whom God was to make known His will to His people, and it was necessary that they should entertain the utmost reverence for him as the ambassador of God, all these miracles are wrought at his word. Nature seems to be entirely at his command. He foretells the punishment to be inflicted on Pharaoh for refusing to obey the direct orders of God delivered by his mouth; and upon his speaking the word, lifting up his rod, or stretching out his hand, what he had foretold forthwith comes to pass. What means could have been better adapted to the ends proposed? What could have conduced more powerfully to dispose this people to receive from the hands of Moses whatever revelation Almighty God should be pleased to make?

VI. But the goodness of Almighty God did not stop here. No sooner are the people gone from Pharaoh, than immediately He exerts His Almighty power in their behalf, by performing more stupendous miracles than any they had hitherto seen. He had resolved, for His own wise ends, to conduct them through a wild and barren desert, where there was neither path nor any human guide to lead them. To supply the latter, He sends an angel from heaven as their conductor. This heavenly spirit, in order more effectually to assist and benefit the favoured people committed to his care, assumes a visible form peculiarly adapted to their wants. "The Lord went before them by day in a pillar of a cloud, and by night in a pillar of fire, to give them light, to go by day and by night," Exod. xiii. 21.

He shows them the way they are to go. He protects them from the scorching heats of the sun by day, and by his splendour dispels the darkness of the night. He makes known to them the proper time for proceeding on their journey, and when and how long they ought to take their rest: "When the cloud was taken up from the tabernacle, then after that the children of Israel journeyed; and in the place where the cloud abode, there the children of Israel pitched their tents; at the commandment of the Lord, the children of Israel journeyed, and at the commandment of the Lord they pitched; as long as the cloud abode upon the tabernacle they rested in their tents," Num. ix. 17, 18. What sentiments of confidence and love must not this continued proof of the divine goodness have produced in this people!

VII. No sooner had Pharaoh and his servants heard that the Israelites had fled, than, thinking only of the loss of their service, and forgetting all the scourges they had suffered, they repented of what they had done: "Why, say they, have we done this, that we have let Israel go from serving us?" Exod. xiv. 5. Pharaoh, therefore, immediately resolves to pursue them with his army, and bring them back to their former slavery. His people readily agree to the proposal, and he comes, with all his hosts, upon the Israelites, at a place where they are hemmed in by the wilderness and the Red Sea, and where there is no human possibility for them to escape. But God again interposes in their behalf by new miracles. Their heavenly conductor changes his position from front to rear, to be a barrier between his people and their enemies. "And the angel of God which went before the camp of Israel, removed and went behind them, and the pillar of cloud went from before their face and stood behind them; and it came between the camp of the Egyptians and the camp of Israel, and" (see another miracle!) "it was a cloud of darkness to them, but it gave light by night to these; so that the one came not near the other all the night," Exod. xiv. 19, 20.

Next morning, to complete their deliverance, Moses, by God's command, stretched forth his hand over the sea, and immediately it divided into two parts, leaving the dry land in the middle, and the waters standing up as a wall upon the right hand and upon the left. The Israelites, astonished at this visible protection of heaven, boldly enter the untrodden path, and safely pass through to the other shore; the Egyptians, blinded by their passion, and bent upon what they had in view, madly follow, in hopes at last to overtake them; but the time is now at hand appointed for completing the punishment of their obdurate hearts. No sooner are the people of God safely over than Moses again stretches out his hand over the waters, as if to tell them they are now at liberty to return to their usual channel,—" And immediately the sea returned to his strength, and covered the chariots and the horsemen, and all the hosts of Pharaoh —there remained not so much as one of them; and thus the Lord saved Israel that day out of the hands of the Egyptians, and Israel saw the Egyptians dead upon the sea-shore," Exod. xiv. 27, &c. What a visible instance of the almighty hand of God! What a stupendous miracle! What a suspension of the laws of nature! And all this for what end? For that end surely which was actually produced by it. "And Israel saw that great work which the Lord did upon the Egyptians, and the people feared the Lord, and believed the Lord and His servant Moses," Exod. xiv. 31.

These were the great ends which Almighty God proposed by doing such wondrous things, to fill the hearts of His people with a salutary fear of offending Him, and to gain authority and credit with them both for Himself and His servant; and by this means to dispose their minds for receiving with perfect submission that sacred law which He was about to reveal to them by His holy prophet. These, then, are ends which God Himself judges worthy of His interposition by miracles, even of the first order.

VIII. The further we proceed, the more convincing proofs do we discover of this truth in the conduct of divine Providence. The people being now entered into that vast and barren wilderness through which it pleased God to lead them, soon find themselves exposed to the sufferings of hunger and thirst, and the utter want of all the necessaries of life. In this dismal situation, with misery and death staring them in the face, their hearts began to fail. They murmured against Moses for bringing them out of Egypt to kill them, as they said, in the wilderness, Exod. xvi. 3. They looked upon all that had been done as his work alone, and called in question his being sent by Almighty God for their deliverance.

This was doubtless inexcusable, considering the many proofs they had received of the divine mission of their leader. But the mercy of their God again had pity on them; and, condescending to their weakness, He again exerted His almighty power in their behalf, and wrought still more wonderful miracles among them, to convince them that not Moses of himself, but "that He their Lord had brought them out of the land of Egypt," Exod. xvi. 6. "And ye shall know," said He upon this occasion, "that I am the Lord your God," ver. 12. For this purpose He rains down upon them a wonderful food from heaven—a food altogether miraculous, both in the manner of its being given and in all its properties.

In order to try them, however, whether or not they were "really willing to walk in His law," Exod. xvi. 4, and entertained that filial confidence in Him, with which so many wonders wrought in their favour ought to have inspired them, He orders only a certain quantity of this heavenly food to be gathered at a time, so much for each person daily. But as the seventh day was to be kept holy as His Sabbath, and spent in His service, He allows a double quantity for each to be gathered on the sixth day. He also orders that what was thus gathered each day should be used, and that nothing of it should be left till the following morning.

The design of Almighty God in these orders is evident. It was to try their obedience; to root out from their hearts all anxiety and solicitude for the concerns of this life, and to nourish in their souls a perfect confidence and total reliance on the divine providence and protection for everything they stood in need of. Now, observe the miraculous properties of this manna, and how excellently it was adapted to those ends! When the people went out to gather it, "some gathered more and some less" than the measure prescribed; "but when they brought it home and met it, he that gathered much had nothing over, and he that gathered little had no lack. . . . Some of them left of it till the morning, and it bred worms and putrefied; . . . but what remained over" the sixth day, "they laid it up till the morning, . . . and it did not putrefy, neither was there any worm therein;" also it bore without difficulty all the force of the fire, but melted with the slender heat of the rising sun.

Lastly, this miraculous food was rained down upon them every morning of the six days of the week, but "on the seventh day they found none." See here an accumulation of miracles, which continued with that people as a standing proof of the finger of God during the space of forty years that they remained in the wilderness, and even till they ate the new fruits of an inhabited land. Nay, what is still more surprising, a measure of this very manna, which could not continue one night without worms and corruption when kept contrary to the command, was ordered by God to be laid up in the ark before the Lord, where it was preserved sound and incorrupt for ages, that their latest "posterity might see the bread with which God fed them in the wilderness," which was a standing and perpetual miracle among them, Exod. xvi.

IX. The joy which this heavenly boon occasioned was soon checked by want of water, none of which was to be found in that dry and barren desert; upon which they began again to murmur, and immediately a new miracle is wrought to supply them. Moses strikes the rock with his rod, and it is forthwith melted down into a stream of limpid water, sufficient for the whole multitude and their cattle, Exod. xvii.

Again, they began to tire of the manna, and calling to mind the food, both fish and flesh, which they had enjoyed in Egypt, they murmured, and a new miracle is wrought to gratify their desire, and give them flesh in abundance. Moses himself seemed confounded when God promised to supply them with flesh, looking upon it as a thing incredible, considering where they were: "The people," says he to Almighty God, "are six hundred thousand footmen, and Thou hast said I will give them flesh, that they may eat a whole month; shall the flocks and herds be slain for them to suffice them?" But God immediately checks him by only reminding him who He was that promised it. "And the Lord said unto Moses, is the Lord's hand waxed short? Thou shalt see now whether My word shall come to pass unto thee or not;" and accordingly the very next day He sent them flesh to the full, Num. xi.

Finally, to complete the proofs of his affection for them, and thereby to increase their confidence and love of Him, during the forty years He led them in the wilderness He gave such strength and durability to their clothing, that from the day they came out of Egypt, "your clothes," as Moses expresses it to the people themselves, "are not waxen old upon you, and thy shoe is not waxen old upon thy foot," Deut. xxix. 5. In all this we see how much Almighty God thought it worthy of Himself to perform the most amazing miracles, in order to gain the love and confidence of His people, and to dispose them to receive with respect and deference the law which He was about to deliver to them.

X. We come now to the revelation itself; and here we find a new scene opened to our view; a scene of miracles even superior, if possible, in their amazing greatness to any that had gone before. Two days were employed to prepare the people for this great event, and upon the third day God descends in a visible form of fire in the sight of the entire multitude, attended with all the ensigns of majesty which could render His appearance awful. A thick cloud covers the mountain, the sound of trumpets is heard on every side, flashes of lightning burst forth from the clouds, peals of thunder roll, and the whole mountain trembles with violent earthquakes. From the midst God Himself speaks aloud to His people, and pronounces, with His own divine mouth, in the hearing of all the multitude, the sacred law which He was pleased to give them. The people, spectators of this impressive scene, heard with amazement the heavenly voice; and seeing "the thunders and the lightning, and the noise of the trumpets, and the mountain smoking," they were exceedingly afraid, "and removed, and stood afar off, and said to Moses, Speak thou to us and we will hear, but let not God speak to us lest we die," Exod. xx.

Nothing could more effectually serve to convince this

people that their God was the sovereign Lord of heaven and earth, than what they heard and saw upon this occasion. Nothing could imprint more deeply on their minds a veneration and dread of that Almighty Being Who spoke to them. Nothing could more contribute to excite the utmost respect for Moses, whom they saw so highly honoured by their great Creator, and to dispose them to receive from him, with the most religious deference, whatever Almighty God should afterwards be pleased by him to reveal to them. This was one of the principal ends which God had in view in His visible appearance among them, as He Himself says to Moses, "Lo, I come unto thee in a thick cloud, that the people may hear when I speak with thee, and believe thee for ever," Exod. xix. 9. But this deserves to be considered more particularly.

XI. In the first place, we see, in this memorable event, a striking example of the infinite goodness of God, and of His ardent desire of the moral perfection of His rational creatures. What more convincing proof of this than to see this great Being condescend to reveal to them His holy will and law as the proper rule to conduct them to that perfection; and to do this in such a manner, and in such circumstances, as could not possibly fail to give them the most full conviction that it was the God of nature Himself, the sovereign Lord and Master of the universe, Who spoke whilst they saw how entirely all nature was subservient to Him.

But as it would have been too much for human weakness if all the particulars of the religion which God intended for His people had been delivered to them in such a manner, we see, in the second place, with what infinite wisdom Almighty God brings about His ends with undoubted certainty, but at the same time with the greatest sweetness.

The awfulness of His appearance fills their minds with such dread and fear, that they themselves pray that He would never speak to them again in such a manner. What He had already done had fully convinced them that He was their sole and sovereign Lord, and that Moses was sent and commissioned by Him; that, therefore, it would be sufficient if He declared to Moses what further orders He should please to give them, and they would receive them from him as the dictates of God Himself. Now what was this but the very disposition of mind which God required of them, as the end proposed in all these wondrous works which He had wrought? And therefore He approved of what they said, and replied to Moses, "They have well spoken that which they have spoken," Deut. xviii. 17.

Lastly, in this whole series of repeated miracles, we have a convincing proof how much Almighty God esteems the moral perfection of His creatures; that is, the implanting and strengthening in their hearts a firm belief of what He reveals to them as His truth, a fear of offending Him, a filial confidence in His goodness, and a sincere love and obedience to Him as their supreme God and sovereign Lord. We see how much Almighty God esteems these things worthy of His procuring, even by the temporary subversion, if it may be so said, of the most constant laws of nature.

That these were the very ends which God had in view in working so many wonders among His people, is evident from His own repeated declarations. To those above related I shall add the following, as being particularly expressive of this truth. It is taken from Deut. iv., where Moses, exhorting the people to love and serve their God, who had done such great things for them, speaks to them as follows: "Did ever people hear the voice of God speaking out of the midst of fire, as thou hast heard, and live? or hath God essayed to take Him a nation from the midst of another nation by temptations, by *signs*, and by *wonders*, and by war, and by a mighty hand, and by a stretched-out arm, and by great terrors, according to all that the Lord your God did for you in Egypt before your eyes? Unto thee it was showed, that thou *mightest know that the Lord He is God; there is none else beside Him.* . . . Know therefore this day, and consider it in thine heart, that the Lord He is God in heaven above, and upon the earth beneath; there is none else: thou shalt keep therefore His statutes and commandments," &c. In consequence of this, the people unanimously resolved to love and serve their God, Who had done such great things for them; and having declared their firm resolution of doing so, Almighty God, to show how ardently He desired this from them, and that He desired it with a view to their real and lasting happiness, thus expresses Himself to Moses: "O that there were such a heart in them, that they would fear Me and keep all My commandments always, that it might be well with them, and with their children for ever," Deut. v. 29. In all this it is manifest what were the ends which the divine wisdom had in view in the many and amazing miracles wrought among this people.*

* See also Deut. ix. x. xi., Psalm lxxviii. (*alias* lxxvii.), and Psalm cv. (*alias* civ.), through the whole, where the same truth is most beautifully declared.

CHAPTER VI.

OTHER GENERAL ENDS OF MIRACLES, AS DISCLOSED BY REVELATION.

I. WHAT we have seen in the preceding chapter must show beyond all doubt to those who receive the Scriptures as the Word of God, that to procure belief with mankind, when He is pleased to reveal to them His will, and to excite in their minds and hearts those holy sentiments of faith, confidence, love, gratitude, and obedience, are ends truly worthy of the divine interposition by miracles, and are so judged by God Himself. But as this is a most important subject, I must pursue it a little further, and show from the same sacred records a few more of the general ends which God has been pleased to procure by the same means, and which directly or indirectly conduced to the happiness and perfection either of whole nations or of individuals.

II. The miraculous manner in which Almighty God was pleased to reveal and establish His religion, was fully sufficient to convince all then present, and also all who in after-ages should believe upon the tradition and testimony by which it was to be handed down to them. Still the divine wisdom, well knowing the corruption of the heart of man, its impatience of restraint, its readiness to shake off the yoke on the least pretence, foresaw how apt men would be in after-ages to reject the belief of this first miraculous establishment of religion, if not supported by convincing proofs. We find, therefore, that Almighty God, in all succeeding ages, when His religion was in danger of being corrupted or destroyed, was always ready to defend it by the same means by which He had at first established it. He judged its preservation, when in danger, no less worthy His divine interposition than its first establishment among His people.

III. After the death of Joshua and his contemporaries, who had been eyewitnesses of all the glorious things which Almighty God had done for that nation, the memory of those wonders began to wax weak among them: "The people served the Lord all the days of Joshua, and all the days of the elders that outlived Joshua, who had seen all the great works of the Lord that He did for Israel. And Joshua died, and also all that generation were gathered unto their fathers; and there arose another generation after them which knew not the Lord, nor yet the works which He had done for Israel," Judges, ii. In consequence of this, for a great number of years—that is, during the whole period that Israel was governed by judges—they from time to time "did evil in the sight of the Lord, and served Balaam; and they forsook the Lord God of their fathers, Who brought them out of the land of Egypt," sometimes the whole nation, sometimes a considerable part of it, "and followed other gods, and provoked the Lord to anger," *ibid.*

In this juncture Almighty God did not fail to defend His own cause; nay, we may justly say, that He wrought one continued miracle, by literally and daily fulfilling those prophecies which, long before, had been made by Moses. This great man, foreseeing the future infidelity of the people, foretold to them the consequences both of their obedience to the Lord their God, and of their apostasy from His service. He assured them, that if they adhered to Him and to His holy law, every temporal blessing would be their portion. "If you walk in My statutes," says Almighty God to them by the mouth of this holy prophet, "and keep My commandments and do them, then I will give you rain in due season, and the land shall yield her increase. . . . And I will give peace in the land, and you shall chase your enemies, and they shall fall before you by the sword. . . . And I will walk among you, and I will be your God, and ye shall be My people." See the whole passage, Levit. xxvi. ; see also Deut. xxviii. And, on the contrary, if they should forsake the Lord their God, abandon His service and prove disobedient to Him, He assured them that all temporal evils would be sent upon them as the just punishment of their ingratitude ; "But if you will not hearken unto Me, and will not do all these My commandments, I also will do this unto you, I will even appoint over you terror, consumption, and the burning ague, and I will set My face against you, and ye shall be slain before your enemies, and they that hate you shall reign over you," &c., *ibid.*

Now, what is the whole history of the Judges but a literal verification of these prophecies? See the second chapter of that book, which in this respect is an abridgment of the whole. And as the accomplishment of prophecies, which had been uttered long before, is an undoubted proof that God is their author, nothing could more powerfully contribute to convince that people that the religion which they had received from their fathers was from God, than their daily experience of the immediate consequences which exactly followed, according to prediction, as they either adhered to their religion and their God, or became disobedient to Him.

IV. Neither were there wanting several particular miracles during this period, wrought either indirectly or directly for the same end,—as the victory over Siserah, and the manner of his death, foretold by Deborah; also Gideon's fleece, and the deliverance of the people from the captivity of the Midianites, by the miraculous victory which he obtained over them; the circumstances attending the birth of Sampson, his amazing strength, with that most extraordinary miracle of his obtaining water to quench his thirst from the dry jaw-bone of an ass; and Samuel's procuring thunder and lightning in an instant on a clear harvest-day,—from which we see how attentive Almighty God was to defend the purity and truth of His religion by miracles, from the dangers to which it was exposed during this period of the Judges.

These instances now mentioned we shall have occasion to notice afterwards in a more particular manner. But there is also another celebrated passage connected with this period which deserves a little more attention here. Under the government of the high priest Eli, in punishment of the sins of His people, God permitted the ark of His covenant, which was the glory of their nation, to be taken from them, and carried away by the Philistines. This was a subject of triumph and exultation to these heathens, but of the utmost affliction and humiliation to the Israelites. But though Almighty God was pleased thus to punish and humble His people for their sins, He did not fail to vindicate the honour of His religion, and to defend the ark, which was the most sacred testimony of His covenant with them, from the insults of His enemies by repeated miracles. By these the infidels were forced to acknowledge His power and authority both over them and all their gods, and at last to restore the ark with honour to the people.

When it fell into their hands they placed it in the temple of Dagon their god; but next day that idol was found lying flat upon the ground, as it were in an act of adoration before the ark of the Most High God. When raised up by its votaries and put into its place, the day after it was found not only fallen as before, but even broken into pieces upon the threshold; Almighty God disdaining to have an idol standing beside His ark, or placed upon an equal footing with it. He smote all the people of every city and its neighbourhood whither they carried the ark, with sore boils and shameful diseases, which swept them off in numbers, so that the people of that city cried out, " The ark of the God of Israel shall not abide with us, for His hand is sore upon us, and upon Dagon our god." At last when, forced by these chastisements, they resolved to send it home again to the Israelites, they tried the test of a miracle to know whether what had happened to them was from God, on account of the ark, or was only an ordinary accident of life; and God was pleased to grant the very sign which they demanded, to convince them that what had happened to them was from Him in defence of His religion, and of the sanctity of that sacred deposit which, for His own just and wise ends, He had permitted to fall into their hands.

V. During the reigns of Saul, David, and Solomon, no attempt was made against religion, and accordingly in these reigns we find no miracles wrought directly in its defence. But after Solomon's death, when Jeroboam became king of the ten tribes, and endeavoured through his false and worldly policy to carry off his people from the service of God, and lead them to idolatry, immediately we find Almighty God rising up in defence of His religion, and asserting its truth by miracles.

After Jeroboam's defection, the first public solemnity that is mentioned of his idolatry, was the time chosen by God to appear in His own cause. When a number of people were present, the sacrilegious altar prepared, and the king ready to burn incense upon it, a prophet sent by God stood forth, and prophesied against the altar in these words: "O altar, altar, says the Lord; behold, a child shall be born unto the house of David, Josiah by name; and upon thee shall he offer the priests of the high places that burn incense upon thee, and men's bones shall be burnt upon thee," 1 Kings, xiii. This prophecy we find literally accomplished many years afterwards (2 Kings, xxiii. 15).

But that Jeroboam and all the people might know that it was a true prophecy, which should be fulfilled in its proper time, another was made to be accomplished before their eyes, which was, that that very altar against which the former prophecy was made should suddenly be rent in two, and the ashes that were upon it be poured out upon the ground. This is given by the prophet as a sign to convince them of the truth of the former. Before this sign was accomplished, however, another miracle intervened to confirm it still further. The unhappy king, incensed at the prophet for what he had said, "put forth his hand from the altar, saying, Lay hold on him; and his hand which he put forth against him dried up, so that he could not pull it in again to him;" and immediately the other sign was accomplished,—"The altar also was rent, and the ashes poured out from the altar, according to the sign which the man of God had given by the word of the Lord." Then the whole was completed by another miracle; for the king, astonished at what had happened, "said to the man of God, Entreat now the Lord thy God, and pray for me that my hand may be restored to me again; and the man of God besought the Lord, and the king's hand was restored and became as it was before," *ibid.* Now, for what end were all these miracles wrought, but to convince the king and the people of the greatness of their guilt, in leaving the religion of their fathers, and consequently to vindicate that true religion against all the efforts of Jeroboam to destroy it?

VI. Some time afterwards, when a child of this same Jeroboam fell sick, in his anxiety he desired his wife to disguise herself and go to the prophet Ahijah, who had formerly foretold him that he should be made king of the ten tribes, and to inquire what would be the fate of the child. The prophet was now old and had lost his sight; but before the queen's arrival Almighty God disclosed her coming to His servant; told him her object, and the answer to be given. Accordingly, upon her entering the door of his house, he addressed her by name, and reproaching her with her husband's perfidy and ingratitude to God, foretold her, that in punishment of his great sin all his family should be cut off, and not so much as one soul should be left of his posterity; and that in process of time all his people whom he had seduced from their God, should be reduced to the greatest misery, overcome by their enemies, and carried away captives to a strange country. As a sign of the truth of these prophecies, he declared to her, that as soon as she returned and set her foot within the city, her child should die—all which came to pass as foretold. Here again we see miracles proper to God alone, the foretelling things to come, both nigh at hand and in future ages; the first being given and verified as a proof of the certainty of the latter, till it also should be accomplished in its proper time; and all this to defend the true religion, and show those who had abandoned it the enormity of their crime.

VII. The next public and violent attack upon religion was made by that impious prince Achab, who, having married a heathen woman, was persuaded by her to put to death all the prophets of God, and to persecute His servants, in order to destroy religion and force the people to idolatry. In this critical conjuncture the great Elijah, or Elias, was raised up by God as a bulwark to defend His truth, and to stem the torrent of impiety which was threatening to overflow the land. The first step which the prophet took was to inform the king that "there should neither be dew nor rain upon the earth for these years, but according to his word," 1 Kings, xvii. 1; thereby intimating that Almighty God had, in a manner, put the rain and dew in his hands, that while he pleased none should fall, and at his desire it should be sent again upon the earth. What he said was literally fulfilled; not a drop fell for three years and a half, till the prophet obtained it by his prayers.

The consequences of this drought were dreadful; famine and misery devastated the land, destroying both man and beast. What more convincing proof could be given the king of the evil of his ways, and of the truth of that holy religion which he was persecuting? And that this extraordinary power was given to Elias, and this severe scourge sent upon the people for this very end, to convince the king of his wickedness, the prophet expressly told him: "It is not I that have troubled Israel, but thou and thy father's house, in that ye have forsaken the commandment of the Lord, and followed Baalim," 1 Kings, xviii. 18.

VIII. The prophet finding that what he had said and done made little impression on the king, addresses himself to the people; and in order to convince them of the falsity of those pretended gods whom the king had induced them to adore, and that the God of their fathers was the only true God, he challenges them to put the case to a fair trial, and offers, though single and alone, to sustain the cause of God against all the prophets of Baal, who were four hundred and fifty men. The method which he proposed for deciding this grand question was plain to the lowest capacity, and convincingly decisive. It was to refer the case to their gods themselves, and to leave it to them to defend their own cause by performing the miracle demanded for that purpose. He proposed that each side should prepare a sacrifice, and call upon their respective gods, and that the god that answered by fire should be esteemed the only true God.

The proposal was accepted with general applause, and the prophets of Baal dared not refuse the challenge. Accordingly they began first. They took a bullock, cut it in pieces, laid it on wood, but without fire under it, and called upon their god Baal from morning till the time of "the evening sacrifice; but there was neither voice, nor any to answer, nor any that regarded," 1 Kings, xviii. 29. Then Elijah in his turn built an altar to the Lord, and dug a large trench round about it, which he filled with water, that the miracle which he was going to work might be the more evident. Then he put the wood in order, and laid the bullock on the wood, and made a short prayer to God, begging Him to grant the miracle desired, "and let it be known," says he, "this day, that Thou art God in Israel, and that I am Thy servant, and that I have done all these things at Thy word; that this people may know that Thou art the Lord God, and that Thou hast turned their hearts back again." Scarcely had he finished this prayer when immediately "the fire of the Lord fell and consumed the burnt sacrifice, and the wood, and the stones, and the dust, and licked up the water that was in the trench," *ibid.* This was too evident a proof not to have its desired effect. Accordingly all the multitude of the people, confounded and amazed, "fell on their faces, and they said, The Lord, He is God; the Lord, He is God."

IX. It can scarcely be imagined that this stupendous miracle should not have made some impression even on the heart of Achab; and we find that when Elijah, immediately after it, ordered all the prophets of Baal to be put to death as seducers of the people, the king offered no objection. The goodness of God, desirous to improve this seed sown in the heart of Achab, was pleased soon after to work other miracles in his favour, but directly intended at the same time to prove that He was the only true God.

The king of Syria, seeking a cause of quarrel with Achab, sent to him some insidious messages and haughty demands, which, not being complied with, he raised a vast army, and came to besiege Achab in Samaria. Upon this a prophet comes from God to Achab with this message, "Hast thou seen all this greatm ultitude? Behold, I will deliver it into thine hand this day, *and thou shalt know that I am the Lord.*" And that the hand of God might be the more manifest in this victory, it was to be gained only by two hundred and thirty-two men; which happened accordingly, and the enemy were "slain with a very great slaughter." To wipe away this disgrace, the Syrians returned the following year in vast numbers, (before whom the whole army of Israel "was like two little flocks of kids"), and vainly boasted that the gods of the Israelites being gods of the hills, were therefore stronger than they the preceding year; but now they would keep to the valleys, and would surely gain the victory. Here the honour of the true God was attacked by these infidels, and therefore a prophet is sent to Achab with this message, "Thus saith the Lord, Because the Syrians have said, The Lord is God of the hills, but he is not God of the valleys, therefore I will deliver all this multitude into thine hand, and *ye shall know that I am the Lord*," 1 Kings, xx. Achab accordingly gained a complete victory, and humbled the Syrians.

X. These facts speak for themselves, and are the most convincing proofs, that to preserve the true religion which God has once established, is esteemed by Him an object truly worthy of His care, and that it is highly becoming His divine wisdom and goodness to perform the greatest miracles in its defence. Those which we have seen above were directly wrought for this purpose, and intended as proofs of the true religion; but there were many others wrought by Elijah at the same time, which, though performed upon other occasions, were most undoubted proofs of his being a servant of the true God, and that the religion he professed was true.

I must not, however, omit another miracle of this prophet in foretelling the death of king Ahaziah, when he sent messengers in his sickness to inquire of " Baal-zebub, the god of Ekron, whether he should recover of his disease," 2 Kings, i. These messengers the prophet met, and, according to the instructions he had received from an angel, told them to return to their master and tell him in the name of the Lord, " Is it because there is not a God in Israel, that thou sendest to inquire of Baalzebub the god of Ekron? therefore thou shalt not come down from that bed on which thou art gone up, but shalt surely die," *ibid.* ver. 6; and soon after " he died, according to the word of the Lord which Elijah had spoken," ver. 17. Here we see the death inflicted upon him foretold, and happening accordingly in punishment of his impiety in neglecting the God of his fathers, and sending to inquire of an idol about his recovery. These also, then, were miracles wrought in defence of the true religion.

XI. In the reigns of the succeeding kings, as the wickedness of the people of Israel daily increased, Almighty God multiplied His miracles among them, particularly by the hands of Elisha, the successor of Elijah, after this latter had been translated. We find also many particular prophecies made on different occasions with their perfect accomplishment, especially that of the captivity and the dispersion of the ten tribes, the Babylonian captivity, and the destruction of Jerusalem, which were expressly foretold as punishments of the people's sin in forsaking the true religion; and consequently, when literally fulfilled, were so many convincing proofs of its truth. All this shows how attentive Almighty God was during this period of the kings, to work repeated miracles in defence of His true religion.

XII. During the time of the Babylonian captivity, religion was to all human appearance in the utmost danger. The people were dispersed amidst an infidel nation, were not allowed to exist in a body by themselves, were deprived of the public exercise of their religion, and daily exposed to the dangerous example of the heathen nations among whom they dwelt. When we consider the inconceivable proneness of this people to idolatry even in their own country, with all the aids of their religion, it seems next to a miracle that, in the above circumstances, they were not entirely perverted. But their very captivity itself, and the sufferings they endured in it, were a powerful means to preserve them; for they were a convincing proof of the truth of their religion, being a literal accomplishment of the many prophecies concerning it. Neither did God fail during this period to perform surprising miracles, which not only confirmed his people in their religion, but even forced from their greatest enemies the acknowledgment that their God was the only true God, the sovereign Lord of heaven and earth: witness the preservation of the three children in the fiery furnace, of Daniel in the lions' den, and his repeated interpretation of dreams, with their full accomplishment.

XIII. From the rebuilding of Jerusalem to the coming of our Saviour, we find the Jewish nation no less firmly attached to their religion than they formerly had been prone upon all occasions to forsake it. The repeated and fatal effects of their infidelity, and the numberless things which Almighty God had done in proof of His truth, had at last overcome their obstinacy, and attached them most firmly to His service; and therefore, miracles wrought in proof of their religion became less frequent during this last period. Still, even at this time, when the kings of Syria made some violent attacks upon religion, and several of the Jews themselves, blinded by their passions, joined the common enemy, and thereby increased the danger, we see Almighty God no less ready than in former ages to defend His truth, and to work miracles for this purpose. The account of this persecution, and of the miracles which Almighty God wrought upon that occasion, is given at large in the books of the Maccabees, to which, for brevity's sake, I must refer; and from all that we have seen above in this present chapter, I draw this evident conclusion, that to preserve the true religion by miracles when it is in danger is no less worthy of Almighty God than to establish it at the beginning by the same means, and that this is the judgment which God Himself makes, never having failed during the whole course of the Mosaic dispensation, to work great and surprising miracles in defence of His religion, whenever it was exposed to danger.

XIV. Next to the immediate defence of religion itself, there is nothing which Almighty God seems to desire more than that His people should preserve a high respect and religious veneration for persons and things immediately connected with Him, or employed in His service. Hence He has always manifested the greatest jealousy for the honour of the sacred character and authority of the priesthood; for the respect due to those His servants whom He employed as His ambassadors to men; and for the reverence due to all holy things used in His service, as His ark, His temple, the sacred vessels, and the like. And, indeed, wherever there exists a true spirit of religion and piety towards God, this will of necessity show itself in a just respect and veneration for all sacred persons and things immediately connected with Him; and where these are wanting, it may justly be inferred that virtue and piety are declining, and that religion itself is already in danger. Almighty God, therefore, has judged this also an object worthy of His care, and has been pleased, through the whole series of the old religion, to work extraordinary miracles, in order to excite and preserve in His people a high esteem of the sanctity of the priesthood, and a just regard and veneration for holy persons and holy things. At the first establishment of their religion, when their minds were yet gross and rude, and unacquainted with the ways of God, the imprinting these sentiments in their hearts seemed particularly needful, and accordingly at that time we find the infinite wisdom and goodness of God singularly bountiful in working many miracles for that purpose.

XV. Aaron and Miriam, the brother and sister of

Moses, presumed upon a certain occasion to speak against him, and to put themselves upon an equality with him; but their presumption was immediately checked. Almighty God Himself appeared in His glory on the tabernacle, reproved them by name for their crime, declared how much more highly favoured Moses was by Him than they, and said, "Wherefore then were ye not afraid to speak against My servant Moses?" Num. xii. 8. Then departing from them in great wrath, He in an instant smote Miriam with a universal leprosy, from which she was not cured till after seven days, at the earnest prayer of Moses.

XVI. Soon after this Korah and his companions, full of jealousy and envy against Moses and Aaron, for the high dignity of the priesthood conferred on the latter and his family, rose up against him, accusing them of ambition and usurpation, and carried off many of the chiefs of the families to their party, of whom about two hundred and fifty men took upon themselves to provide censers and offer incense before the Lord. Moses was deeply afflicted at their crime, and dreading the fatal consequences, pressingly exhorts them to return to their duty, and avert their impending ruin. But seeing their obstinacy, he foretells their destruction, as the most convincing proof of his being commissioned by God: "Hereby," says he, "shall you know that the Lord hath sent me to do all these works, for I have not done them of my own mind. If these men die the common death of men, or if they be visited after the visitation of all men, then the Lord hath not sent me; but if the Lord make a new thing, and the earth open her mouth and swallow them up, and all that appertain unto them, and they go down quick unto the pit, then ye shall understand that these men have provoked the Lord," Num. xvi. 28.

Scarcely had Moses finished these words, when, lo! they are immediately accomplished: "And it came to pass, as he had made an end of speaking all these words, that the ground clave asunder that was under them, and the earth opened her mouth and swallowed them up, and their tents, and all the men that appertained unto Korah, and all their goods; and they went down alive into the pit, and the earth closed upon them, and they perished from among the congregation," ver. 31, &c. And as for these two hundred and fifty principal men that had presumed to offer incense not being priests, "there came a fire out from the Lord and consumed them," ver. 35.

What an extraordinary interposition of the divine power is here displayed! what surprising miracles! how admirably adapted to convince that rude people of the sanctity of that authority which Moses and Aaron exercised, and to fill their minds with profound respect and veneration for the priesthood, which they saw so signally vindicated by God Himself!

Such, however, was the obduracy of the people, that even these amazing miracles did not effectually cure them; but the more they continue to oppose the sacred authority which God had established among them, the more He proceeds by miracles to confirm it. The following morning, when the first emotions of fear and amazement had subsided, the people were deeply afflicted at the death of so many chiefs of their families, and looking on Moses and Aaron as the authors of that calamity, they raised a general murmur against them. Moses well knew that God would not permit this to pass unpunished; nay, God Himself threatened them with utter destruction, and accordingly a plague began. Moses ordered Aaron immediately to offer an atonement for the people, which he did. God was appeased, the plague was stopped; but, in the short time it lasted, no less than fourteen thousand of the people were consumed by it. What an instance of the divine vengeance! what a miraculous interposition of the divine power! what a convincing proof of the divine commission of Moses and of the sanctity of the priesthood!

But that these things might be fully established, and no ground left again to call them in question, Almighty God condescends to add another miracle, to be continued as a lasting proof to future generations. He orders twelve rods to be provided, one for each of the tribes, with the name written upon it, and Aaron's name upon the rod of Levi. These were ordered to be laid up in the tabernacle before the ark; and the point in question, whether Almighty God had chosen Aaron and his family to be his priests, or they had usurped that high dignity of themselves, was put to this miraculous test, as God Himself appointed, "The man's rod whom I shall choose shall blossom," Num. xvii. 5.

Nothing surely could be more above all the powers of nature than that a dry rod, without even being put into the earth, and that in the short space of one night, should send forth leaves and blossoms; and yet the very next morning, when the rods were examined, "The rod of Aaron was budded, and brought forth buds, and bloomed blossoms, and yielded almonds!" ver. 8. This was so convincing that it fully satisfied the people, and stopped their murmuring, and the blossomed rod was ordered by Almighty God to be laid up in the ark of the testimony, as a proof to all future ages of the authority and sanctity of the priesthood.

XVII. As we proceed in the history of God's people we find repeated examples of the surprising miracles of various kinds performed in testimony of the sanctity of the priesthood and of holy things, and in order to excite in the people a high esteem and veneration for them. When under the command of Joshua they arrived at the Jordan, which was the boundary of Canaan, the land of promise. It was in the harvest season, and the river had so overflowed its banks that the people could not pass. On this occasion Almighty God was pleased to work new miracles in favour of His people. In these he had several ends in view, as related, Jos. iii. iv. One was to convince the people still more of the divine favour and protection, and consequently to increase their love and confidence in Him. Joshua therefore said to the people, foretelling the miracle that was to be performed, " Hereby ye shall know that the living God is among you, and that He will without fail drive out the Canaanites," Jos. iii. 10; see also chap. iv. ver. 24.

Another end was to establish the authority of Joshua, to convince the people that God was with him, and consequently to engage them to a perfect submission and obedience to him. Thus Almighty God Himself says to him, " This day will I begin to magnify thee in the sight of all Israel, that they may know that as I was with Moses, so I will be with thee," Jos. iii. 7; see also chap. iv. ver. 14. The miracle which was wrought for this purpose, Joshua foretells to the people in these words: " Behold, the ark of the covenant of the Lord of all the earth passeth over before you into Jordan. . . . And it shall come to pass, as soon as the soles of the feet of the priests that bear the ark of the Lord, the Lord of all the earth, shall rest in the waters of the Jordan, that the waters of Jordan shall be cut off from the waters that come down from above, and they shall stand upon a heap," Jos. iii. 11, 13.

This was literally performed, as related at large in the

following verses, the waters below running down, and those above standing firm, leaving a dry passage for the whole people through the channel of the river: "And the priests that bare the ark of the covenant of the Lord stood firm on dry ground in the midst of Jordan, and all the Israelites passed over on dry ground, until all the people passed clean over Jordan," ver. 17. But when all had passed over, the priests were then ordered to come out of the river: "And it came to pass, when the priests that bare the ark of the covenant of the Lord were come out of the midst of Jordan, and the soles of the priests' feet were lifted up unto the dry land, that the waters of Jordan returned into their place, and flowed over all his banks as they did before," Jos. iv. 18.

By this miracle, which was a renewal of what had been done in the preceding generation by dividing the Red Sea (Jos. iv. 23), what respect, esteem, and veneration must not have been excited in the people towards the priests and the ark of the covenant, who were the immediate instruments by which it was performed, and to whom it is in a particular manner attributed! "As soon," says Joshua, "as the soles of the feet of the priests that bare the ark shall rest in the waters, the waters shall be cut off," which was accordingly done; and as long as they stood in the Jordan, the division of the water continued; and the moment their feet were out of the Jordan, its waters returned to their place as before. Could anything serve more to exalt them in the sight of the people? could anything more effectually show the sanctity of the priesthood, and the respect due to the ark?

XVIII. To create and maintain this respect for holy things, Almighty God had prohibited all save the priests, even the Levites themselves, from touching the ark, or looking into the Holy of Holies. When the different offices were appointed for the families of the Levites, and the sons of Kohath were ordered to be the bearers of the sanctuary, and the altars, and the holy vessels, and other instruments used at the altar, the priests, the sons of Aaron, were expressly commanded to cover up all these things, before the others came to carry them, and they were forbidden under pain of death to touch them, or even to see them uncovered. Thus, after having given orders to the priests in what manner everything was to be covered, the Scripture says, "After that the sons of Kohath shall come to bear it, but they shall not touch any holy thing, lest they die," Num. iv. 15. And a little after, "but they" (viz., the sons of Kohath) "shall not go in to see when the holy things are covered, lest they die," ver. 20.

This law was evidently made in order to excite in the people a just respect and veneration towards all holy things belonging to the service of God; and we find that in after-ages those who transgressed the law were severely and often miraculously punished. Besides what happened to the Philistines while the ark of God was in their possession, observe what is related when they sent it back to the Israelites. Its first arrival was among the Bethsamites, who were filled with joy on seeing it return; but in their joy they had the curiosity and presumption to open and look into the ark, a crime so displeasing to God, that He immediately "smote them with a very great slaughter, to no less a number than fifty thousand, threescore and ten men," 1 Sam. vi. 19. In like manner, when David was bringing up the ark in a numerous procession, and with great solemnity, to the place which he had prepared for it, the oxen which drew the carriage on which the ark was placed, became unruly, and kicked so, that it was in danger of being overthrown. Upon this Uzzah, one of those who drove the carriage, " put forth his hand to the ark of God and took hold of it, for the oxen shook it; and the anger of the Lord was kindled against Uzzah, and God smote him there for his error, and there he died by the ark of God," 2 Sam. vi.

What an impression must not this have made on the hearts of all the people! what an idea must it not have given them of the sanctity of God, and of everything belonging to His service! what sentiments of reverence and veneration must it not have excited in their minds towards these holy things! David himself was so deeply affected with fear and dread, that he dared not venture to take the ark to himself, as he had proposed, seeing the great respect which God required to be paid towards it.

Another miraculous instance of the like nature in vindication of the respect due to holy things, we have in Balshazzar, king of Babylon, who, in the midst of his banquet, ordered the holy vessels which his father had carried away from the temple of Jerusalem, to be brought, that he and his concubines and nobles might drink out of them. This profanation of these holy vessels did not long pass unpunished. A man's hand appears to the king, writing upon the wall over against him. He is immediately seized with excessive fear at the miraculous sight. Daniel the prophet is called in to read and explain the writing, and he assures the king that his ruin is at hand, in punishment of his sacrilege; that this miraculous handwriting was sent by God to foretell his impending destruction on that account. And that very night the prediction was literally fulfilled, Dan. v.

From these and other examples recorded in the Scriptures, we see that Almighty God esteems the exciting and preserving in the hearts of His people a respect and veneration for the priesthood, and for all holy things, to be an end worthy of procuring even by miraculous exertions of His almighty power. Of this we shall have occasion to say more when we come to consider the instruments of miracles; and here we will only add a few examples of miracles wrought to convince mankind of the sanctity of holy persons not priests, and to procure to them and to their words credit and authority when Almighty God is pleased to commission them to declare His will to others.

This we have already partly seen, both with regard to Moses and Joshua; but there is another striking instance of it connected with the latter. When Joshua had gained a great victory over the combined armies of five kings, not only did Almighty God assist His people in a miraculous manner to discomfit their enemies, "by casting down great stones from heaven upon them" to destroy them, but also, as the day was far spent, and time failed the Israelites for the pursuit, Joshua, full of confidence, "spoke to the Lord, and said in the sight of Israel, Sun, stand thou still upon Gibeon, and thou moon in the valley of Ajalon. And the sun stood still, and the moon stayed, until the people had avenged themselves upon their enemies. . . . So the sun stood still in the midst of heaven, and hasted not to go down about a whole day. And there was no day like that, before it nor after it, that the Lord hearkened unto the voice of a man," Jos. x. 10, &c. What respect and veneration must not the people have conceived for a man at whose desire God was pleased to stop the general course of nature, and suspend for a whole day the laws of the universe! What opinion must they not have formed of his sanctity and power with God, Who was pleased in so wonderful a manner to hearken to his voice!

XIX. Again, when the people of Israel became tired of being governed by judges, and demanded a king to reign over them, the holy prophet Samuel was exceedingly afflicted, and looked upon their demand as a rejection of God Himself, and a withdrawal of themselves from His authority. Being instructed by God, however, Samuel provided them a king of God's own choosing, and on the day when this king was presented to them, before resigning his charge, he expostulates with them on their ingratitude to God, shows His infinite goodness in condescending to their desire, and then promises on the part of God, that notwithstanding this their sin, if they will only in future "fear the Lord, and serve Him, and obey His voice," all will yet be well with them. But "if they did not obey His voice, but rebelled against His commandment, that then the hand of the Lord would be against them, as it had been against their fathers." Immediately, to confirm his words, and to convince the people of the greatness of their crime, he works an extraordinary miracle, which he even foretells beforehand: "Is it not wheat harvest," says he, "to-day?"—that is, a clear, fine harvest-day—"I will call upon the Lord, and He shall send thunder and rain, that ye may perceive and see that your wickedness is great which ye have done in the sight of the Lord in asking you a king. So Samuel called unto the Lord, and the Lord sent thunder and rain that day; and all the people greatly feared the Lord and Samuel. And all the people said unto Samuel, Pray for thy servants unto the Lord thy God, that we die not," &c., 1 Sam. xii.

Here we have a miracle performed to prove the truth of the prophet's words. This it not only did, but also increased the people's veneration for the holy servant of God, and convinced them of his power with God, so that they greatly feared him, and earnestly recommended themselves to his prayers.

XX. In like manner, when king Ahaziah in his sickness sent messengers to Baal-zebub, the god of Ekron, to inquire if he should recover his health, Elijah, meeting the messengers by the way, sent them back to inform the king he would surely die, because, forsaking the God of Israel, he had sent to inquire of an idol; upon which the king sent a captain and fifty men to bring the prophet prisoner to him. When the captain with his men came to the prophet, he accosted him with an air of authority, "Thou man of God, the king hath said, Come down;" to which the prophet immediately replied, "If I be a man of God, then let fire come down from heaven, and consume thee and thy fifty; and immediately there came down fire from heaven, and consumed him and his fifty," 4 Kings, i. Upon this the king sent another captain with his company upon the same errand, and the same thing was repeated with him also.

Here, then, is a great miracle performed. Fire comes down from heaven in an instant, at the voice of a man, once and again, and destroys a hundred people, in order to prove the sanctity of Elias, and that he truly was a man of God. In the same manner, when he raised the widow's son from the dead, and delivered him into his mother's hands, the natural and immediate effect it produced was to convince her of the sanctity of the prophet; for, receiving her son alive from his hand, in a transport of joy and admiration she said, "Now by this I know that thou art a man of God, and that the word of the Lord in thy mouth is true," 3 Kings, xvii. 24.

XXI. Again, when Elisha returned from accompanying his master Elijah, who had been taken up to heaven, arriving at the Jordan, and having in his possession the mantle of Elijah, which he had dropped at parting, in order to obtain a passage through the river, " He took the mantle of Elijah that fell from him, and smote the waters, and said, Where is the God of Elijah? and when he also had smitten the waters, they parted hither and thither, and he also went over," 4 Kings, ii. 14.

Nothing could give this prophet a greater idea of the sanctity of his master, than to see that the elements were not only obedient to himself in person, but even to the touch of the mantle that had once belonged to him, accompanied with the invocation of God for his sake. This last miracle no less effectually convinced the sons of the prophets, who were spectators of it, that Elisha himself was a holy servant of God, and had succeeded as prophet in place of his master who was gone; for " when the sons of the prophets, who were to view at Jericho, saw him, they said, The spirit of Elijah doth rest on Elisha; and they came to meet him, and bowed themselves to the ground before him," *ibid.*, verse 15.

It were endless to mention every example of this kind. The above are more than sufficient to show what is here intended; and indeed the convincing mankind of the sanctity of God's holy servants, and procuring credit and respect for them, is a natural consequence that may be expected from all miracles wrought by them; but the above examples clearly show that it is one of those ends which Almighty God sometimes directly intends by them.

XXII. Another end which we find the divine wisdom had in view in miracles was, to convince idolaters that He was the only true God of all the earth, when at any time He sought to make known and propagate His true religion among them, or to punish them for their impieties and blasphemies against it. Thus, when Naaman the Syrian was miraculously cured of his leprosy by washing seven times in the Jordan, as the prophet Elisha had desired him, "he returned to the man of God, he and all his company, and came and stood before him, and he said, Behold, now I know that there is no God in all the earth but in Israel," 4 Kings, v. 15. Here we see the happy effects of this miracle in convincing Naaman of the falsity of the superstition in which he had been brought up, and in bringing him to the knowledge and service of the only true God. On the other hand, the glorious deliverance of king Hezekiah from the impious Sennacherib, was foretold and executed in a miraculous manner, in order to punish that prince for his haughty and impious blasphemies against the true God, and to convince him and all his host that the God of Israel, whom he had blasphemed, was the sovereign Lord of the earth, and that all the power and strength of his numerous armies were wholly in the hands of this Supreme Being, and a mere nothing before Him. See the whole history, 4 Kings, xvii. xix., and Isaiah, xxxvi. xxxvii.

XXIII. It is commonly noticed as a remarkable instance of the divine providence, that whilst, by the dispersion of the ten tribes, and the captivity of the Jews in Babylon, God justly punished His people for their repeated crimes and frequent rebellion against Him, He at the same time made use of this to convey to these other nations a knowledge of Himself, of His religion, and of the sacred books, and thus to dispose them for receiving, in process of time, the Redeemer and His doctrine, when He should afterwards be sent among mankind. To do this the more effectually, we find that

He wrought the most glorious miracles during the Babylonian captivity, which extorted, even from His inveterate enemies, a signal confession of His almighty power, and of His being the only King and sovereign Lord of the earth.

The impious and haughty Nebuchadnezzar, seeing the firm resolution of the three holy youths in refusing to comply with his idolatry, and to worship the golden statue that he had set up, was filled with indignation, and in his fury expressed his pride and arrogance in this blasphemous manner,—"Who is that God that shall deliver you out of my hands?" But when he saw them walking loose in the midst of the fiery furnace, confounded and amazed he called them out, acknowledged them for servants of the most high God, and broke out into this glorious attestation of His divinity: "Blessed be the God of Shadrach, Mesach, and Abed-nego, who has sent His angel and delivered His servants that trusted in Him. . . . . Therefore I make a decree, that every people, nation, and language, which speak anything amiss against the God of Shadrach, Mesach, and Abed-nego, shall be cut in pieces, and their houses made a dunghill; because there is no other God that can deliver after this sort."—See Dan. iii. 28, 29.

Again, when the prophet Daniel had related to the king his dream, which he had forgotten, and which none of the wise men among the Chaldeans could discover, and when he showed him also the meaning and interpretation of it, the king was so amazed that "he fell on his face and worshipped Daniel, and commanded that they should offer an oblation and sweet odours to him. And the king answered unto Daniel and said, Of a truth it is that your God is a God of gods, and a Lord of kings, and a Revealer of secrets, seeing thou couldst reveal this secret," Dan. ii. 46, 47. Another example to the same purpose we have in the preservation of Daniel in the lions' den, which made such an impression on Darius, another heathen and idolatrous prince, that he wrote to all his subjects as follows : " Peace be multiplied unto you : I make a decree, that in every dominion of my kingdom, men tremble and fear before the God of Daniel ; for He is the living God and steadfast for ever, and His kingdom that which shall not be destroyed, and His dominion shall be even unto the end. He delivereth and rescueth, and worketh signs and wonders in heaven, and in earth, who hath delivered Daniel from the power of the lions," Dan. vi.

XXIV. I shall now briefly sum up what we have seen in this and the preceding chapter. We find, from undoubted facts related in the sacred Word of God itself, that God has been pleased to perform many great and astonishing miracles at different times and in various places, for the following ends : First, to convince mankind that the doctrine which He revealed to them by those who wrought these miracles in His name, was truly His doctrine, and thereby to engage them the more readily to receive, and the more steadfastly to embrace it. Secondly, to defend His revelation once made, and to preserve the religion which He had given to His people from all attempts in after-ages to corrupt or destroy it. Thirdly, to assert His own honour against all false gods and their idolatrous worship. Fourthly, to engage His people to believe and trust in Him, to love Him, to obey Him, and to serve Him only, and thus to promote the sanctification and perfection of their souls. Fifthly, to assert and vindicate the sanctity of His priesthood, and of all those holy things made use of in His immediate worship, and to procure due respect and veneration to them. Sixthly, to show the sanctity of those holy persons whom He sends from time to time into the world, as His messengers to men, and to gain due respect and credit to them, that by their words and examples others may be excited to greater piety and fervour. Seventhly, to convince idolaters and those who know Him not that He is the only true God, when at any time He is pleased to communicate the knowledge of Himself and of His holy will to them. From all this we draw the obvious and natural conclusion, " that since Almighty God has been pleased to work the most stupendous miracles for gaining these ends, it was most worthy of Him to do so; and as it was so then, it is no less so now, and will be at all times whenever the like ends may require it."

CHAPTER VII.

THE PARTICULAR ENDS OF MIRACLES KNOWN FROM REVELATION.

I. WHEN we consider the importance of the general ends of miracles related in the two preceding chapters—ends in which the glory of the Supreme Being, and the sanctification and happiness of whole nations, were so intimately concerned—we are not surprised that a God of infinite goodness should condescend to exert His almighty power for objects so worthy of Himself. But it may seem somewhat wonderful if we find that He has been no less liberal in performing the most surprising miracles, even when only the sanctification and happiness of particular persons were immediately concerned. And, indeed, it is from this supposed disproportion between the end and the miracle performed, as if the former were not worthy of the latter, that free-thinkers draw objections against the existence of particular miracles.

Their mistake arises from their ignorance or inattention to three very important truths, and evidently shows how superficial is their investigation of these matters, notwithstanding the air of authority and self-sufficiency with which they dogmatise concerning them. These truths I shall here display, because they serve as so many principles to illustrate the ends of miracles, and at once invalidate every objection against their existence, drawn from the pretended insignificance of these ends.

II. First, the intrinsic value of one single soul is immeasurably greater, and more esteemed by Almighty God, than the whole inanimate creation. This is a truth which we have seen in a certain manner proved by natural reason; but it is only revelation which can place it in its full and proper light, as only He who made the soul, and therefore perfectly knows its real value, can give us a just and adequate appreciation of it. And the idea which Almighty God gives us in His Holy Scriptures of the high value and intrinsic worth of a rational soul is indeed noble and sublime.

In the first place, He assures us that, with regard to our bodies and our worldly interest, the whole is not equal nor comparable to one soul: "What will it profit a man," says Jesus Christ, "to gain *the whole world* and lose his own soul? or what will a man give in exchange for his soul?" Matt. xvi. Alas! the world is but a fleeting shadow which must end with time, but the soul will exist for ever. There is, then, as great a difference between the value of the whole world and the worth of an immortal soul, as there is between time and eternity.

2dly, We learn from Scripture that the devil, who is termed in holy writ "the god of this world," and "the ruler of the powers of darkness," puts such an immense value upon souls, that his continual employment is to go about like a roaring lion seeking to destroy and secure them to himself, and that he is willing to give all the treasures of this world for a single act of worship from one soul. When our blessed Saviour was pleased to submit to the humiliation of being tempted by Satan, after other means had failed, that wicked spirit at last takes Him up to a high mountain, and there " showed unto Him all the kingdoms of the world in a moment of time. And the devil said unto Him, All this power will I give Thee, and the glory of them; for that is delivered unto me, and to whomsoever I will I give it. If Thou, therefore, wilt worship me, all shall be Thine," Luke, iv.

What an idea does not this give us of the high worth of a single soul above all the material world, when we see this wicked spirit, who knows the value of both, giving so great a preference to the former! But even this is little, or rather nothing, compared to the esteem which Almighty God Himself has shown for the soul of man, in sending his own only Son, equal to Himself, to redeem mankind from misery, at no less a price than the last drop of His precious blood, shed in the midst of the most cruel torments!

When we consider the infinite dignity of the person of Jesus Christ, His innocence and sanctity, and the inestimable value of His precious life, we cannot fail to conceive the most exalted idea of the worth of the human soul. We see that glorious Being submitting to the utmost humiliation, concealing His sanctity and innocence under the outward appearance of a sinner, and laying down His precious life in the midst of torments, for no other end than to save our souls, and redeem us from that interminable misery which we had deserved by sin. What shall I say of the solicitude and care which Almighty God everywhere expresses throughout His Holy Scriptures for our happiness? His ardent desire for our salvation? which are the most endearing proofs of the high value and esteem which He sets upon the soul of man.*

* The following beautiful lines of Dr Young, in his 'Night Thoughts,' are very much to our purpose here :—

If, therefore, in the judgment of Jesus Christ Himself, the whole world is not to be compared to one soul, can we be surprised that Almighty God should cause a change or alteration in the ordinary course of the inferior creation, when the perfection and happiness of a soul can be by that means promoted? If He sets so high a value on the soul of man as to lay down His own life to redeem him, can we wonder that He should suspend for a time the laws which govern inanimate matter, or cause any unusual change in it, in order to secure the salvation of a soul which has cost Him so much.

To accomplish the redemption of mankind, "He spoke much, and did more, and suffered most of all," as a certain holy man observes; but to perform the most stupendous miracle, He has only to will, and immediately His will is obeyed. If, then, He has actually done the greater to gain souls, can we be surprised that He should do the less? And is it not most worthy of Him to do what costs Him only to will it, in order to secure an end for which He has already done and suffered so much, even a cruel and ignominious death? If deists and freethinkers would attentively consider this, instead of ridiculing miracles, because they profess to see no great and general good end to be procured by them, they would easily be convinced that it is most worthy and becoming the majesty of God to perform even the most surprising miracles, to suspend the whole order, and all the laws of

> " Know'st thou th' importance of a soul immortal?
> Behold this midnight glory, worlds on worlds!
> Amazing pomp! redouble this amaze;
> Ten thousand add; add twice ten thousand more;
> Then weigh the whole; *one soul* outweighs *them all*,
> And calls th' astonishing magnificence
> Of unintelligent creation poor."
> —*Complaint*, Night VII.

nature, when the perfection or happiness of one single soul can be the better secured by so doing.

Secondly, Another cause of their mistaken judgment is their ignorance or forgetfulness of two objects which the divine wisdom has in view in working miracles—the general or universal ends common to all miracles, and the particular ends in various individual cases. The general and universal ends which God has ultimately and principally in view in every miracle, and indeed in all His works, as we have seen above, are—first, His own glory, and then the salvation of souls. The former is invariably the consequence of every true miracle, because it necessarily manifests to the world the power, wisdom, goodness, or justice of God. But besides, it also promotes the perfection and salvation of souls, by exciting in the hearts of all who see, or afterwards come to know it, sentiments of gratitude, love, and confidence in the divine goodness, or a salutary fear of the divine judgments. The particular and inferior ends of miracles are those good and salutary effects which are more immediately intended, and directly produced by them, either for the benefit or punishment of those concerned, which vary with different circumstances, but are always conducive and subservient to the above general ends, as the bestowing temporal favours, or the inflicting temporal sufferings. Of these the former naturally excite the most grateful sentiments of love, confidence, praise, thanksgiving, and other such holy virtues, in the hearts of those who see or know of such miracles, and especially of those who experience the beneficent effects of them; and the latter tend no less powerfully to rouse sinners from their lethargy, to move them to repentance, and to inspire all who see or hear of them with a salutary fear of the divine justice, and a dread of offending their Creator.

CHAPTER VII.

A miracle may be performed in behalf of a single person only, and seem directly to tend to his good alone; yet, when known to others, it becomes a more general good, and, if published to the world, a universal benefit, producing the best effects, manifesting the glory of God, and promoting the good of souls, even to the latest posterity. Witness the miracles of this kind recorded either in holy writ or in the genuine lives of the saints, which it is impossible to read, with a faithful heart, without being moved to sentiments of piety. Here, then, lies another great source of the mistaken judgment and false reasoning of deists. They overlook the general and most valuable ends necessarily found in all true miracles, which are, the displaying, in a sensible and affecting manner, the perfections and glory of the Supreme Being, and thereby promoting the perfection of the soul of man. Instead of observing this, they are perpetually grovelling on the earth. They confine their thoughts to the immediate sensible effects produced by miracles; and because they do not always discover in them some remarkable result relating to present happiness, they conceive that what they see is unworthy of God, beneath the dignity of the divine majesty, and by no means deserving of miraculous interposition. The falsity of such reasoning is manifest from what has been said above, and will appear still more when we come to the facts themselves.

Thirdly, Another cause of their mistake lies in supposing that the ideas of the Supreme Being regarding miracles are similar to their own. Miracles in the eyes of man are something exceedingly great and wonderful, the effects of a power altogether inconceivable to us; and they naturally fill our minds not only with wonder and amazement, but also either with joy and pleasure, or with fear and dread, according as they affect ourselves or others.

Hence, according to our ideas, a miracle is an arduous work requiring a power superior to anything we know; and the more uncommon or extraordinary in our eyes is the thing done, the greater effort of power appears to be involved. From this we speak of greater and smaller miracles, according as they seem to require a greater or less effort of power in their performance. But can any reasonable person imagine that they appear in this light to Almighty God? How preposterous the idea! With regard to God, there is no difference between what we term the greatest and the smallest miracle; between annihilating a mite and annihilating the universe; between creating a grain of sand and creating a world. To Him the one is as easy as the other. A single act of His will equally suffices to perform them both. Nor to Him can anything be wonderful, because He perfectly knows all that possibly can be done in creatures, and actually sees everything that will be accomplished in them to all eternity. Hence to Him nothing can possibly be new, nothing wonderful, nothing can be miraculous in His eyes; "the works of all flesh are before Him," says the wise man, "and there is nothing hidden from His eyes: He sees from eternity to eternity, and nothing is wonderful in His sight," Ecclus. xxxix. 24, 25. This great truth many entirely overlook, and argue as if they imagined that miracles made the same impression upon God that they do on man; that what we call a greater miracle is to Him more difficult than a smaller; that therefore the one is more precious in His eyes than the other, and requires a proportionably more valuable end to be gained before He can be induced to perform it.

Perhaps few persons would distinctly express, or even deliberately entertain, these ideas; but they seem to lurk in the minds of many, and to influence their judgments.

For how many immediately conclude miracles to be false because they do not perceive what seems to them a sufficient proportionate end? The folly of this is evident, both from the principles of reason and from the many express facts declared in Holy Scripture. These demonstrate that Almighty God has been pleased to perform many miracles for the benefit even of particular persons, and where the immediate end would seem, according to modern ideas, to be but unimportant, but which very much conduced to promote the great end of all miracles, and continue to this time to display the infinite goodness or justice of God, and to fill the hearts of sincere Christians with devout affection towards their Creator. These we shall divide into different classes, according to the nature of the particular ends immediately and directly intended by them.

III. The first class comprises those cases where Almighty God, communicating any truth, giving any commission, or making any promise to His servants, was pleased to convince them by miracles that these were from Him, and not a delusion. We have seen above how He acted in regard to Moses when He appeared to him in the wilderness, in the burning bush, and gave him the commission to deliver His people out of Egypt. He was pleased to perform miracles upon this occasion by turning the rod of Moses into a serpent, by making his hand leprous, and then restoring both to their former state, for no other immediate end than to convince Moses that it was God Himself who was giving him this commission, and to inspire him with confidence in the divine protection for power to perform it with success.

IV. Another beautiful example of this we find in the call of Gideon to be the deliverer of the people of God from the tyranny of the Midianites. After the angel had

ENDS OF MIRACLES FROM REVELATION.

conversed with him, and told him that he should "save Israel from the hands of the Midianites," and encouraged him by the promise of his protection—"Surely I will be with thee, and thou shalt smite the Midianites as one man"—Gideon, doubtful if this were really a messenger from heaven, asked a sign: "If now," says he, "I have found grace in thy sight, then show me a sign that thou talkest with me." Then going into the house he made ready the flesh of a kid, and brought it out, with unleavened cakes and a measure of flour, and a pot of broth, and presented them to the angel. The angel desired him to lay them upon the rock, and "pour out the broth, and he did so. Then the angel of the Lord put forth the end of the staff that was in his hand, and touched the flesh and the unleavened cakes; and there arose up fire out of the rock, and consumed the flesh and the unleavened cakes. And the angel of the Lord departed out of his sight," Judges, vi.

Here we see a miracle—a flame of fire brought from the rock in an instant by the touch of the angel's staff, and consuming the offering—for no other immediate end than to satisfy a single person, and to convince him that the commission he had received was from God Himself. Were we to rest here, our modern infidels might descant upon the fact, by depreciating the end obtained—by observing that the miracle was needless, that the end could have been obtained without it, as was done with several of the other judges whom God raised up about this time to deliver His people, and encouraged to undertake that work by the ordinary impressions which He made in their minds without any miracle whatever.

Doubtless Almighty God could have done this also in Gideon's case; neither was He at all obliged to do it by a miracle: but here is an established fact which shows that He does not think it unworthy of Himself to condescend to the desires of His servant, and to work miracles for giving satisfaction even to a single person, and for convincing him that it is He Himself who is speaking with him. We ought not, however, to rest on this immediate end alone, but to consider the impression which this miracle made in Gideon's mind; how it disclosed to him the infinite goodness and condescension of Almighty God—how it filled him with fear of His divine majesty—and with what superior confidence and courage it inspired him to undertake the great work to which God had called him.

These were glorious ends, worthy of the Almighty to procure by repeated miracles, if necessary; and, in fact, we find that He did perform repeated miracles on this very occasion, the more effectually to procure them; for when Gideon, some time after, had gathered together his army to fight for his people, being desirous of further assurance from heaven, he " said unto God, If Thou wilt save Israel by mine hand, as Thou hast said, behold, I will put a fleece of wool in the floor; and if the dew be on the fleece only, and it be dry upon all the earth beside, then shall I know that Thou wilt save Israel by mine hand, as Thou hast said. And it was so; for he rose up early in the morning, and thrust the fleece together, and wringed the dew out of the fleece, a bowl full of water. And Gideon said unto God, Let not Thine anger be hot against me, and I will speak but this once: let me prove, I pray Thee, but this once with the fleece; let it now be dry only upon the fleece, and upon all the ground let there be dew. And God did so that night; for it was dry upon the fleece only, and there was dew on all the ground," Judges, vi.

What a field for sneers and ridicule is here! How

unworthy, would our modern deists say, of the Almighty to be occupied with such trifles! How far beneath the majesty of God to alter the ordinary course established in nature for gratifying the idle desires of a person who ought rather to have been punished for his incredulity after what he had already seen! "I believe too much in God," says Rousseau, "to credit so many miracles so little worthy of His nature." But a pious soul would draw a very different conclusion, and would read, in these facts, the infinite goodness and condescension of God, His paternal indulgence towards His servants, His high esteem of a single soul, which He is ready to gratify even by working repeated miracles: and from these considerations would be filled with sentiments of praise, thanksgiving, confidence, love, and gratitude, towards such infinite goodness. Nor is there any reason to doubt but that this was the effect produced in the mind of Gideon; and the same effect it continues to produce to this day in all pious souls, who, firmly believing the sacred truths revealed by God, read his inspired Scriptures with reverence and devotion. Another example somewhat similar to this we have in the angel that appeared to the parents of Samson and foretold his birth, though his mother had been till that time barren. When they were offering sacrifice to the Lord, "the angel did wondrously" before them, "and ascended up in the flame of the altar," to convince them that he was a messenger from God, and that what he had said was true. —See Judges, xiii.

V. The miracle performed by Isaiah the prophet before king Hezekiah deserves particular notice here. This good king had fallen sick, and was threatened with death; but, upon his tears and prayers, God was pleased to add fifteen years to his life, and He sent the prophet

Isaiah to inform him that in three days he should be able to go to the house of God. But Hezekiah, anxious for a proof of the truth of this prophecy, "said unto Isaiah, What shall be the sign that the Lord will heal me, and that I shall go up into the house of the Lord the third day? And Isaiah said, This sign shalt thou have of the Lord, that the Lord will do the thing that He hath spoken: shall the shadow go forward ten degrees, or go back ten degrees? And Hezekiah answered, It is a light thing for the shadow to go down ten degrees: nay, but let the shadow return backward ten degrees. And Isaiah the prophet cried unto the Lord, and He brought the shadow ten degrees backward, by which it had gone down in the dial of Achaz," 4 Kings, xx.

With what a stupendous miracle are we presented! The ordinary course of nature suspended! the diurnal* motion of the heavens not only retarded or stopped, as was done when at Joshua's command the sun stood still, but absolutely reversed, and a motion diametrically opposite impressed upon them! And all for what end? To satisfy a single person of the certainty of an event which, in the short space of three days, he would have seen verified by the fact itself.

Here human reason is lost in amazement, and infidelity would sneer at this relation, and rejecting it with disdain as a palpable absurdity. "Can reason ever believe," will the deist say, " that the Supreme Being has nothing else to do than attend to the idle curiosity of such worms as we are? to gratify every foolish desire of man, much less to work miracles for such an end? But to suspend

---

* The intelligent reader will easily perceive that I express myself here in the Scripture style, which on this subject accommodates itself to the appearances which these things make on the eyes of the beholders.

ENDS OF MIRACLES FROM REVELATION. 149

the universal laws of the whole creation, to alter the course of the heavens, to undo in a manner His own work, to gratify the impatience of a single person, which the short space of three days would have satisfied in the natural course of things, without any miracle at all; how ridiculous to believe such a tale, so unworthy of God! What proportion is there between the superlative greatness of the miracle here said to be wrought and the end gained by it? Does the Almighty do anything without some end worthy of Himself, and worthy of the means He uses? and do we see any such end here?" Such are the impious arguments daily used in similar cases not only by deists, but even sometimes by those who profess themselves Christians.

It is indeed strange to observe their unreasonable conduct. If the miracle recorded be in their eyes small or trifling in itself, they reject it upon this very account— "it is unworthy of God to be employed in such trifles." If the miracle be great and stupendous, and which evidently none but God can perform, then "it is ridiculous," they say, "to suppose that God would do such things without some great end proportionate to the greatness of the means he uses." The cause of their mistake, however, is evident from the principles already laid down; for in the end they consider only the immediate secondary effect, failing to consider how much a miracle, wrought for an immediate end, tends farther to manifest the divine perfections, God's esteem and love for the soul of man, and to excite in the hearts of those who see it the most excellent affections towards such infinite goodness. And these, the natural consequences of all miracles, are ends worthy of anything which God may perform in the material creation, whether great or small. Now, who can doubt but that these ends were exceedingly promoted by the miracle above related? Nay, who is there to this day that reads the account of it in the Holy Scripture with a faithful and pious heart, and does not feel himself penetrated with affections of admiration, reverence, piety, and love? The effects, then, were not confined to Hezekiah and Isaiah alone, or to those present when the miracle was wrought; but the fact being recorded in holy writ, its effects have continued in numbers of souls to this day, and will never cease to be produced in many more as long as the world endures. Now, will unbelievers say that these are not effects worthy to be procured even by the greatest miracle?

Again, with reference to the thing done, their mistake lies in this—they do not consider that, whether the miracle be great or small, stupendous or less surprising, it is the same to God. To Him the one is as easy as the other. He has only to will, and what He wills is instantly accomplished. But the more extraordinary the miracle, the more effectually does it promote the great and ultimate ends of all miracles—the glory of God and the good of souls. I might here mention other examples of this class, as that Zacharias being struck dumb, in proof of the truth of what the angel Gabriel declared concerning the birth of his son St John the Baptist; but the above are amply sufficient.

VI. In the second class, I shall relate those cases wherein we find Almighty God condescending to work miracles in favour of particular persons as a reward of their virtues, particularly their acts of charity, their confidence in His goodness, and constancy in His service.

When Elijah the prophet was forced to leave his retreat in the wilderness, Almighty God ordered him to go to Zarephath, where he had commanded a widow woman to feed him. This poor woman, by the long continuance of the famine, was reduced to a handful of meal and a little oil in a cruse, and was just going to make the last cake for herself and son, and then resign herself to death, when the prophet met her, and desired her to bring him a little water, and bake a cake first for him, and then for herself and son. Considering her condition, this was a hard demand, and a severe trial of her charity. It is true, indeed, that the prophet at the same time foretold her in the name of God that "her meal should not waste, nor her oil fail, till the Lord sent rain upon the earth;" but he was a stranger, and she a heathen woman of Sidon, not belonging to the people of Israel. She did not then know him to be a prophet, and an impostor might have said the same thing to gain his end. Nevertheless the poor woman, seeing him a stranger and in distress, did as he desired, and first made a cake for him. In reward of her charity, Almighty God multiplied her handful of meal and her cruse of oil to such a degree "that she, and he (Elijah), and her house, did eat many days; and the barrel of meal wasted not, neither did the cruse of oil fail, according to the word of the Lord which He spake by Elijah," 3 Kings, xvii. Here we have a miracle the immediate and direct end of which was the rewarding an act of charity, and the supplying the wants of the prophet.

Probably our modern freethinkers would not in their wisdom deem this an end worthy of so great a miracle; but we see that Almighty God did, and performed it for this very purpose. But if they should differ in opinion upon this point from the God that made them, let them not be so rash as to reject the belief of this miracle upon the ground that they see no worthy end. Let them reflect that what they judge unworthy was only the immediate inferior and particular end; and that the ultimate end of all miracles, the manifesting the glory of God and the procuring the perfection of souls, were most admirably promoted by this glorious miracle. Let them consider what effect it must have had on the heart of the prophet himself, and of the poor widow and her family. Neither were its effects confined to that family alone. Being recorded in holy writ, it continues to produce the same in all believers, and to be an admirable incentive to the holy virtues of hospitality and charity, so pleasing in the eyes of God, and so profitable to those who practise them.

But the goodness of God did not stop here. It happened some time after that the widow's son fell sick and died, and the afflicted mother had recourse to the prophet in her sorrow. He, full of compassion and gratitude, carried the dead child to the upper chamber where he lay, and prayed God to restore the child to life. And observe the argument he used to induce God to grant his petition: "O Lord God," says he, "hast Thou also brought evil upon the widow with whom I sojourn, by slaying her son?" Mark "with whom I sojourn," the person who has been so hospitable, so charitable to me. This was too strong a motive not to influence the mercy of our God to yield; and therefore, upon the prophet's praying that his soul might return, "the Lord heard the voice of Elijah, and the soul of the child came unto him again, and he revived; and he delivered him alive unto his mother," 3 Kings, xvii. This also shows that Almighty God deems it worthy of Himself to perform the greatest miracles to reward the virtues and charitable actions of His servants.

VII. Another beautiful example of this we see in what the prophet Elisha did for the Shunammite woman, his charitable hostess. She, seeing the prophet often passing by, "constrained him to turn into her house, and eat bread;" and, conceiving a high opinion of him as a man of God, "she said unto her husband, Behold now, I perceive that this is a holy man of God that passes by us continually: let us make a little chamber, I pray thee, and let us set for him there a bed, and a table, and a stool, and a candlestick; and it shall be when he cometh to us, that he shall turn in thither," 4 Kings, iv.

This is the description which the Scripture gives us of the hospitality and charity of this good woman, and of her regard for those whom she believed to be servants of God. The prophet was not insensible of her kindness; and, desiring to show his gratitude, called to ask what he could do for her in return; and understanding by his servant that though she was a woman of condition, and well provided for, yet she had no child, and that her husband was advanced in years, he immediately prophesied that within a year she should have a son, which was fulfilled accordingly; "for the woman conceived and bare a son at that season that Elisha had said unto her," verse 17; and thus the blessing which of all others her heart desired, was bestowed upon her in a miraculous manner, in reward of her hospitality and charity to God's servant.

The divine goodness to her did not stop here. This very child, being grown up, fell sick and died, and, at the prayer of the prophet, was miraculously restored to life—as in the case above mentioned, a still farther confirmation of how agreeable her conduct was to Almighty God, and how ready He is to reward acts of charity and mercy. Again, when Almighty God had resolved to send a famine upon the land, which was to last for seven years, Elisha foretold it to his benefactress, advising her to leave her country during that time, which she did accordingly. And after seven years were passed, and plenty restored to the land, the goodness of God so ordered that, Elisha being then dead, his servant was relating to the king the wonderful actions of his master, and especially the raising this woman's son from the dead, at the very instant of time when the woman and her son, being returned to their own country, presented themselves to the king to petition that their lands, which had been seized in their absence, might be restored. "And Gehazi said, My lord, O king, this is the woman, and this is her son whom Elisha restored to life." Such an effect had this providential concurrence of favourable circumstances upon the king, that "he appointed unto her a certain officer, saying, Restore all that was hers, and all the fruits of the field, since the day she left the land even until now," 2 Kings, viii. Observe here what a chain of benefits is miraculously bestowed upon this woman in reward of her charity, as the more immediate end proposed by them, but which at the same time most admirably displayed the infinite power and goodness of God, and cannot fail to produce the most excellent effects in the hearts of all who believe them.

VIII. The deliverance of the three children from the fiery furnace, and of Daniel from the lions, belong also to this class. The confidence which the three holy youths had in God is plain from their heroic answer to Nebuchadnezzar, when he ordered them, under pain of being thrown into the fiery furnace, to fall down and adore the idol which he had erected, adding this impious vaunt, "And who is that God that shall deliver you out of my hands?" Dan. iii. 15. To this they replied, "Our God Whom we serve is able to deliver us from the burning fiery furnace, and He will deliver us from thine hand,

ENDS OF MIRACLES FROM REVELATION. 155

O king," verse 17. And their constancy in the service of their God they express in the following verse in these beautiful words: "But if not, be it known unto thee, O king, that we will not serve thy god, nor worship the golden image that thou hast set up." That their miraculous preservation was intended directly as a reward of these their virtues, is acknowledged by the king himself, when, after calling them out of the furnace, he said, " Blessed be the God of Shadrach, Mesach, and Abednego, who has sent His angel and delivered His servants who trusted in Him, and yielded their bodies, that they might not serve nor worship any god except their own God," *ibid.*, verse 28.

As to Daniel, when the king came next morning to the den of lions, and cried to him, "O Daniel, servant of the living God, is thy God, whom thou servest continually, able to deliver thee from the lions?" Daniel immediately answered him, "My God hath sent His angel, and hast shut the lions' mouths that they have not hurt me; forasmuch as before Him innocency was found in me," Dan. vi. 20, &c. And upon this, by the king's command, "Daniel was taken up out of the den, and no manner of hurt was found upon him, because he believed in his God," verse 23.

IX. To the third class belong all the examples in holy writ where the immediate end was only to supply the various bodily wants of particular persons, and that sometimes in things so unimportant as to unassisted natural reason might seem trifling and unworthy of divine interposition. Samson is employed by Almighty God to deliver His people from the yoke of the Philistines, and to fight their battles against these their enemies. For this purpose he is endowed with amazing strength, with which he performs wonders. He goes out against his enemies all alone. With no other arms than the jaw-bone of an ass, he enters the battle, gains an entire victory, and kills a thousand men with his own hand. But, scorched by the heat of the day, and exhausted by fatigue, he is upon the point of perishing himself of thirst. Does the Almighty forsake His servant in this extremity? By no means. He even works a miracle to relieve him; for upon his crying to Him for help, He "clave a hollow place that was in the jaw-bone of the ass," which he had thrown out of his hand; and lo! it sends forth a stream of water to quench his thirst and refresh him.—Judges, xv.

X. The great Elias is ordered to flee to the desert from the face of his persecuting enemy, who sought his life only on account of his steady adherence to the service of his God. This may be thought to have been only flying from one death to another, from the sword of Achab to famine in the wilderness. But God is his protector, and works an unheard-of miracle to sustain him. He commands the wild ravens to provide for His servant, and accordingly they bring him every day a piece of meat and a loaf of bread, whilst the brook supplies his drink; and this miraculous provision continued to be brought him daily so long as he remained in that desert. At another time the same great prophet was again in the wilderness, destitute of all human assistance, and an angel is sent with a cake of bread and a bottle of water to feed him, and such strength communicated to him by this miraculous food that he needed nothing more for the space of forty days thereafter.

XI. A poor widow is oppressed by her husband's creditors, and having nothing wherewith to pay, they seize upon her two sons to carry them off for bond slaves. In her distress she flies to the prophet Elisha, and reminds him that her husband had been a good man, as he himself knew, and one that feared the Lord. The prophet, moved with compassion, asks what she had in the house, and she answered she had nothing but a pot of oil. Then he said, "Go borrow thee vessels abroad of all thy neighbours, even empty vessels; borrow not a few. And when thou art come in, thou shalt shut the door upon thee and upon thy sons, and thou shalt pour out into all those vessels, and thou shalt set aside that which is full." Accordingly they proceeded, and the oil was so multiplied in her hands that it continued to flow in abundance, and never stopped till they had no more empty vessels. Then the prophet told her to sell this miraculous oil and to pay her debts, and that she and her sons might live upon the rest.—4 Kings, iv.

XII. Again, "The men of the city said unto Elisha, Behold, I pray thee, the situation of this city is pleasant, as my lord seeth; but the water is very bad, and the ground barren. And he said, Bring me a new cruse, and put salt therein; and they brought it to him. And he went forth unto the spring of the waters and cast the salt in there, and said, Thus saith the Lord, I have healed these waters; there shall not be from thence any more death or barrenness. So the waters were healed unto this day, according to the saying of Elisha which he spake," 4 Kings, ii. 19.

XIII. In the time of a great dearth the same holy prophet "came to Gilgal, and a number of the sons of the prophets were sitting before him. And he said to his servant, Set on the great pot, and seethe pottage for the sons of the prophets. And one went out into the field to gather herbs, and found a wild vine, and gathered there of wild gourds his lap full, and came and shred them into the pot of pottage; for they knew them not. So they poured out for the men to eat. And it came to pass, as they were eating of the pottage, that they cried out, and said, O thou man of God, there is death in the pot. And they could not eat thereof." The prophet, unwilling to lose so great a quantity of food in the time of famine, immediately performs a miracle to cure it, by only casting a little meal into the pot: "And he said, Then bring meal. And he cast it into the pot; and he said, Pour out for the people, that they may eat. And there was no harm in the pot," 4 Kings, iv.

Again, during the same famine, a present was brought to Elisha of twenty loaves of barley, and some full ears of corn, which he immediately ordered to be given to the people. "And his servant said, What, should I set this before a hundred men?" But Elisha replied, "Give the people, that they may eat; for thus saith the Lord, They shall eat, and shall leave thereof." And accordingly these loaves were so miraculously multiplied, that "they did eat, and left thereof, according to the word of the Lord," 4 Kings, iv.

XIV. The two holy prophets, Elijah and Elisha, were walking together to the place where the former was to be taken up. On their way they came to the river Jordan, which they had no human means of passing; and, after standing a little by the river, "Elijah took his mantle and wrapt it together, and smote the waters, and they were divided hither and thither, so that they two went over on dry ground," 4 Kings, ii. And the same miraculous division was repeated in favour of Elisha alone, when he was returning home, after his master had been taken from him.` Lastly, to mention only one other instance under this class, when the sons of the prophets were cutting wood on the banks of the Jordan, in order

ENDS OF MIRACLES FROM REVELATION.

to enlarge their dwelling, the head of one of their axes fell into the water. The poor man was greatly afflicted at this misfortune, and cried to Elisha, who was present with them, "Alas, master! for it was borrowed." Elisha, pitying the poor man's case, " said, Where fell it? and he showed him the place. And he cut down a stick, and cast it in thither, and the iron did swim. Therefore said he, Take it up to thee; and he put out his hand and took it," 4 Kings, vi. Many other instances might be brought, from the curing diseases, delivering from dangers, and the like; but these are obvious throughout the whole Scripture, and what I have here related are fully sufficient for my purpose.

XV. In all the examples related under this class, and others that might be mentioned, the immediate end directly intended by Almighty God, was the relieving the temporal wants of particular persons; and that not only in the greater concerns of life, as supplying them with food when they were perishing, or the delivering them from imminent dangers, but even in their smaller wants: such are the two cases last mentioned. The end proposed by these miracles was not the confirming any point of doctrine disputed, or authorising any new revelation; neither was it directly to manifest the sanctity of His servants, though this also was a consequence of some of them. The only end directly and immediately intended was, as we have seen, the relieving the temporal wants of particular persons in distress.

We must conclude, therefore, that in the judgment of God Himself, the relieving the temporal necessities of mankind, even of particular persons, is an end worthy to be procured, by miracles even the most extraordinary. At the same time, it is an admirable and well-adapted means to secure the other more important ends common to every miracle, the glory of God and the good of souls; for nothing can give us a more lively sense of the infinite goodness and power of God than the beneficent effects of miracles—nothing can contribute more powerfully to excite affections of gratitude, confidence, and love towards our kind and bountiful Benefactor. The important end of miracles is to manifest the goodness, power, and other attributes of God, and to promote the sanctification of our souls. Now, what can contribute more to this than to see the Almighty condescending to work miracles to supply even the most trifling wants of His servants; or to find Him, on the other hand, overturning, in a manner, all the laws of the universe, and reversing the very nature of things, in order to defend those that trust in Him? The trifling smallness, if I may use the expression, of the miracles wrought in the one case, and their amazing greatness in the other, equally contribute to the same great end—namely, the manifesting in the most striking manner the infinite love of God to man; and those who object to miracles on these considerations, show themselves ignorant of the nature of true love, and of the tender feelings of the human heart.

True love esteems nothing little, nothing trifling, nothing unworthy of attention, that can serve or please the object of affection. It braves dangers, despises hardships, and cheerfully undergoes all labours, however great, or even seemingly above its strength, when required by the interest or happiness of the beloved object. Such is the nature of the human heart, that it cannot resist the influence of such conduct; for whether we perceive a continual attention in another to please and oblige us on all occasions, however trifling, or see him doing great things for our service, in either case we are equally convinced of the sincerity of his affection, and our heart is naturally inclined to make to him a suitable return of love.

How convincing, then, how affecting a proof is it of the infinite love of God to man, to behold Him, the sovereign Lord of all things, condescending to use both these means of gaining our hearts to Himself! On the one hand, He shows such an amiable attention to all our wants, as even miraculously to supply them; and on the other, He performs the greatest miracles when the necessities of His servants require them. What effect must not this have upon a grateful soul!—what tender and affectionate feelings must it not necessarily excite in the breast of man towards that supreme Being, Who gives us such affecting proofs of the sincerity of His love, and uses such means to gain our affections! But what insensible, what inhuman hearts must not they have who can resist these proofs—nay, who even dare to despise and ridicule this conduct of their Creator, to call it in question and absolutely deny it; and that upon the very grounds which are the most convincing proof of the sincerity, as well as of the greatness, of His love and affection to His creatures!

XVI. The fourth and last class which I shall here notice, comprises cases of a different immediate tendency, though no less conducive to the great general ends of miracles. Besides showing the almighty power of God, they manifest the severity and rigour of His justice, striking the hearts of sinners with a sense of their danger, and inspiring a salutary fear of offending Him. Some miracles of this class have for their immediate object the correction of the sinner, not his destruction; whilst others destroy the delinquent, and serve chiefly as a warning to others. In both we find that the divine wisdom operates as in the preceding cases, sometimes accomplishing these ends by the weakest instruments, which, in the language of modern infidels, would be called unworthy of God, and beneath His majesty; as the flies, frogs, lice, and other vermin by which He punished Pharaoh; the hornets by which He drove out the Canaanites before His people, and the like; and at other times performing the most surprising miracles for the same purpose—equally, however, in both cases manifesting His own power and sovereignty. By the former He convinces mankind that he stands in no need of creatures to accomplish His ends, or to punish those who offend Him, while the weakest instruments serve in His hand equally as the greatest; and by the latter He shows the immensity of His power, as all created nature becomes subservient to His will, when He pleases to employ it.

XVII. The first example I shall notice is that of Lot's wife. When the angels had led Lot and his family out of Sodom, they commanded them to flee with all speed to the place appointed for them, that they might not be involved in the destruction of that devoted city, and expressly forbade them so much as to look behind them. "Escape for thy life," says the angel; "look not behind thee, neither stay thee in all the plain; escape to the mountain, lest thou be consumed." Lot's wife, solicitous for the friends and goods she had left behind in Sodom, moved by curiosity, and unmindful of, or disregarding, the order of the angel, looked back, and immediately the hand of God was upon her in a most miraculous manner,—"she became a pillar of salt;" a lasting monument of the severity of God's justice upon those who disobey Him! Gen. xix.

Here we may observe that the immediate end obtained

by this miracle regarded only Lot and his two daughters, who alone at that time knew the prohibition given, the transgression committed, and the punishment inflicted. Here, then, we see a miracle proper to the almighty power of God alone—the instantaneous change of a living person into a pillar of salt—performed to the utter destruction of that person in punishment of her sin, where the immediate end directly intended was a warning to three souls only; and consequently that this, in the judgment of God, is an end worthy to be procured even by the greatest miracle. But then it must be owned that the good effects were not confined ultimately to these three, but extended to all in after-ages who should hear and believe what is here related, as displaying the dreadful consequences of sin, the severity of the divine judgments, and exciting in their hearts a salutary fear of offending their great Creator.

This is the very use that Jesus Christ Himself makes of this example in the Gospel, when, foretelling the revelation of the Son of Man, which will be to each one in particular at the hour of death, He exhorts us to take off our affections from creatures, as the best disposition for that day. "Remember," He says, "Lot's wife," Luke, xvii. 32; intimating, that as her affection for what she possessed and was obliged to leave behind in Sodom, prompted her to look back contrary to the command given, and brought on her punishment, so likewise, if our hearts and affections be bound to the things of this world when we are forced to leave all behind us, and to appear before the Son of Man at His revelation to us at death, this attachment will become an occasion of our offending God, and bring upon us likewise ruin and destruction.

XVIII. The beautiful history which the Scripture

gives us of Balaam and his ass deserves a particular place here, as displaying a miracle performed for no other immediate and direct end than to correct a person for a sin committed. When the second messengers of Balak came for Balaam, upon his consulting God whether he should go or not, the answer he received was, "If the men come to call thee, rise up and go with them." Balaam being himself desirous of going, instead of waiting till they should come and call him, "rose up in the morning and saddled his ass, and went with the princes of Moab."

It would do an injury to the sacred Scripture to give what follows in any other than its own words, as they have something particularly affecting in them: "And God's anger was kindled because he went: and the angel of the Lord stood in the way for an adversary against him. Now he was riding upon his ass, and his two servants with him. And the ass saw the angel of the Lord standing in the way, and his sword drawn in his hand; and the ass turned aside out of the way, and went into the field; and Balaam smote the ass to turn her into the way.

"But the angel of the Lord stood in a path of the vineyard, a wall being on this side, and a wall on that side. And when the ass saw the angel of the Lord, she thrust herself unto the wall, and crushed Balaam's foot against the wall; and he smote her again. And the angel of the Lord went further, and stood in a narrow place, where there was no way to turn either to the right hand or to the left. And when the ass saw the angel of the Lord, she fell down under Balaam; and Balaam's anger was kindled, and he smote the ass with a staff. And the Lord opened the mouth of the ass, and she said unto Balaam, What have I done unto thee that thou hast smitten me these three times? And Balaam said unto the ass, Because thou hast mocked me: I would there were a sword in mine hand, for now would I kill thee.

"And the ass said unto Balaam, Am not I thine ass, upon which thou hast ridden ever since I was thine, unto this day? Was I ever wont to do so unto thee? And he said, Nay. And the Lord opened the eyes of Balaam, and he saw the angel of the Lord standing in the way, and his sword drawn in his hand; and he bowed down his head, and fell flat on his face. And the angel of the Lord said unto him, Wherefore hast thou smitten thine ass these three times? Behold, I went out to withstand thee, because thy way is perverse before me; and the ass saw me, and turned from me these three times: unless she had turned from me, surely now also I had slain thee, and saved her alive. And Balaam said, I have sinned," &c., Numb. xxii.

This beautiful narrative needs no comment. Modern infidelity may indeed here find occasion to sneer at the seeming disproportion between the thing done and the end to be gained—at so much pains being taken for the correction of Balaam which might have been accomplished in a simpler manner, by the angel appearing to himself for instance, and telling him that he did wrong. Infidelity may have recourse to its own vain and human ideas of what it is becoming God to do, or not to do, and tell us that His infinite wisdom will surely go always by the nearest, plainest, and most simple way, to gain its ends, and that we are not to suppose that Almighty God will use so many unnecessary means for what He could do by one alone, &c. Yet the pious and faithful Christian opposing this plain fact, supported by the authority of God Himself, to all these vain speculations, rejects the weak ideas of human reason, and in this extraordinary miracle, discovers new and convincing proofs of the infinite goodness and condescension of God towards His creatures, finding in it the strongest incentives to love, praise, and adore His divine bounty, and humbly to obey His holy will.

XIX. The disobedient prophet slain by a lion is another instance of a miracle performed together with prophecy, in punishment of disobedience to the orders of God, though in a matter seemingly of small importance, but intended as a warning to us to be careful perfectly to obey the divine orders, whether the matter be great or small. This prophet, after going down to Bethel, and there delivering his prophecy against Jeroboam and his altar, and performing two great miracles in confirmation of it, was persuaded, by the lying testimony of another prophet, to go to his house and eat and drink with him, contrary to the express command of God, who had absolutely forbidden him to eat bread or drink water there.

But "it came to pass, as they sat at table, that the word of the Lord came unto the prophet that brought him back; and he cried to the man of God that came from Judah, saying, Thus saith the Lord, Forasmuch as thou hast disobeyed the mouth of the Lord, and hast not kept the commandment which the Lord thy God commanded thee, thy carcase shall not come into the sepulchre of thy fathers," 1 Kings, xiii. This prophecy was soon fulfilled; for, "when he was gone away" upon his ass to return home, "a lion met him by the way and slew him; and the carcase was cast in the way, and the ass stood by it; the lion also stood by the carcase. . . . Men passed by and saw this;" yet the lion never offered to hurt them, but stood by the carcase till the other prophet came to take it away to bury it; and neither "ate the carcase nor tore the ass," *ibid.*, ver. 28.

Here we see a wild lion commissioned by God to execute His justice on this disobedient prophet, and performing His orders in the most exact and perfect manner, without turning to the right hand or to the left; nay, forgetting his natural ferocity, and perhaps the keen stings of hunger, he kills the prophet as he was ordered, but neither tears the carcase nor destroys the ass, nor does hurt to any that passed by, but guards the dead body till the proper person came to bury it, and then returns to the woods whence he came.

XX. The miraculous punishment of Gehazi, servant to Elisha the prophet, must also be particularly observed. When this avaricious man had followed Naaman to obtain money from him upon his being cured of his leprosy; returning to his master, "Elisha said unto him, Whence comest thou, Gehazi? And he said, Thy servant went no whither. And he said unto him, Went not mine heart with thee, when the man turned again from his chariot to meet thee? Is it a time to receive money and to receive garments?" &c. "The leprosy therefore of Naaman shall cleave to thee and to thy seed for ever. And he went out from his presence a leper white as snow." 4 Kings, v. The prophet, though absent, saw all that passed; and no sooner does he pronounce sentence upon his covetous servant, than immediately the punishment is inflicted! What a demonstration of the divine justice! What a severe correction of Gehazi! What a lesson and warning to others!

XXI. These facts speak for themselves, and prove that Almighty God Himself judges it becoming His divine majesty, and worthy of His infinite wisdom, to perform amazing miracles, even where the immediate end proposed is only to benefit particular persons, to supply their wants, to deliver them from dangers, or even to gratify their wishes. Objections formed against any miracle, then, from the pretended insignificance of such ends, can never be admitted by a Christian without impeaching the divine wisdom in all the above examples, and in many others recorded in the sacred Scriptures. It is no less manifest how unworthy of a rational philosopher all such objections are, as they proceed only from a real or pretended ignorance of very obvious truths, which totally invalidate every objection that can be brought against them.

CHAPTER VIII.

THE INSTRUMENTS USED IN PERFORMING MIRACLES.

I. AT first sight this subject may not seem to require any special treatment; but under it we shall find several particulars, which will serve to illustrate the nature of miracles, and to show the proper meaning of certain expressions in the Holy Scripture. Besides, as the enemies of religion urge the apparent weakness and insignificance of the instruments used in working miracles, as an argument against their existence, it is proper to examine this objection in order to test its true value. There is also another question which deserves particular attention, and on which the Christian world is much divided; which is, how far any respect or veneration is due, or may lawfully be paid, to instruments which the divine wisdom is pleased to employ in working miracles. Under this head, then, I propose to consider these three things in order: 1. What are the instruments which God uses for performing miracles, and how they act. 2. What weight against the existence of miracles the argument has which is drawn from the lowliness of the instruments. And 3. Whether any respect and veneration may lawfully be paid to them?

II. That Almighty God may make use of creatures as

instruments for working miracles, or may perform them without any such instrument, if He thinks proper, cannot be called in question. But what He actually does use, or has used for this purpose, can be known only from experience, and principally from what He Himself has revealed to us in His Holy Scriptures. Now there we find that sometimes He makes use of His rational creatures, sometimes of irrational, and at other times of those that are inanimate; each of which we shall consider separately.

The rational creatures used by God as His instruments in working miracles, are either angels or men. When an angel is said to perform a miracle, this may be understood in two ways. If the act performed be not a miracle absolutely, but only such with relation to man, and consequently within the natural compass of an angel's power, then the expression means that the angel is the efficient cause, and performs it immediately by his own strength, according to the orders which he has received from God. But if it be an absolute miracle superior to all created power, and therefore proper to God alone, then the expression signifies that the angel acts merely as an instrument, fulfilling some condition which God appoints; and God Himself immediately performs the miracle.

Of the former kind we have an example in the deliverance of Daniel from the lions; for when the king came early in the morning to the den, to inquire if he was still alive, he answered, "O king, live for ever! My God hath sent His angel, and hath shut the lions' mouths, that they have not hurt me." Here we see that the angel was sent by God to defend His servant, and restrain the fury of those raging animals that they should not hurt him; a thing which there is no reason to think exceeds the natural powers of an angel. Other examples of this kind are frequent in Holy Writ.

Of the second kind it is not so easy to give examples; because, not knowing exactly to what extent an angel's natural power can reach, we are unable to determine how far those miracles related in the Scripture as done by angels, were within their natural strength or not. We know not, for example, if an angel can himself raise a flame of fire in an instant from a rock. It would seem, indeed, more probable that he cannot—that this is a miracle proper to God alone; and if so, then we have an example of this second kind in Gideon's offering, when the angel appeared to commission him to deliver the people of Israel from the slavery of the Midianites. For when he brought out flesh, and bread, and broth, and laid them upon the rock before the angel, immediately upon the angel's touching it with the end of his staff, "there rose up fire out of the rock, and consumed the flesh and the unleavened cakes," Judg. vi. 21. Now, if this was the immediate work of God, then the angel's part, as God's instrument, was only to perform the outward condition appointed of touching the offerings with his staff, and the effect, the work of God Himself, immediately ensued.

We have, indeed, one pretty certain example of this in the pool of Bethsaida, of which the Scripture says, "that an angel went down at a certain season into the pool and troubled the water; whosoever then first after the troubling of the water stepped in, was made whole of whatsoever disease he had," John, v. 4. The instantaneous cure of diseases is the work of God alone; and consequently all these cures performed at this pool were done by Him; the angel acting as God's instrument, at the appointed season "went down and troubled the waters," which was the part allotted by God to him as a condition prerequired to the performing these cures.

III. When a miracle is said to be performed by men, the expression ought always to be understood in the latter sense, that God performs the miracle by them as His visible instruments, upon their doing what He appoints.

Thus we are told in the Scripture, that "God wrought special miracles by the hands of Paul," Acts, xix. 11; where we see that God wrought the miracles, and St Paul was only the means or instrument by which He did so. It is in this sense, therefore, that we are to understand these other expressions of Scripture, where the working of the miracle is attributed immediately to man, as in the Acts, ii. 43, where it is said, "And many wonders and signs were done by the apostles;" for it cannot be said that the apostles did these things by their own natural strength as the efficient causes, but that Almighty God performed them by their means.

IV. The co-operation which Almighty God requires from man, when He uses him as His instrument in working miracles, is both internal and external. The internal consists in a strong faith and confidence in God, the disposition of soul that God always gives to those by whom He works miracles; it being the ground upon which the grace of miracles is founded. Thus our Saviour assures us that "all things are possible to him that believes;" and that a strong faith is "able to remove mountains," because it powerfully moves and engages God to do what it so firmly expects from Him. Hence it is, that those whom God employs to work miracles, know themselves, from this interior confidence, that the miracle will be wrought, and generally foretell it, by which a double lustre is added to the miracle, and its authority enhanced.

The external co-operation of man takes place in many

THE INSTRUMENTS OF MIRACLES. 173

different ways, of which the following declared in Holy Writ are the principal:—First, By command: thus Joshua commanded the sun to stand still, and it did so; upon which the Scripture adds, "And the Lord hearkened to (or obeyed) the voice of a man," Josh. x. 14; showing by this expression that God was the efficient cause by whom the sun was stopped, and that He did it at the desire of Joshua His servant. Elias, also, once and again commanded fire to come down from heaven, and he was instantly obeyed. And when St Peter cured the lame man, he spoke also by command,—"In the name of Jesus Christ of Nazareth, rise up and walk," Acts, iii.

Secondly, By prayer, of which there are many examples throughout the Scripture. Thus, when Moses promised that Pharaoh should be delivered from the frogs and flies, besides the confidence he had in God, expressed in his positive and absolute declaration to Pharaoh, he also had recourse to prayer as the external condition which God required: "And Moses cried unto the Lord, because of the frogs which he had brought against Pharaoh; and the Lord did according to the word of Moses, and the frogs died," &c., Exod. viii. 12, 13. Again, "And Moses entreated the Lord; and the Lord did according to the word of Moses, and he removed the swarms of flies," *ibid.*, verses 30, 31.

Samson in his thirst cried unto the Lord, and He most miraculously supplied him with water, Judg. xv. In like manner, Samuel, full of confidence that God would perform the miracle of sending thunder and rain at his desire, first foretold it boldly to the people, and then "cried unto the Lord, and the Lord sent thunder and rain" in a moment, 1 Sam. xii. 18. Elias, in his competition with Baal's prophets, had scarcely finished his prayer when "the fire of the Lord fell and consumed the burnt-sacrifice, and the wood," &c., 3 Kings, xviii. Thus, also, the miracles wrought on Gideon's fleece, the sun's going back ten degrees, and many others related in the Holy Scripture, were obtained by prayer as the external condition required on the part of man.

Thirdly, By touching. Thus the sick were cured by the laying on of hands; and Elijah and Elisha, when they raised from the dead the sons of the two women with whom they dwelt, both prayed and stretched out their bodies upon the dead corpse, and they were immediately restored to life. And of Elijah the Scripture says, "And the Lord heard the voice of Elijah, and the soul of the child came to him again, and he revived," 3 Kings, xvii. 22—distinguishing, as we have done above, what belonged to God from what was done by the prophet.

Fourthly, By prayer and command united. Thus, when St Peter raised up Tabitha from the dead, "he prayed; and turning himself to the body, he said, Tabitha, arise: and she opened her eyes; and when she saw Peter she sat up," Acts, ix.

Fifthly, By affirming the thing to be so. Thus, the moment Elisha said to his servant, "The leprosy of Naaman shall cleave unto thee," that instant he was immediately seized with it, "and he went out from his presence a leper white as snow, 4 Kings, v. 27.

Sixthly, By affirming it in the name of God; so Elisha said to the widow of Zarephath, "Thus saith the Lord, The barrel of meal shall not waste, neither shall the cruse of oil fail, until the day that the Lord sendeth rain upon the earth," 3 Kings, xvii. This last is very common among the prophets, and is a kind of prophecy flowing from their strong faith.

V. In these cases we see the different ways in which men co-operated immediately as instruments in the hand of God for working miracles; but in many other cases He required that those by whom He wrought miracles should use other inanimate creatures for this purpose as inferior instruments. Thus he commanded Moses to smite the waters of Egypt with his rod, that they might be turned into blood, Exod. vii. 20; and to stretch out his rod over the Red Sea, that it might be divided, Exod. xiv. 16; and to smite the rock that it might send forth water, Exod. xvii. 9. Aaron also is commanded to stretch out his hand with his rod over the streams, that the frogs might come up, Exod. viii. 5; and to strike the dust of the earth with his rod, that it might become lice, *ibid.*, verse 17.

The respective parts which God and His servants acted in these and other similar cases, is particularly distinguished in the plagues of hail and locusts, where, after relating what God commanded, the Scripture adds, " And Moses stretched forth his rod towards heaven, and the Lord sent thunder and hail," &c., Exod. ix. 9. And again: " And Moses stretched forth his rod over the land of Egypt, and the Lord brought the east wind, and the east wind brought the locusts," Exod. x. 13.

VI. God has been pleased to use many different creatures in the hands of His servants as inferior instruments for working miracles, and often such as appear the meanest and most insignificant in the eyes of man. What more so than ashes? yet Almighty God commands Moses to take ashes from the furnace and "sprinkle them towards heaven"—that is, throw them up into the air—in order to produce the plague " of boils breaking out on man and beast throughout all the land of Egypt," Exod. x. 8, 9. So Elijah, smiting the waters of Jordan "with his mantle, they were divided hither and thither," and he and Elisha "went over on dry ground," 4 Kings, ii. 8. A handful of salt cast into the springs of poisonous and unwholesome waters by Elisha both healed the waters and rendered the country fertile, which before was barren, 2 Kings, ii. 20. A little meal thrown into the pot of pottage, by the same prophet, cured it of the poison of the noxious herbs which had been inadvertently put into it, 4 Kings iv. A piece of wood cut from the tree and cast into the Jordan by the same holy man, caused the heavy lump of iron that had fallen into the river to swim on the surface of the waters, 4 Kings, vi. From these, and many other similar examples, we see that Almighty God has often made use of the lowest creatures as instruments in the hands of His holy servants to perform the most surprising miracles.

VII. Having thus seen that the divine wisdom makes use of His rational creatures in miracles, and what part they act in them, I now proceed to consider the examples in the Holy Scriptures, which disclose to us the manner in which irrational creatures are used by Almighty God for the same end: and on this we may be brief; for in whatever way the learned world may account for what is called instinct in the brute creation, certain it is that they have not free will as man has to resist the impressions of the Creator. They are in this respect more immediately under His influence, and whatever He is pleased to require of them they are immediately obedient to His holy will.

When Almighty God requires anything of man, He not only manifests His will to him externally, but must also assist him to perform it by the internal influence of His grace. It is true that when He absolutely wills that man should comply, He infallibly obtains his com-

THE INSTRUMENTS OF MIRACLES.   177

pliance without prejudice to his liberty; but man too often resists the will of his Creator—nay, does the very reverse of what he knows his Creator requires of him. But with irrational creatures it is not so. As they are incapable of knowing and understanding the will of their Master, they are also incapable of resisting the impressions which He is pleased to make upon them, however contrary these may be to their natural dispositions and instincts. And the miracles which God performs by these creatures generally consist in causing them to act in a manner contrary to their natural habits, in order thereby to obtain such ends as the divine wisdom has in view.

The Holy Scripture points out some examples of this kind, where Almighty God was pleased to make use of irrational creatures, causing them to act in an extraordinary manner for promoting His designs on men. First, for correcting sinners. Thus He gave to Balaam's ass the power of speech, and enabled her to argue in a rational manner, in order to convince that wicked prophet of his unreasonable conduct.

Secondly, For punishing sinners. Thus he sent swarms of hornets upon the people of Canaan to destroy them by their stings, and foretold that He would do so to punish those wicked nations, and to convince His own people that He fought for them—see Exod. xxiii. 28, Deut. vi. 20, and Joshua, xxiv. 12. In like manner, after the dispersion of the ten tribes, when the new inhabitants came to dwell in their land, the Scripture says: " And so it was that at the beginning of their dwelling there they feared not the Lord; therefore the Lord sent lions among them, which slew some of them," 2 Kings, xvii. 25.

In both cases the Scripture assures us that these

hornets and lions, in leaving their own places in such numbers, and attacking whole nations of people, contrary to their natural habits, as no one was injuring or destroying them, were employed by God to punish those sinful people. Several other examples we have also in the locusts, frogs, flies, lice, &c., with which the Egyptians were scourged; for though these miraculous punishments were brought about by means of Moses and Aaron, which led me to notice them in the former class of the rational instruments, yet it was not what Moses and Aaron did, but the immediate influence of the will of God upon these creatures, which determined them to torment the Egyptians, whilst they had no power to hurt the people of God. They are therefore proper examples here also, to show how God is pleased to cause the very brutes themselves to act in a miraculous manner when He pleases for His own wise ends. Another example we have in the fiery serpents which He sent among His people as a punishment of their murmurings against Him.

Thirdly, For bestowing favours upon His faithful servants. Thus He commanded the ravens to feed Elijah in the wilderness; and these creatures, obedient to the divine will, though in opposition to their nature, never failed, during the time the prophet remained there, to bring him bread and flesh twice every day.

VIII. The last class of instruments used immediately by Almighty God Himself in working miracles, are inanimate creatures. These are of different kinds, as we find in Scripture, but chiefly these four—holy relics, holy images, holy places, and holy things, consecrated to the external worship of God, by which we find many surprising miracles performed, and related both in the Old and New Testaments. Here, however, before we consider the examples themselves, it will not be amiss to explain what is meant by the word holy, for there seems to be some ambiguity in the term.

God is essentially holy, the source of all holiness, and the nearer any creature approaches to God the more holy must it be. Holiness, therefore, in the general acceptation of the word, signifies separation from creatures and union with the Creator. This separation and union may be effected in various ways, according to the nature of the thing which we call holy; and it is from this difference in the nature of the separation from creatures, and of the union with God, that the different senses of the word holy take their rise.

IX. The word holiness or sanctity, when applied to rational creatures, is the same as Christian virtue and perfection; for the more the heart of man is detached from the inordinate love of creatures, and the more he is united in affection to God, the more holy, the more virtuous he is, and the nearer to perfection. By this expression, then, a holy person, is understood one who is a friend of God, highly favoured by Him, adorned with His holy grace, separated in affection from all irregular or inordinate ties to any creature, and united, by a holy resignation of his will, to his Creator. In this sense holiness or sanctity implies a great purity of heart and love of God on the part of man, and a reciprocal affection on the part of God towards him, adorning his soul in a special manner with His divine grace and all holy virtues.

X. Another tie by which man becomes united to God is his being employed by God as His minister and ambassador to man, and receiving that sacred authority and spiritual power, which are necessary for acting in that character. Here the union with God is manifest, and also the separation which it naturally implies in such a person from every worldly or secular employment which could in the least degree interfere with or hinder the discharge of the duties of the high station to which God has called him. Thus St Paul, speaking of his apostleship, says that he was "called to be an apostle, separated unto the Gospel of God," Rom. i. —that is, separated from all secular concerns, and dedicated to the service of God and of His Gospel; and, writing to Timothy, he calls the ministers of the Gospel soldiers of Jesus Christ employed in fighting His battles: "Thou, therefore, labour as a good soldier of Jesus Christ. No man that warreth entangleth himself with the affairs of this life, that he may please him who has chosen him to be a soldier," 2 Tim. ii. 4.

For this reason the ministers of God are always esteemed holy; and undoubtedly they are so in the sense here explained—that is, in the character they bear, and in the powers and authority with which God has invested them. But as the union with God, and separation from creatures in this case, are very different from those in the preceding, so our idea of the holiness resulting from them is also different. The one is *holiness of person*, the other *holiness of character*. The former may and often does exist without the latter; but the light of reason shows that the latter ought always to be accompanied by the former. Yet this is only a moral congruity, not an absolute necessity; seeing that the character and all its powers may exist, and are holy, though there be no holiness of person; nay, it is much to be regretted, and is too often the case, that the sanctity of the person does not correspond with the character.

XI. If, now, we consider the meaning of the term holiness when applied to inanimate things, we shall find various ideas implied in it, according to the different relations which these creatures have with God.

In the first place, some things are set apart for the external worship of God, and dedicated entirely to His service, such as the ark, the temple, churches, altars, sacred vestments, sacred vessels, and the like, which are therefore called and esteemed holy. Their separation from other creatures consists in this, that they are no more to be employed to profane uses, nor by common hands; they no longer belong to this world, nor to worldly purposes; and they are not to be handled or treated in a light and careless manner, but with due respect as things belonging to God and united to Him, by being entirely appropriated to His service.

Secondly, There are certain things which Almighty God has Himself expressly appointed and ordained to be used in His Church as the constant and undoubted means of bestowing the greatest of all blessings upon us —His heavenly grace, both for cleansing our souls from the guilt of sin and strengthening us against relapse. These are His holy sacraments, to the pious and devout use of which He has annexed these valuable graces. These, therefore, are justly esteemed exceedingly holy, inasmuch as they are separated from all profane uses, and can never be abused or treated with disrespect without the highest guilt being thereby incurred; and their union with God is extremely close and intimate, as they are the never-failing channels of conveying His divine grace to our souls.

Thirdly, There are other things which, being by human appointment set apart for similar uses, are esteemed sacred and holy by Christian people. For, seeing that divine Providence makes use of inanimate creatures as the means of bestowing many blessings on man; and knowing that prayer—particularly the public prayer of the Church—is most powerful with God, the Christian world, from the earliest ages, has set apart as *holy* certain things blessed by the priests of the Church, imploring the divine goodness to be pleased, in virtue of these prayers, to grant special favours to those who use them with pious dispositions. Now creatures thus blessed are esteemed holy according to St Paul: " Every creature is good, and nothing to be refused, if it be received with thanksgiving; for it is sanctified by the word of God, and by prayer," 1 Tim. iv. 4, 5. By these are meant holy water, holy oil, blessed candles, ashes, palms, and the like. Their separation from other creatures, and union with God, consist in this, that they are set apart by the Church as means of conveying the effects of her prayers to her children, and of obtaining for them some special blessing; and therefore they are not to be used for profane purposes, but to be treated with the respect due to things set apart for the divine service.

Fourthly, With regard to places, besides temples and churches, which are solemnly dedicated, and therefore justly esteemed holy, we find other places called holy for a different reason. Thus, where God has been pleased at any time to manifest Himself or His will to man, either by Himself or by an angel, the place where this occurred is called holy, and a due respect commanded to be paid to it, as being sanctified by the divine presence. Thus Moses at the burning bush, and Joshua when the angel appeared to him, were ordered to put off their shoes from their feet, for the place whereon they stood was holy ground. See also what a sublime idea Jacob had of the holiness of that place where God had appeared to him in his dream: "How dreadful," says he, "is this place! this is none other but the house of God, and this is the gate of heaven," Gen. xxviii. 17. The holy Mount Sinai, or Horeb, was ever after called the *Mount of God*, and esteemed most holy, because there God appeared with so much majesty to His people when He gave them the ten commandments. In like manner, St Peter calls Mount Tabor, on which he saw the transfiguration of his Master, the *holy mount*. Again, if God is pleased to give more manifest and uncommon signs of His presence, and of His power and goodness, by bestowing favours on man in particular places, they are also justly esteemed and respected as holy. Under this head also are included those places where the chief mysteries of man's redemption were accomplished, as, in the esteem of all Christians, they acquire a particular holiness on that account. Now the holiness of those places—that is, their separation from others, and their union with God—is easily perceived, but is of a different kind from those of the former classes.

XII. In the above cases, the holiness of these creatures seems to be something inherent in them, on account of their immediate and intrinsic relation to God; but there are two other things also esteemed holy, where the holiness seems to be more extrinsic, and rather in the esteem of men than in the things themselves, as not resting in them, but being referred to something else—and these are holy images and holy relics.

When relics consist of any part of the body of a saint, they seem to inherit a considerable degree of intrinsic holiness, that body having been sanctified by the superabundant graces of God with which its soul was adorned; having been the temple of the Holy Ghost, and the abode of that blessed soul to which it once was, and will again be united, to reign with Christ in glory. But when the relics are not parts of a saint's body, but only things that had belonged to him, as clothes, books, &c., or things that had touched his body, the holiness attributed to them is more of an extrinsic kind, and acknowledged only in as far as they relate to, or have connection with, a servant of God. Such also is the case with the holiness which men attribute to the pictures or images of Christ and His saints. If at any time, however, God should be pleased by relics or holy images to produce any miraculous effect, they thereby acquire another kind of sanctity, of the same nature with that of holy places, or other things made use of by Almighty God as His instruments for bestowing benefits by miracles on men. They become holy for a double reason, both as being used by God for this end, and also from their relation to the sacred persons to whom they belong. Here we must not forget the Holy Scriptures, which are justly esteemed exceedingly holy, being dictated by the Holy Ghost, and containing His sacred truths, and thereby having a most intimate connection with God.

From what has been said, it is easy to understand the different senses in which these several things are esteemed and called *holy*, and the various grounds upon which this appellation is given them. We return now to relate the examples of miracles which the Word of God presents to us as wrought by means of inanimate holy things.

XIII. First, with regard to holy images, we have a beautiful example related, Numb. xxi., where we are told, that when the people, upon a certain occasion, murmured and "spoke against Moses," in order to punish this their great sin, "the Lord sent fiery serpents among the people, and they bit the people, and much people of Israel died," ver. 6. The people, upon this, repented of their crime, cried to God for mercy, and the remedy which He Himself appointed was this: "And the Lord said unto Moses, Make thee a fiery serpent, and set it upon a pole; and it shall come to pass, that every one that is bitten, *when he looketh upon it, shall live.* And Moses made a serpent of brass, and put it upon a pole; and it came to pass, that if a serpent had bitten any man, *when he beheld the serpent of brass, he lived,*" ver. 8, 9.

Here we see a holy image commanded by God Himself to be set up in the sight of the people, and an extraordinary miracle performed, not once or twice, but innumerable times, by simply looking upon it. I call this image holy for two reasons: first, on account of its relation to Jesus Christ, of whom it was a type, as He Himself assures us in these words,—"As Moses lifted up the serpent in the wilderness, even so must the Son of Man be lifted up: that whosoever believeth in Him should not perish, but have eternal life," John, iii. 14, 15.

Here it is intimated, that as those who had been bitten by the fiery serpents, and were in danger of temporal death, were immediately cured by only looking on the brazen image which Moses lifted up in the camp, so all those who should in after-times be bitten by the infernal serpents, by temptations to sin, and thereby be in danger of eternal death, should find a speedy and a certain remedy by looking with a lively faith upon Jesus Christ raised upon the cross. For this reason, then, the brazen serpent was a lively image of Jesus Christ, and justly esteemed holy on account of this relation to Him. But it also deserves that appellation in a more immediate manner, because Almighty God was pleased to make use of it as an instrument by which He performed a multitude of most surprising miracles, proper only to God Himself—that is, the immediate cure of the envenomed bite of the fiery serpents, which otherwise brought certain death, and that by only looking on the image which God had ordered to be set up among His people.

Here I cannot forbear observing that this is a convincing proof that the true sense of what Protestants call the second commandment, but which, in reality, is only an explanation of the first, is by no means to forbid the making of pictures or images, even of holy things, and for religious purposes. For can it be imagined that had God given such a prohibition, He would Himself, and that so soon after, have given orders to Moses to act in direct opposition to it? Such a supposition would be injurious to the divine wisdom. The true meaning, then, of that part of the commandment, can only be what the words themselves clearly express—the forbidding to make images, in order to bow down to them, or to serve them as gods, by which they became idols; and those who thus served them became guilty of idolatry.

XIV. With regard to miracles wrought by relics, we have several most striking instances in the Holy Scripture. When Elijah himself divided the waters of Jordan by smiting them with his mantle, it was then but the instrument in his hand by which God performed that miracle. But when Elisha returned with his master's mantle, and smote the waters with it, and said, "Where is the Lord God of Elijah?" the mantle then was truly and properly a relic; and the miracle of dividing the waters of the Jordan, which immediately ensued, was performed by Almighty God precisely by means of this mantle as a relic, upon account of its connection with His holy servant Elijah, to whom it formerly belonged, and in whose name He was called upon to perform it.

Another extraordinary miracle—a miracle of the highest class—was performed by the bones of this same great prophet Elisha, some time after his death—namely, the raising a dead man to life. It is thus related in the Scripture: "And Elisha died, and they buried him. And the bands of the Moabites invaded the land at the coming in of the year. And it came to pass, as they were burying a man, that, behold, they spied a band of men; and they cast the man into the sepulchre of Elisha: and when the man was let down, and touched the bones of Elisha, he revived, and stood up on his feet," 4 Kings, xiii. 20, 21. Here there was no prayers used, no means applied, not even the smallest thought or expectation of such a thing, as the dead man being restored to life, which, therefore, is attributed solely to his touching the relics of the holy prophet.

In the New Testament, also, we have some remarkable examples of the same thing—where we are told, that "aprons and handkerchiefs that had touched the body of St Paul were brought unto the sick, and the diseases departed from them, and the evil spirits went out of them," Acts, xix. 12. Nay, so liberal was Almighty God in working miracles, that even the very shadow of St Peter passing over the sick cured them: for "by the hands of the apostles were many signs and wonders wrought among the people—inasmuch that they brought forth the sick into the streets, and laid them on beds and couches, that, at the least, the shadow of Peter passing by might overshadow some of them," Acts, v. 12, 15. And the poor woman with the bloody flux in the Gospel, by only touching the hem of our Saviour's garment, was immediately made whole.

XV. We have seen above, several examples of miracles

wrought by means of holy things dedicated to the service of God, particularly the ark of the covenant; the wonders performed by it in the passage of the people over the Jordan (Jos. vi. and vii.), the miraculous effects wrought by it among the Philistines; the falling of their idols before it; the misery and destruction of that people through all their cities wherever it went; and the miraculous punishments which were immediately inflicted by Almighty God upon those of His own people who profaned it. We have also taken notice of the miracles wrought in Babylon upon Belshazzar the king, when he profaned the sacred vessels which his father had carried off from Jerusalem, Dan. v.

Under this head of holy things I shall add only one more example of a constant and standing miracle among the people of God by means of holy water, which never failed when the circumstances concurred in which it was appointed by God to be performed. It is related in the fifth chapter of Numbers, and was appointed by Almighty God for ascertaining the innocence, or discovering the guilt, of any woman whom her husband suspected of being unfaithful to him. "If the spirit of jealousy come upon him, and he be jealous of his wife, whether she be defiled or not; then shall the man bring his wife unto the priest, and he shall bring her offering for her; . . . and the priest shall bring her near, and set her before the Lord. And the priest shall take holy water in an earthen vessel; and of the dust that is in the floor of the tabernacle the priest shall take, and put it into the water; . . . and the priest shall charge her by an oath, and say unto the woman, If . . . thou hast not gone aside to uncleanness with another instead of thy husband, be thou free from this bitter water that causeth the curse: but if thou hast gone aside, and if thou be defiled, then the priest shall charge the woman with an oath of cursing; and the priest shall say unto the woman, The Lord make thee a curse and an oath among thy people; . . . and this water that causeth the curse shall go into thy bowels. . . . And the woman shall say, Amen, amen. And the priest shall write these curses in a book, and he shall blot them out with the bitter water. And he shall cause the woman to drink the bitter water that causeth the curse; and the water that causeth the curse shall enter into her and become bitter . . . . And when he hath made her to drink the water, then it shall come to pass, that if she be defiled, and have done trespass against her husband, that the water that causeth the curse shall enter into her and become bitter; . . . and the woman shall be a curse among her people."

XVI. We come now finally to consider the examples of miracles wrought in holy places, or to show that Almighty God is pleased to make use of some places in preference to others, in which He displays His munificence and liberality towards mankind, by performing miracles in their favour, and bestowing other benefits upon them.

The first remarkable instance of this kind which chiefly deserves our notice, is what happened at the dedication of the Temple. This place being chosen by Almighty God as His own house, in which He was to dwell among men, He was resolved to be most liberal in bestowing His favours upon such as should there have recourse to Him for help; and that this might be known to all, He was pleased, that when king Solomon made the prayer of dedication, he should particularise the different kinds of favours which people might expect.

Solomon therefore begins his prayer by begging "that His eyes may be open upon this house day and night." That if any injury be done a man, and the case be brought before the altar in this house, that "He would judge His servants—requiting the wicked, and justifying the righteous." That if the people be overcome by their enemies, and return, and confess, and pray in this house, He would "hear their prayer and forgive their sin, and bring them again to their own land." That when the heavens are shut, and there is no rain, and consequently famine and misery, on account of their sins, if "they pray towards this place, and turn from their sins, that He would hear their prayer, forgive their sins, and send them rain" in its season. In time of dearth, or pestilence, or blighting, or mildew, or whatever sore or sickness there be, then "what prayer or what supplication soever of any man, or of all Thy people Israel, when every one shall know his own sore, and his own grief, and shall spread forth his hands in this house; then hear Thou from heaven Thy dwelling-place, and forgive, and render to every man according to all his ways, whose heart Thou knowest." Also, "when strangers come and pray in this house, hear Thou from heaven, and do according to all that the stranger calleth to Thee for, that all people may know that this house which I have built is called by Thy name. If Thy people go out to war, and pray unto Thee—towards this house; hear Thou their prayer—and maintain their cause. If they sin against Thee, and Thou be angry with them, and deliver them over before their enemies, and they carry them away captives, yet, if they turn and pray unto Thee—and return to Thee with all their hearts, and pray towards this house, which I have built for Thy name; then hear Thou their prayer, and maintain their cause, and forgive Thy people which have sinned against Thee."

Now it is evident, that if this prayer was heard, and

if Almighty God was always ready to grant the fervent prayers of His people made in this holy temple, or even made towards it, in all the circumstances here mentioned, or whatever other favour they might need, this will prove a striking example of the truth in question, that God is more ready to hear our prayers, and to bestow benefits upon us in some particular holy places, chosen by Himself, than in others.

This prayer of Solomon was granted, and God determined to bestow all these favours mentioned upon those who should ask them from Him in this His holy temple, or even turned towards it. This Almighty God was pleased to evince by a glorious miracle. For no sooner had Solomon ended his prayer than the "fire came down from heaven and consumed the burnt-offering; and the glory of the Lord filled the house: and the priests of the Lord could not enter into the house of the Lord, because the glory of the Lord had filled the Lord's house. And when all the children of Israel saw how the fire came down, and the glory of the Lord upon the house, they bowed themselves with their faces to the ground and worshipped." Not only did God give this miraculous proof of His having heard Solomon's prayer, but He also "appeared to Solomon by night, and said unto Him, I have heard thy prayer, and have chosen this place to Myself for a house of sacrifice. If I shut up the heaven that there be no rain; if I command the locusts to devour the land; or if I send pestilence among My people: if My people shall humble themselves and pray, and seek My name, and turn from their wicked ways; then will I hear from heaven, and forgive their sin, and will heal their land. Now Mine eyes will be open, and Mine ears attentive to the prayers that are made in this place; for now have I *chosen* and *sanctified this house,* that My name may be there for ever, and Mine eyes and mine heart shall be there perpetually."—See the whole at large, 2 Chron. vi. vii. Here, then, we have a proof of Almighty God's choosing one particular place in preference to any other, wherein to bestow His choicest blessings upon man, and confirming this His choice by a miracle performed before a vast multitude of people.

XVII. Again, when Naaman came to the prophet Elisha to be cured of his leprosy, and stood before his door with his horses and chariots, "Elisha sent a messenger unto him, saying, Go and wash in Jordan seven times, and thy flesh shall come again unto thee, and thou shalt be clean," 4 Kings, v. 10. Upon this, Naaman, not knowing the counsel of the Almighty, and despising the thought of God's working miracles more in one place than another, was exceedingly angry, and said, "Are not Abana and Pharpar, rivers of Damascus, better than all the waters of Israel?" &c. But he did not consider that his cure was not to be the effect of any natural quality of the water, but of the immediate power of God, Who was pleased upon this occasion to exert that power by the water of the Jordan, and by no other. Accordingly, when, by the persuasion of his servants, he obeyed the prophet, and bathed seven times in the Jordan, he was immediately restored to perfect health. By this he was convinced that his cure was the work of God, Whom he acknowledged as the only true God, and Who bestows His favours upon man when, how, and where He pleases.

Another similar example we have in our Saviour's giving sight to the man born blind; for, after anointing his eyes with the clay which He had made, He said to him, "Go, wash in the pool of Siloam. And he went and washed, and came seeing," John, ix. 7. The incredulous of this age would perhaps smile, and say that he might as well have washed anywhere else, as all that could be intended by washing was only to remove the clay which had been put upon his eyes. But every serious Christian will form a very different opinion, and say that had he washed elsewhere he would not have received his sight; because the cure was not owing to any particular virtue either in the clay or in the water, but to the immediate operation of God, Who had resolved to work this miracle at the pool of Siloam, and nowhere else.

But the most remarkable example is that of the pool of Bethsaida with its five porches, where many miracles were performed, and perfect cures wrought of the most inveterate and otherwise incurable diseases; for, as the Scripture tells us, "An angel went down at a certain season into the pool and troubled the waters; whosoever then first, after the troubling the waters, stepped in, was made whole of whatever disease he had," John, v. 4. Now, as this never failed at the particular season when the angel descended, we have an admirable example of a particular place chosen by Almighty God where a continual series of never-failing miracles was performed, and nowhere else.

XVIII. Having considered the various kinds of instruments used by the divine wisdom in performing miracles, and the way in which they act, we must now examine the argument drawn from the lowliness or insignificance of these instruments. If I were arguing this point with Christians, who believe the sacred Scriptures to be the Word of God, and dictated by the Holy Ghost, it would be soon and easily decided. These sacred oracles assure us, that the ordinary conduct of divine providence is to bring about the greatest events by the weakest instruments, thereby to confound the pride of man, and that no flesh might glory in itself. "The foolishness of God," says St Paul, " is wiser than men, and the weakness of God is stronger than men. God hath chosen the foolish things of the world to confound the wise, and hath chosen the weak things of the world to confound the things that are mighty; and base things of the world, and things which are despised, hath God chosen; yea, and things that are not, to bring to nought things that are, that no flesh should glory in His presence," 1 Cor. i. 25, 27, 28.

Nothing gives a faithful soul a more exalted idea of God than these words, wherein we see how infinitely superior He is to all creatures. He needs no help, He requires no instruments to perform His work, and when He is pleased to employ any such, He generally uses those which bear the least proportion to the end proposed, thereby to confound human prudence, and to display His own divine perfections. This every pious Christian knows, and is so far from being scandalised at the apparent meanness of the instruments used in performing miracles, or from having the most distant thought that this could be turned as an argument against their existence, that he rather regards it as a proof of their reality, because most conformable to the ordinary ways of divine providence, and showing most clearly God's almighty power. Besides, such a person well knows that the Scripture is full of examples of the most stupendous miracles wrought by the lowest instruments; and as he is sensible that the best way to learn what it is fitting that God should do, is to consider what He has already done, he concludes that nothing is more becoming the infinite majesty of God than to perform the greatest miracles by the weakest means.

Is it not amazing, then, to hear persons who pretend to be Christians, even zealous Christians, advancing this very argument against the existence of particular miracles, and joining the common enemy in undermining Christianity? The only cause I can discover for such unreasonable conduct is what the holy prophet David said of the Israelites upon a similar occasion: "They were mingled among the heathen, and learned their works," Ps. cvi. 35. Daily exposed to hear the blasphemous railleries of half-learned unbelievers against religion, and reading with avidity their impious books, they seldom or never examine what is the real worth of their reasons, or investigate the solid grounds of Christian truth; but, dazzled by the wit and pompous language under which the impieties of libertines are couched, they come insensibly to adopt their mode of thinking, and to look upon their apparent arguments as unanswerable. Were it not for this or some such delusion, I cannot see how a serious Christian could ever be imposed upon by the argument we are at present treating, or draw from it a conclusion so contrary to fact, so injurious to Almighty God, and so nearly bordering upon blasphemy. For it arraigns the divine wisdom of folly, in having frequently made use of the weakest and seemingly most inadequate instruments to perform the most glorious miracles.

XIX. But let us consider what can be said to show the weakness of this argument, when proposed by those who disbelieve the Scriptures. In the first place, I would ask those gentlemen to show me wherein the strength of their argument precisely lies—to point out the connection between the reason alleged and the consequence drawn from it; for I confess that I cannot discover it. I easily see, in the way that they propose it, a sneer, a jest, a turn of ridicule; but any solid connection of reason I perceive none.

A miracle is related to have happened, and is attested

by evidence as convincing as could be desired by any reasonable person in such matters. But the instruments used are, in the eyes of human wisdom, lowly and insignificant; and immediately the existence of the miracle and all its evidence are, upon this account, rejected with a sneer, and the person treated with contempt who should dare after this to believe it. Nay, without bestowing a thought upon the evidence for its existence, no sooner have they a glimpse of what they choose to call meanness in the instrument used, than they reject the whole with contempt as a manifest imposture. Is this reason? is this philosophy?

Before I can approve their conclusion, I must again insist upon their showing the connection of this their argument. "The instrument to us seems mean and insignificant; therefore the miracle, with all its evidence, is falsehood and imposture." The only thing that can be alleged to give at least a shadow of reason in this matter, is one or other of these arguments: First, there is no proportion between the means used and the effect; therefore it is impossible that the effect should have been produced. Secondly, it is unbecoming the divine wisdom to use such means to produce such amazing events; therefore the miracles never took place.

The first of these proceeds upon a supposition manifestly false, that the means or instruments used have some physical influence, or in some way co-operate to the effect produced, or that God uses them as helps for that purpose. From what we have seen above, and from the light of reason itself, it is evident that this supposition is unfounded and ridiculous; and therefore the conclusion drawn from it is equally so. The second argument is contrary to common-sense itself, since it is plain that nothing gives us a higher, a more noble idea, of the wisdom and power of God, than to see Him acting in a manner so much superior to all the wisdom of man; and were there any proportion between the means used in miracles and the effect produced, the power of God would disappear. They would cease to be miracles, as a proportionate cause could be assigned for the thing done. But when there is no such proportion—nay, when we clearly see the most evident disproportion between the means applied and the effect produced—we are then naturally led to admire the infinite power of God, who produces such amazing effects by means so totally inadequate.

Besides, though the things which appear to us to concur in the performance of miracles be termed instruments or means, yet it is not in the strict sense of the word that they are so called; for in no respect whatever do they physically concur in producing the miracle —this is solely the work of God. What we call means, might perhaps with greater propriety be termed external signals in the eyes of men, to make the finger of God more evident; or, if you please, they may be called *conditions* which Almighty God required to be performed externally by man, upon the performance of which He Himself alone, or His holy angels commissioned by Him, immediately worked the miracle: consequently, as Almighty God may prescribe any condition that He pleases, and is very far from looking upon those things as low or insignificant which appear so to man, it is unreasonable to say that it is unbecoming in God to use any of them for the above purpose. Whatever different esteem man may put on ashes and on gold, they are equal before God; and consequently, it is as becoming Him to use the one as to use the other in the performance of the greatest miracle. We must conclude, then, that the argument against the existence of a miracle drawn from the apparent lowliness or insignificance of the instrument, is a mere sophism which proves nothing; that it is altogether unbecoming a philosopher to advance it; and that in the mouth of a Christian it borders upon blasphemy.

XX. I come now to the last point to be examined under this head of instruments used in performing miracles—namely, whether any respect or veneration may lawfully be given to those creatures which Almighty God makes use of for this purpose. This has been much debated among Christian writers, and therefore, in order to throw as much light as possible upon it, I shall begin by examining the proper meaning of the words, respect, veneration, worship, and the like. In doing this, we must carefully distinguish three things first: the judgment which we form of the excellence or worth of any object; secondly, the value or esteem which we put upon it on that account; thirdly, the external signs, either in words or actions, by which we manifest to others the ideas we entertain. These three things are naturally connected with each other, for according to our judgment of anything we esteem and value it; and when we entertain a high opinion of any object, we naturally express this outwardly by words or actions.

These three things, then, seem to be included in the general idea expressed by the words, respect, veneration, worship, or adoration. Hence, therefore, we may lay down this general rule to regulate our inquiries: "When the judgment which we form of the excellence of any object is just; when we value and esteem it as it deserves; and when we manifest outwardly, by words or actions these our interior dispositions—this is a just and laudable respect, which common-sense itself teaches to be not only lawful, but strictly due, and which we ourselves never fail to exact from others, when we know or even think we are possessed of any such valuable quality."

XXI. To understand this more perfectly, we must remark that our opinion of the valuable qualities of the object is the cause of the respect which we manifest. This opinion or judgment is seated in the understanding, and it is chiefly upon the justness or falsity of this judgment that the nature of the subsequent respect depends. For if I know a nobleman, for instance, to be what he is, and form a true judgment of his dignity, and of the respect which I owe to him conformably to this judgment, then this respect when given is just and proper. But if, by a false judgment, I mistake him for a king, and consequently have the interior esteem, and show the outward respect which is due only to royalty, then the respect which I pay to him is unjust. It by no means belongs to him. But then it is clear that this is solely owing to my mistaken judgment. On the other hand, when, by a false judgment, I look upon the object as not having the excellence which it really possesses, this produces a want of due respect, or a respect false by defect, as the former is by excess.

The esteem of the object, subsequent to the judgment which we form of its possessing such and such excellences, is not a necessary consequence of that judgment, nor does it always exist in the same degree in every person. This is an act more of the will than of the understanding, and is always a consequence of, and in proportion to, our love and affection for the excellences of which we think the object to be possessed. Thus, two men equally know all the properties and qualities of gold; but yet their estimation of it may be very different. The one whose heart is fixed upon his treasures prefers them to everything else, sets the highest value on them, and is ready to sell his very soul for their sake. The other, whose love and affections are placed upon other objects, puts very little value upon gold. A pious Christian and a libertine deist both know that a consecrated chalice is dedicated to the service of Jesus Christ upon His altars. The Christian esteems it highly on this account, and treats it with such respect that he does not dare to touch it irreverently, because his love and esteem for Jesus Christ cause him to love and respect anything so nearly connected with Him. The deist, on the other hand, who has no regard for Jesus Christ, pays no more respect to a chalice consecrated to His service than to any common cup. In these examples, and many others that might be adduced, both persons form the same true judgment that the object possesses certain qualities: but to one these qualities are valuable because he loves them—to the other they are of little or no value, because he has no affection for them; and of course, though the judgment be the same, the subsequent esteem or value put upon the object is very different.

Such is our natural constitution, that when the soul is strongly affected, it communicates this affection to the body, producing certain outward movements which correspond with these inward affections, and are demonstrations of them. Thus, joy, grief, fear, &c., never exist in any considerable degree in the soul without exciting their corresponding signs in the body; and in like manner, when we entertain a high esteem of any object, this will not fail to show itself both in our words and actions. But these outward signs of respect or veneration are by no means an immediate consequence of our knowledge that such and such particular excellences exist in the object, but are always the result of our love and esteem, and in proportion to them, for they are the natural expression of our feelings; and hence, the greater such love and esteem are, the more ardent will naturally be the external expressions.

As the excellences of different objects vary in degree and kind, the motives of respect arising from them, and consequently the respect itself, must be of various kinds. Thus the motive of our esteem and respect for magistrates and princes proceeds from the civil dignity and authority which they possess. This is a civil excellence, and the respect paid them with the outward signs by which it is expressed is termed civil veneration. The respect of children for their parents is the result of that natural power and authority which parents have over them; and as the influence of this motive is the work of nature itself, the respect paid to parents, and all external expression of it, is called natural respect or veneration. The motive of our respect for holy persons and holy things is their connection with Almighty God. This is its general character, and hence it is called religious respect, religious worship, or religious veneration.

Lastly, The motives of the respect and veneration which we pay to God Himself are His own divine perfections, upon account of which, knowing Him to be infinitely above all creatures, and worthy of being infinitely esteemed and beloved by us, we do esteem and respect Him above all things whatever. This motive is divine, and therefore the worship and veneration which we pay to God, and all the external acts by which we express our inward dispositions towards Him, are called "divine worship, and acts of divine worship." Here we must observe, that no external act of respect (sacrifice alone excepted) is in the least degree expressive of the judgment which we form concerning the nature of the excellences in the object to which we pay respect or veneration. This judgment is the motive of our respect. It determines the nature of it; and no external act of respect, except sacrifice, precisely of itself, and abstracting from the circumstances in which it is performed, has any determinate signification of any one kind of worship more than another—as all such external acts are indiscriminately used to signify natural, civil, religious, and divine worship, according to the object. All that these external actions naturally represent is, a desire to testify esteem, respect, and veneration; and the more earnestly and affectionately we perform them, the more we show the depth of our internal feelings. But these external acts do not disclose the cause of our internal feelings, and therefore from external acts alone we can never pronounce with certainty on the motives which produce them. Hypocrisy can perfectly imitate all these external signs of the internal affections. It may use them in mockery and ridicule, as well as from respect and veneration, as was the case when the soldiers bowed the knee before our Saviour and saluted Him, "Hail, King of the Jews!"

This observation deserves particular attention, because it is from overlooking it that the adversaries of the Catholic Church obstinately persist in their uncharitable accusations of idolatry and superstition; for, seeing the ardent and affectionate manner in which her children perform many outward acts of respect towards holy relics and the pictures and images of Jesus Christ and His saints, they immediately conclude that they look upon these things as gods, and pay them the worship due to God alone; a conclusion as unreasonable as it is unjust. These outward acts show indeed the sincerity of their regard and love of the objects and the persons to whom they relate; but they by no means explain their judgment of the nature of the excellences for which they love them. This can only be known by their own words; and upon all occasions Catholics constantly declare their belief of these objects to be quite the reverse of what is laid to their charge.

XXII. After this minute explanation of the idea contained in the words, respect, worship, and veneration, it will be easy to determine the question—whether any respect or veneration may lawfully be given to holy persons and holy things, and in particular to those which the divine wisdom is pleased to use as instruments in working miracles, or in bestowing any particular favour on man.

We have only to apply the above observations, particularly the rule there mentioned, and we shall immediately see the justice of the following conclusions: 1. That all holy persons, places, and things, deserve to be judged holy, according to the explanation which we have given of the word—that is, as separated from other creatures and common uses, and united to God by one or other of the above kinds of union. 2. That in consequence of this they are in themselves more valuable, and deserve a higher esteem, and that a greater respect and veneration should be paid to them than to other persons, places, or things of the same kind, which have no such union or connection with the Deity. 3. That, therefore, actually to entertain that esteem for them in our heart, and to show it outwardly by our words and actions, is not only lawful, but a debt strictly due, seeing that they do possess these excellences of separation from other creatures, and union with the Creator, which justly deserve to be so valued and esteemed. 4. That as their union with God is the only motive on which this superior veneration is grounded, it therefore follows that the honour and respect paid to them ultimately terminates in God, and is, strictly speaking, an act of worship paid to Him.

XXIII. These conclusions are not only clear and evident; they are the very voice of nature itself. Suppose that any person had in his possession Elijah's mantle, or the handkerchiefs and aprons which had touched the body of St Paul, and that the same miracles recorded in the Holy Scriptures had been wrought in himself or others by their means, would he regard them no more, or put no greater value upon them, than upon any others of the same kind? Would not nature itself dictate to him to value and esteem them above treasures of gold and silver? Would he not, both in word and action, show his esteem and veneration for them? Certainly he would; and let any man ask his own heart what he would do were the case his own, and I feel assured he will give the same answer.

When the people of God were bitten by the fiery serpents, and found an immediate remedy in looking at the brazen serpent, with what respect, reverence, and veneration must they not have regarded that image! We need only examine our own heart to know what they did on this occasion. So true it is, that when we know a thing to be connected with Almighty God, especially if He has used it as an instrument of bestowing extraordinary favours on mankind, if we have any sense of religion in our hearts, and our minds be not warped by passion or prejudice, we naturally conceive a high esteem and religious veneration for it; and this feeling as naturally manifests itself outwardly in our words and actions.

XXIV. Here I cannot omit citing the authority of one who, as all the world knows, is no friend to Popery or miracles; I mean the celebrated Dr Middleton. The 'Observator,' one of the Doctor's antagonists, had advanced, that "if God works a cure by dead men's bones, it does not follow that the bones are to be worshipped." If this gentleman means that such bones are not to be worshipped as gods, or divine honour paid them, no one will dispute the point with him. But if he means that, in the case proposed, no respect, no veneration of any kind is to be given, all the above reasoning, and the voice of nature itself, cry out against him. Of this Dr Middleton is so sensible, that in his remarks on the 'Observator' (page 23), he answers with warmth to the above assertion—"But, in fact, it immediately did follow, has, and must follow, in confusion of his silly hypothesis."

XXV. But we require no such testimony, having the high authority of the Holy Scriptures themselves; for in these sacred oracles we find repeated instances of the most profound external acts of respect, worship, and veneration paid to holy persons and holy things, especially to those chosen by Almighty God as His instruments in performing miracles. When Obadiah was sent by Ahab to seek for water, and met the holy prophet Elijah by the way, "he knew him, and fell flat upon his face," 1 Kings, xviii. 7. The sons of the prophets, when they saw Elisha divide the waters of Jordan, and pass through on dry land, said,— "The spirit of Elijah doth rest on Elisha; and they came to meet him, and bowed themselves to the ground before him," 4 Kings, ii. 15. After the defeat of the people of God at Ai, "Joshua rent his clothes, and fell to the earth upon his face *before the ark of the Lord* until the eventide, he and the elders of Israel, and put dust upon their heads," Jos. vii. 6.

Remark here how profound an external act of worship is paid to the ark, an inanimate object! In the days of Samuel, when the Israelites were defeated the first time by the Philistines, they said,—" Let us fetch the ark of the covenant of the Lord out of Shiloh unto us, that when it cometh among us it *may save us* out of the hands of our enemies," 1 Sam. iv. 3. Here, in Scripture language, the saving the people is attributed to the ark.

Omitting other examples, I shall only add, that in order to see how religious worship to holy persons and holy things was sanctioned and even required by Almighty God, we have merely to recall the miraculous punishments inflicted on those who failed in this duty. See above, chap. vi. § xiv., &c. From these authorities we justly conclude, "that it is consonant to right reason, agreeable to the dictates of nature, and required by Almighty God Himself, that due respect and religious reverence be paid, for His sake, to all holy persons and holy things, especially to such as He is pleased to use as instruments for manifesting His own glory, and promoting the good of man, in working miracles."

XXVI. Before I leave this subject, it will be proper to examine a question that naturally occurs here—whether God at any time employs wicked men as His instruments for performing miracles.

That those who are the servants and favourites of God, and honoured with the gift of miracles, may fall even into the most grievous sins, is not called in question. St Peter was sent with his fellow-apostles to heal the sick, to cast out devils, and to perform other wonders, and yet we know how he afterwards fell. Neither do we inquire whether wicked men, by the agency of evil spirits, may not sometimes perform prodigies and wonders. This is readily granted. The Scriptures are explicit upon this point. Such prodigies, however, are by no means true miracles, but lying signs and wonders. Neither are such men instruments in the hands of God in these cases, but instruments of the devil. What we are here to inquire is, whether Almighty God at any time makes use of wicked men, who openly lead wicked lives, and whilst they are in a state of enmity with Him, as His instruments to work real miracles, and in what manner, or on what grounds He does so. In order to form a correct judgment, I shall first consider such examples as we find in the Holy Scriptures, and then examine what light they throw on this question.

XXVII. The first example is that of Balaam. Concerning him commentators are not unanimous whether he really was a prophet of the most high God, though a wicked man; or if he was, and always had been, a magician or soothsayer. Some few are of the former opinion, but the Fathers in general and best commentators regard him as having always been an impious magician. However this may be, it cannot be called in question, that if he ever had been a servant of God and a true prophet, such he was not when sent for by the king of Moab, as the Scripture expressly calls him then a "soothsayer," Jos. xiii. 22; and his building seven altars, and ordering a set number of victims on each, were acts of idolatry and superstition done on the high places of Baal, in his honour, and seeking knowledge from him by such enchantments. In Numb. xxiv. 1, they are expressly called enchantments, and Balaam is said to have given them up in despair; because, instead of obtaining what he desired, he always found that God opposed him and blessed Israel. Besides, wherever he is mentioned in other parts of Scripture, he is spoken of with horror and detestation as one of the worst of men—see 2 Pet. ii. 14, 15, and Jude, ver. 11. Yet we find that he was inspired by God not only to pronounce a solemn benediction upon the people of Israel, but also to make a most solemn prophecy of the Messiah, and to foretell the future fate of several of the people in that country.

The next example is that of Saul, who not only when he was in friendship with God and innocent, was filled with a prophetic spirit and prophesied with the other prophets, as related, 1 Sam. x. 10; but also afterwards, when he was cast off by God for his sins—nay, when he was resolved to kill David, had sent several parties for that purpose, and afterwards went himself—was filled with the prophetic spirit and prophesied, 1 Sam. xix. 23.

The third example is that of Judas, who "was a thief," John, xii. 6; and Christ knew from the beginning that he "should betray Him," John, vi. 64—yea, upon a certain occasion said of him that he was a devil: "Have not I chosen you twelve, and one of you is a devil? now He spake of Judas Iscariot," John, vi. 70. Yet notwithstanding this He sent him out with the others on their mission, and gave him, as well as them, the power of working miracles: "And when He had called unto Him His twelve disciples, He gave them power against unclean spirits, to cast them out, and to heal all manner of sickness, and all manner of diseases; . . . and He commanded them, saying, Heal the sick, cleanse the lepers, raise the dead, cast out devils," &c., Matt. x. 1, &c.

The fourth example is of Caiphas, who, though a

cked man, and at that very time plotting the destrucion of Jesus Christ, yet even then prophesied the necessity of His death for the salvation of the whole world.

Besides, our blessed Saviour Himself expressly says: "Many will say to me in that day, Lord, Lord, have we not prophesied in Thy name? and in Thy name cast out devils? and in Thy name done many wonderful works? And then I shall profess to them that I never knew you; depart from me, ye that work iniquity," Matt. vii. 22.

Lastly, St Paul evidently supposes the power of working miracles even in wicked men who are devoid of charity, when he says, "Though I should have all faith so as to remove mountains, and have not charity, I am nothing," 1 Cor. xiii.

XXVIII. Let us now examine these several examples, and see what conclusion can be drawn from them. First, with regard to Balaam, nothing is more common in the Holy Scripture than to find Almighty God turning the impiety of wicked men against themselves, either the more effectually to convince them of their error, or to exalt His servants; and in these cases, as the royal prophet says, "He bringeth the counsel of the heathen to nought, and maketh the devices of the people of none effect," Ps. xxxii. 10.

In the case before us, Balak wished Balaam by his enchantment to imprecate ruin and destruction on the people of God. Balaam was most desirous of complying with the king's request, and accordingly had recourse to charms and incantations for this purpose. But Almighty God interposed in behalf of His chosen people, disappointed all the effects of Balaam's enchantments, and instead of allowing the devil to assist him, sent His own angel to make known to Balaam the impossibility of what he wished, to reprove his avarice and impiety, and to put words in his mouth concerning Israel quite the reverse of what Balak wished. For "the Lord put a word in Balaam's mouth, and said, *Return unto Balak, and thus thou shalt speak,*" Numb. xxiii. 5. And again, when a second attempt was made, "The Lord met Balaam, and put a word in his mouth, and said, Go again unto Balak, and speak thus," ver. 16.

These words were not only a solemn benediction of Israel, but also a prediction of what was to be done in future ages by their posterity against the people of Balak and their neighbours, who had joined with him against the people of God, in just punishment of their impiety. For in the place where that prediction is made, as well as in the last benediction of Israel, Balaam declares, that what he is about to say are the words that he had heard: "He hath said, who heard the words of God, who saw the vision of the Almighty," &c., chap. xxiv., ver. 4. And again, "He hath said, which heard the words of God, and knew the knowledge of the Most High, who saw the visions of the Almighty," ver. 16.

From these observations it seems that Balaam was not properly God's instrument in working a miracle, but rather the subject on whom the miracle was wrought—being compelled in direct opposition to his wish to bless the people of God, and to relate the evils that were to come upon these nations, as the angel had declared to him; and consequently, it cannot be inferred from this example that Almighty God ever makes use of wicked men living openly in sin as instruments of working miracles.

XXIX. With regard to Saul, it must be observed, 1st, That the word prophesy does not always in Scripture imply the foretelling things to come, nor by prophets are we always to understand those who foretell such things. By prophets are often meant those who are deputed to sing the praises of God, or bodies of religious men who lived together, and were employed in that office, celebrating the divine praises both by vocal and instrumental music. The hill of God, where Saul met with a company of these men, was probably so called from their residing upon it; and Samuel foretold him that he would there meet them with psaltery, and pipe, and harp, before them, 1 Sam. x. 5.

This appears further in 1 Chron. xv. 16, 17: "And David spake to the chief of the Levites to appoint their brethren to be singers with instruments of music, psalteries, and harps, and cymbals, sounding, by lifting up the voice with joy. So the Levites appointed Heman the son of Joel, and of his brethren Asaph the son of Berechiah." Now this their employment is in another scripture expressly called prophesying; thus, chap. xxv. 1, "Moreover, David and the captains of the host separated to the service of the sons of Asaph, and of Heman, and of Jeduthun, who should *prophesy with harps, and psalteries, and cymbals.*" Again, verse 2, of the sons of Asaph it is said, that they were "under the hands of Asaph, who prophesied according to the order of the king." Here it is evident that the word prophesy cannot mean the foretelling future things, which neither the king could command, nor any one do at his bidding; but must signify celebrating the praises of God for which they were appointed.

Secondly, We may observe that, when Saul met a company of these holy men, and is said to have prophesied with them, it is only meant that Almighty God filled him with an extraordinary devotional affection, which made him forget all worldly concerns, and join in singing the praises of God in an ecstatic manner. In this there was certainly no miracle wrought by Saul; but if there was anything miraculous, the miracle was done in him by the change which the Holy Ghost wrought in his heart—a thing not more wonderful than is done daily in the conversion of wicked men to a good life.

Thirdly, The second time this happened to Saul was when he was in a sinful state, and actually resolved to commit a grievous sin. The whole conduct, therefore, of Almighty God on this occasion, shows both His infinite care of His servants and His earnest desire for the conversion of sinners, which were the ends He had in view in what happened. Saul being determined upon the death of David, no sooner heard that he was at Najoth with Samuel and the prophets, than he sent a party to take him; but immediately on their arrival they were filled with devotion, and forgetting the orders of the king, joined with the others, and prophesied—that is, sang the praises of God. The king hearing this, sent a second and a third party, to whom the same thing happened.

Here Almighty God manifested His power to Saul, which ought to have convinced him how vain it was to fight against God, or to think to destroy David, whom God protected, and had decreed should succeed him in the kingdom. But Saul, blinded by passion, went himself in person to destroy David. When he came near the place, however, God was pleased to work the same change in him, and even in a manner more extraordinary than in his guards, by divesting him for a time of his fury against David, and exciting him to join in celebrating the divine praises.

From this it is evident, that whatever there was miraculous in this change, Saul was only the subject on whom it was wrought. And as his prophesying did not consist in foretelling things to come, but only in singing the praises of God, it is plain that he was by no means made use of by Almighty God as an instrument of working any miracle in the sense in which we have explained that word, and in which it is naturally understood.

XXX. The next case is that of Judas, concerning whom it is certain, first, that he was at last an impious man, and died a reprobate. Secondly, that Jesus Christ knew from the beginning what he would do, and how he was to die. Thirdly, that in conjunction with the other apostles, he received the commission and power of working miracles, when he was sent with them to preach the approach of the kingdom of heaven, and to prepare the people for receiving our blessed Saviour; and there is no reason to doubt that he exercised that power with his brethren.

So far this is certain. But it is not evident from the sacred writings that Judas was actually wicked, leading a sinful life, and at enmity with God, when he was called by Jesus Christ to the apostleship, and received the power of working miracles. For, according to the sacred chronologists, the apostles were sent on their mission with that power very soon after their vocation; and consequently, all that can with certainty be concluded from his case is, that though he was used by God as an instrument in working miracles, yet he afterwards became a reprobate. It is by no means clear that he actually was wicked and in disgrace with God when he received and exercised that power; nay, it seems more reasonable to conclude that at first he was not so, as it is scarcely to be supposed that Jesus Christ would have chosen such a person, raised him to so high a dignity, and have bestowed such powers upon him. At least, if he was then wicked, it could only have been in the dispositions of his heart, and not in his outward conduct and actions; for no such thing is laid to his charge in the Gospel; and as our Saviour's enemies made such a reproach to Him that He kept company with publicans and sinners, they undoubtedly would have cried out much more against Him had one of His own disciples been of that class.

All that follows then from the case of Judas in this supposition is, that the ministers of the Church, whose office it is to preach the Gospel, acting in that quality, may receive the power of working miracles, when the confirmation of their mission or of the truths they preach requires it, for the good of others, whilst they themselves live without reproach in the eyes of the world, even though they should be wicked in the sight of God, and finally end in reprobation.

XXXI. The case of Caiphas comes next to be considered. It is thus related in the Gospel: "Then gathered the chief priests and the Pharisees a council, and said, What do we? for this man doth many miracles. If we let Him thus alone, all men will believe in Him; and the Romans shall come and take away both our place and nation. And one of them named Caiphas, being the high priest that same year, said unto them, You know nothing at all, nor consider that it is expedient for us, that one man should die for the people, and that the whole nation perish not. And this spake he not of himself; but being high priest that year, he prophesied that Jesus should die for that nation," &c., John, xi. 47, &c.

From this account it appears, first, that what Caiphas said was, in its natural signification, a consequence of the preceding deliberation of the council, and the wicked dispositions of their hearts against Jesus Christ. All alleged the danger of letting Him alone, both for themselves and their nation. Caiphas therefore concluded that it was expedient He should die. Secondly, that Caiphas himself had no knowledge of the prophetic import of his words, and was very far from intending it. Thirdly, that the Holy Ghost prompted him to express his thoughts in such words as might at the same time signify both what he maliciously intended against our Saviour, and what Almighty God designed, in foretelling His death for the salvation of mankind. Fourthly, that this was done solely in consequence of his character of high priest, and not of his person: for as the holy Fathers in general explain it, " Prophetiæ donum eo tempore non homini, sed sacerdotio concessit Deus." Fifthly, that it does not appear from the Scripture that Caiphas was bad at this time as to his moral character in the eyes of the people, nor looked upon in that light; for the horrid crime he was guilty of with regard to Jesus Christ was proposed to the people as zeal for the cause of God, and for His law. Sixthly, that in consequence, Caiphas, a wicked man, and an open enemy of Jesus Christ, was no more an instrument in the hand of God in pronouncing this prophecy, than the ass was in pronouncing Balaam's correction and reproof—that is, was a mere material instrument. The sacred character of the priesthood, however, may be a sufficient motive to induce Almighty God to make use of His ministers as instruments in working miracles for His own glory or the good of others, even though they themselves be wicked in His sight, but while this does not appear to the eyes of the world.

XXXII. If now we consider our Saviour's words, Matt. vii. 22, "That many shall say unto Him in that day, Lord, Lord, have we not prophesied in Thy name?" &c., we shall easily see all that can be gathered from them. For we must observe, that though these persons have died in disgrace with God, and will be eternally separated from Him, though they had wrought miracles in His name, yet the Scripture does not say that they were actually wicked men and open sinners when they wrought these miracles. Their having wrought these miracles in His name shows they had the true faith, and were members of His Church; and we find, from the example of the sons of Scæva, that those who have not true faith, and are not members of the Church, though they pretend to work miracles in the name of Jesus Christ, not only are unable, but expose themselves to no small danger by attempting it; see Acts, xix. 13 *et seq.*

Now, if those of whom our Saviour here speaks had true faith, and if in Scripture there is no proof they actually were wicked when they wrought these miracles, we may charitably suppose they were then good men, although afterwards they fell into sin and died impenitent. In this supposition our Saviour's words have their full force, showing us that true piety does not consist in any outward exercise of devotion, as prayer, which He declares in the preceding verse: "Not every one that says to me, Lord, Lord, shall enter into the kingdom of heaven;" nor even in any of those extraordinary graces called *gratis datæ*—that is, given not for the sanctification of those who have them, but for the good of others, as the gift of miracles—for many who have received those gifts will be at last condemned,—but that it consists in doing "the will of God in all things;" for, "he that does the will of My Father Who is in heaven, he shall enter into the kingdom of heaven."

It is, indeed, true that the answer which our Saviour tells us He will give to such persons, "I never knew you," may seem to imply that they had always been wicked; but this consequence is not just; for as it is certain that they had the true faith of Christ and were Christians, they must at some time or other have been in the state of grace and friendship with God, at least after baptism, and till they had lost their baptismal innocence. Besides, it even appears a shock to piety to suppose that Jesus Christ would use as instruments for working the great miracles here related, many who had always been impious men and His enemies; wherefore the words "I never knew you" can only signify that knowledge of approbation and love which Jesus Christ has of those who He foresees by persevering in His favour will be His for ever. Of such He says, "My sheep hear my voice, and I know them, and they follow me; and I give unto them eternal life, and they shall never perish," John, x. 27, 28. With this knowledge it is certainly true that Christ never knew those that perish, though in their former life they had been far advanced in perfection, and even so as to work miracles and to prophesy.

What I have here advanced only tends to show that if we merely consider the words of Scripture there does not appear any certainty from them that those of whom our Saviour speaks were actually in a state of sin, much less that they were openly wicked, when they performed the miracles related; and consequently, that this passage is not a full and direct proof that God ever does make use of wicked men as instruments of miracles.

XXXIII. The last passage from St Paul, where he says, "Though I should have all faith, so as to remove mountains, I am nothing," 1 Cor. xiii., plainly supposes that that strong faith, on which the gift of miracles is founded, may exist in such as are devoid of charity and in disgrace with God; and in this sense it is commonly understood by the holy Fathers and interpreters of Holy Writ.

XXXIV. Coming now to apply these remarks, we must observe that there are two distinct questions—first, whether the gift of miracles can be bestowed on wicked men who lead openly sinful lives; secondly, whether Almighty God does actually sometimes make use of such men as His instruments.

XXXV. The first question is easily solved. The power of miracles is a free gift of God, not due to any merit of the recipient, not necessary for his own immediate sanctification, nor given for that end, but for the good of others, for the manifestation and confirmation of the truth. We see no reason, therefore, to suppose that this power cannot in certain circumstances be bestowed even on wicked men; that is, that Almighty God may not, if He pleases, work miracles even by means of wicked men when His own glory and the good of souls can be promoted thereby. Some of the above texts of Scripture strongly insinuate that this may sometimes be done, and the holy Fathers and commentators acknowledge it.

But as to the second question, Whether Almighty God in fact does make use of wicked men, known as such, as His instruments, in working miracles, I answer—first, that according to the ordinary course of the laws of providence this is very seldom, if ever, the case; secondly, that there is scarcely one positive proof from Scripture that this is ever done; thirdly, that there are several strong reasons why, except in very singular and extraordinary circumstances, God should not do so.

These reasons are—First, because true miracles not only show the truth of that doctrine in proof of which they are performed, but also naturally impress the mind with a strong sense of veneration for the person who performs them, and persuade us of his power with God.

Now it does not seem probable that the divine wisdom and goodness will confer upon persons openly vicious a gift naturally tending to lead others to esteem and reverence them as His friends. Secondly, the gift of miracles naturally procures authority to the possessor; and therefore, were it conferred on a man openly wicked, even in one instance, it might enable him to impose upon *the many*, and lead them to wickedness. Thirdly, the openly sinful lives of wicked men could not fail greatly to detract from the authority of any miracles performed by them, exciting a strong suspicion in the mind that their miracles were not true, but either fictitious or the work of Satan, and not of God; for as miracles give a double lustre to virtue and sanctity, so a holy and virtuous life confirms and enhances the authority of miracles. I answer, fourthly, that if at any time Almighty God makes use of wicked men to perform miracles, this is only, as far as can be collected from Scripture in the examples of Judas and Caiphas, under the following conditions,—when the person performing the miracle is himself a true believer, though a wicked man; for if not a true believer, no miracle will be performed, though attempted even in the name of Jesus, as we see in the sons of Scæva;—when he is adorned with the character of a public minister of God, as Judas and Caiphas were; and then the power is granted to the character, not the person, as is expressly noticed in the case of Caiphas;—when, though wicked in the sight of God, he does not appear so in the eyes of the world; for, as we have seen, above, there is no proof from Scripture that any such were ever used by God as instruments of working miracles;—when the end of these miracles is solely to confirm or make known the truths of God.

CHAPTER IX.

THE AUTHORITY OF MIRACLES.

I. WE now come to an important subject, which requires to be treated with the most careful accuracy—the authority of miracles. The enemies of religion have tried every means to weaken the force of the arguments in its favour from the evidence of miracles. Sometimes they have endeavoured to disprove the possibility of miracles, and having failed there, they have attacked their actual existence. But finding this line of argument unsuccessful, they have had recourse to the weak plea of denying their authority; pretending, with an air of triumph, that though the existence of miracles should be acknowledged, they can prove nothing, nor can the truth of any doctrine be shown from them—both because miracles have been alleged and wrought in proof of opposite doctrines, and also because, according to Christian writers, the sanctity of the doctrine taught is given as a criterion by which to judge and prove the truth of the miracle wrought in its favour. This point, therefore, must be particularly considered, and the objections brought against the authority of miracles carefully examined. But I must premise a few observations.

II. First, then, we must observe that Mr Hume's remarks in his essay against miracles, page 182 (in the note), "That a miracle may be discoverable by men or not," but "that this alters not its nature or essence," is untrue in the Christian idea of a miracle; for as a miracle is an "extraordinary effect produced in the material creation," which material creation is essentially the natural object of our senses, every extraordinary effect produced in it must in itself be "discoverable" by us, whether, in fact, we do discover it or not.

It is true, indeed, that the Christian religion proposes to us several operations proper to Almighty God as matters of faith which are not discoverable by our senses—as "the incarnation of the Son of God," "the union of the divine and human natures in one person," "the conception of Jesus Christ in His mother's womb without her having the knowledge of man," and the like. But these the Christian world never looked upon as miracles in the ordinary and proper sense of that word; and if we reflect attentively, we shall find that they can no more be classed with miracles than the creation of the world at the beginning, or the daily creation of the soul of man and uniting it to the body. These also are operations of the almighty hand of God, and above the power of all created agents; but it is plain that they do not enter into our idea of a miracle.

The above truths do not fall under the cognisance of our senses. We know them only by revelation; they are objects of faith—mysteries which the Christian religion proposes to our belief; but they are not miracles. However, if Mr Hume or any other chooses to call them so, I offer no objection; but they can have no authority as proofs. Their revelation must itself be proved, along with the other truths of Christianity, by miracles properly such, according to the explanation we have given—miracles which are of their own nature discoverable by men, and fall under the observation of our senses.

Secondly, If the fact proposed be evidently a relative miracle, or such as can be performed by creatures of a nature superior to man, whether good or bad, or if there be any solid reason to suspect it is so, or that it may be only the effect of natural causes, it can never serve as a proof of doctrine without further evidence; nor can it make that impression upon the mind which the persuasion of its being a true miracle necessarily does; because the suspicion must always remain, that "perhaps the thing done is owing to natural causes, and is no miracle; perhaps it is the work of Satan and not of God." Only such miracles, therefore, as are known to be from God, and performed either by Himself or by His holy angels, commissioned and authorised by Him, can be used as having any authority in proof of doctrine.

Thirdly, We have seen above that true miracles naturally make a deep impression on the mind, excite a lively sense of the divine presence, veneration and reverence towards God, love and gratitude, confidence in His goodness, fear of offending, and the like. Now the present inquiry is not how far, or by what means they thus affect the heart of man: that is a fact which is known by experience, and is not called in question. But as some of the principal ends intended by Almighty God from miracles were to convince mankind of the divine commission of those sent by Him to inform them of His will, to prove that the doctrine proposed by such teachers is divine, or to defend some tenet formerly revealed and believed to be from God, when it is called in question or denied, the present inquiry is precisely this, "How far true miracles are a sufficient and rational proof to convince the world of the truth of any of these three points, and what authority they have for this purpose?"

Fourthly, With regard to the nature of the doctrine to be proved, we must carefully observe that this kind of proof is not intended to convey a distinct idea of the different parts of the doctrine proposed, or of their mutual connection and relation with each other, as in the case of proofs drawn from internal evidence. Nay, strictly speaking, the authority of the proof from miracles does not fall directly upon the doctrine itself, but upon its revelation; for the immediate object of this kind of proof is to show that the doctrine proposed is revealed by Almighty God. The truth of the doctrine, however, is no less certain on this account, but rather more so; because it is absolutely impossible and repugnant to our idea of God to suppose that He can ever authorise or propagate a falsehood. If, therefore, the authority of miracles can prove that the doctrine attested by them is the doctrine of God, and revealed by Him, it must follow that that doctrine is essentially true.

Fifthly, Those natural truths which are known by the light of reason, and which the human understanding is capable of comprehending, do not require to be revealed by God to convince mankind that they are true; and therefore neither are they, strictly speaking, the proper objects of proof from miracles. Almighty God may indeed, if He pleases, make even natural truths the subject of revelation, in order to manifest them more clearly to mankind, or to give us a deeper conviction of their certainty. But the proper objects of proof from miracles are either such supernatural truths as exceed the comprehension of the mind of man, and cannot be known or proved by natural reason, or they are positive institutions of the divine will requiring something of us which, depending solely on the divine pleasure, can be known only by God communicating them to us.

III. These observations show the precise state of the present question of the authority of miracles. For we see that the miracles required in this proof are such only as are certainly from God, either performed immediately by Himself or by commission from Him; and this at once precludes every objection from miracles having been performed in proof of opposite doctrines, as it is evidently impossible that God can perform miracles in attestation of falsehood. In such a contest, therefore, as that between Moses and the Egyptian magicians, the wonders on the one side cannot be from God, and are not true miracles, but lying signs of Satan, which need deceive no one. For Almighty God is bound by His own divine perfections to prevent such delusions being undiscoverable, as we shall find when we examine the criterion.

From the above observations, we also see what class of doctrines stand in need of proof from miracles; and these are even the divine commission of persons sent by God to communicate His will to man, or such supernatural truths concerning God and spiritual things, as are in themselves incomprehensible to the human understanding, and undiscoverable by natural reason; or, in fine, such positive institutions as God may be pleased to appoint, and which He requires us to receive and observe. This obviates the objections from the incomprehensibility of the doctrine, since it is chiefly such doctrine that requires this proof. The precise state of the question therefore is, "Whether miracles known to be performed by God, or by angels commissioned by Him, in order to prove any of these points, be a just and rational proof to convince mankind that they are in reality the truths of God, and revealed by Him." This is the subject of our present inquiry; and even the light of reason clearly shows that such miracles are a full and convincing proof of the divine revelation of those doctrines for which they are wrought, and oblige all to whom these doctrines are so proved to receive them as truths stamped with the seal of heaven, and attested by God Himself.

IV. The principles which guide our reason in this matter are taken from our ideas of the infinite perfections of the Supreme Being. From these we evidently see, that if God be infinitely good, it is impossible that He can directly concur or employ His almighty power in defence of lies, to the inevitable delusion of His rational creatures whom He loves so much, and whose happiness is so dear to Him. If He be infinitely true and holy, it is impossible He should ever attest, authorise, or propagate falsehood. He must essentially love truth. If He be infinitely wise, He can never act against Himself, either by employing His power against His own veracity, holiness, or wisdom, or by depriving Himself of the most appropriate external means of convincing mankind of whatever He thinks proper to make known to them.

These are principles evident to the light of reason, and essentially connected with our idea of a supreme and infinitely perfect Being. Now, to come to our case; let us suppose that a person appears in the world declaring that he is sent from this Supreme Being, and commissioned to instruct mankind in His divine will, and appeals to God Himself to attest his being thus sent and commissioned. In this case, how can Almighty God give the attestation required so fully as to satisfy His rational creatures, and exclude all suspicion of delusion? It is plain that there are no external means, but by exerting His omnipotence and performing miracles. And it is no less evident that this attestation He never can give if the person who appeals to it be not in fact sent and commissioned by Him. Miracles, in this case, are the voice of God attesting that what His servant says is true. They are the broad seal of heaven authenticating the commission given by God to those whom He sends as His ambassadors to men, and which a God of goodness and truth can never give where the commission is not true and real.

Again, let us suppose that this person proposes a doctrine previously unheard of and unknown, but which he professes to have received from God by revelation, with orders to teach it to men, and appeals again to the same divine attestation. It is evident that if this new doctrine has not been revealed to him, it is impossible God should ever work a miracle in its favour; for this, as in the former case, would be to attest a lie, to authorise a falsehood, to exert His power against His own sanctity, and thereby positively to concur to the deception and delusion of His creatures; in fine, to render precarious and uncertain the only proper external means of convincing mankind of His will. In the third place, let us suppose any received point of doctrine believed to have been originally revealed by God is called in question and denied; and that in defence of its having been revealed, an appeal is made to God as in the two preceding cases, to attest it by miracles; it is clear that if it was not revealed, Almighty God never would, nor ever could, give the required attestation.

It is evident, then, that if it be known that Almighty God works a miracle, in order to attest either the commission of His servants or the revelation of the doctrines which they propose or defend, that this must be a full

THE AUTHORITY OF MIRACLES. 227

and absolute proof of the veracity of the commission, and of the revelation of the doctrine. And observe, that though the divine attestation by miracles should be denied, which may sometimes happen as we shall afterwards see more fully, and though this denial considered merely in itself is not a full proof that the contested doctrine is false, because God is not always obliged to work miracles when required, in defence of doctrines which have been formerly sufficiently revealed, yet, when He is pleased in any of the above cases actually to work the miracle, it is then absolutely impossible, and utterly inconsistent with the divine perfections, that the doctrines so attested should not be from God. The authority of miracles in proof of doctrine, therefore, as above explained, is absolute and conclusive.

The above reasoning may be well illustrated by a parallel case among men. When a person is sent as an ambassador from one sovereign to another, he must have his credentials properly authenticated before he is received in that character by the sovereign to whom he is accredited. This is done by a commission signed and sealed by his master, importing that he is sent and authorised by him. These credentials are an absolute proof, and procure all credit to what he says in his master's name. But as there is a possibility that an ambassador so sent may exceed his commission; if he should at any time make some extraordinary and apparently unreasonable demand, notwithstanding his credentials, his conduct may be called in question. If, therefore, upon this he should produce another commission signed and sealed as the former, and actually authorising him to make the said demand in his master's name, this would protect him from all suspicion of fraud, and prove that his demand, however extraordinary, was not an invention of his own.

The application is obvious: Almighty God makes choice of some faithful servant to whom He reveals His will, and sends him as His ambassador to declare the same to men. He appears among them, declares his commission, and appeals to the miracles which God works by him, and at his desire, as the credentials of his mission. These miracles, therefore, are the signature of God, the seal of heaven, by which his commission is authenticated, and which necessarily procure to him due credit and respect.

But if, among the doctrines which he teaches, he at last proposes some things extraordinary, and not only hitherto unheard of, but incomprehensible and apparently contradictory, which, however, he declares he received from God, and to which he requires entire submission, men hesitate —they begin to suspect. "He is sent from God, say they —we cannot doubt of it; but he is a man, and perhaps in these things he exceeds his orders. It is true, it does not seem consistent with the goodness of God to give His divine attestation to prove that any teacher is sent by Him to the world, and yet permit him, under the sanction of His character, to teach falsehood; but, on the other hand, though this man has proved beyond dispute that he is sent by God to declare His will to man, yet these points which he proposes are so shocking, and in appearance so contrary to common-sense, that we know not what to think."

If, to allay their fears and dispel their doubts, he should produce another commission of the same nature as the former, equally signed and sealed with the finger of God— that is, if he again should have recourse to miracles to prove the very points at which they take alarm, and if God should work the miracles requested—this must immediately remove their doubts, and effectually convince them, not only that this person was sent from God, but that these very incomprehensible doctrines which he teaches were the truths of God revealed to His servant. This we find is the very thing that Almighty God has done.

Jesus Christ appears in Judea and announces Himself a teacher sent by God, the great Prophet so long expected to be the Saviour of the world. St John the Baptist being then in prison, and hearing of His fame, sends two of his disciples to inquire if He is the Messias. His answer is an appeal to His credentials sealed by Almighty God, the numberless miracles He daily wrought, to which there could be no reply. Among His doctrines one was, that He, as man, had received power from God to forgive sins upon earth; and He takes the following occasion to declare this to the people. "They brought to Him a man sick of the palsy lying on a bed; and Jesus said unto the sick of the palsy, Son, be of good cheer; thy sins be forgiven thee."

Immediately some of those best versed in the law were startled at this doctrine, "and they reasoned in their own hearts, Why doth this man thus speak blasphemy? Who can forgive sins but God alone?" Jesus Christ perceiving in spirit what passed in their hearts, immediately produces new credentials to prove this very point, that He as man had received from God the power of forgiving sins, which He here exercised; and works two stupendous miracles for this purpose, first by showing them that He knew what was passing in their hearts: "Why do ye reason these things in your hearts?" and then by a single word restoring the sick man to perfect health. "That ye may know," says He, "that the Son of Man hath power on earth to forgive sins (He saith to the sick of the palsy), I say to thee Arise, and take up thy bed, and go thy way unto thy house; and immediately he arose, took up the bed, and went forth before them all." This was enough— all murmurs ceased: the people "were all amazed, and glorified God, saying, We never saw it in this fashion," Mark, ii.; or, as St Matthew expresses it, "They glorified God that had given such power unto men," Matt. ix.

V. Other examples might be brought both of our Saviour and His apostles; but the above are sufficient for illustrating our present subject. I shall only observe further, that the learned author of the 'Dissertation on Miracles' against Hume, seems to have done injustice to his cause, and greatly weakened the authority of the proof from miracles, by the manner in which he pretends to account for the connection between any doctrine and the miracles wrought in attestation of it.

He supposes "a man of unblemished character to advance doctrines in religion, unknown before, but not in themselves apparently impious or absurd;" and to affirm at the same time "that they were revealed to him by the Spirit of God. It must be owned," says the Doctor, "there is a very strong presumption against the truth of what he says." This presumption "does not arise from any doubt of the man's integrity," for we suppose him of unblemished character; nor does it arise "from any absurdity or immoral tendency we perceive in the doctrine itself," for we suppose it has none such; but it "ariseth principally, if not solely, from these two circumstances—the extreme uncommonness of such a revelation, and the great facility with which people of strong fancy may in this particular impose upon themselves."

He then supposes further, that this man pretends to have also received from God the power of working miracles; and observes, that "we have precisely the same presumption against his being endued with such a power, as against his having obtained such a revelation. Two things," says he, "are asserted, and there is one presumption, and but one, against them, and it equally affects them both; whatever proves either assertion removes the only presumption which hinders our belief of the other."

Lastly, he supposes that the man actually works the miracles before us, and consequently removes this only presumption, and thereby manifests a divine communication, upon which he concludes thus: "We have now all the evidence which the integrity of the person could give us, as to any ordinary event attested by him, that the doctrine he delivers us from God is from God, and therefore true."

According to this hypothesis, miracles give no other certainty of the divine origin and revelation of the doctrines in proof of which they are wrought, than the word of an honest man! It is true, indeed, our author proceeds to affirm that in the case he has proposed, "we have more evidence of the revelation than for any common fact vouched by a person of undoubted probity;" because, says he, "as God is both almighty and all-wise, if He hath bestowed on any so uncommon a privilege (as that of working miracles), it is highly probable, that it is bestowed for promoting some end uncommonly important; and what more important end than to reveal to men that which may be conducive to their present and eternal happiness?"

I leave this highly probable argument to have whatever weight it may possess, and only observe that the author, after answering an objection that might be alleged, seems to lay very little stress upon it; for he thus draws his final conclusion: "And now the connection between the miracle and the doctrine is obvious; the miracle removes the improbability of a supernatural communication, of which communication it is in fact an irrefragable evidence. This improbability, which was the only obstacle, being removed, the doctrine hath, at least, all the evidence of a common fact, attested by a man of known virtue and good sense."—See 'Dissertation on Miracles,' part ii., sect. 3.

I shall not say whether this connection, as here explained, will appear as obvious to a deist as the learned author would have us believe; but this I think is evident, that the explanations he has given will render miracles of no service to the Christian religion. For, in the first place, the Christian religion proposes to our belief doctrines which certainly did appear absurd to the heathen world at its first appearance; for the Word of God assures us, that the doctrine of the Cross "is a scandal to the Jews and a folly to the Gentiles." In the second place, these doctrines to this day appear absurd and contradictory to deists and unbelievers, a numerous and learned body, who, for this very reason, reject and ridicule them. Thirdly, the apostles who first taught these doctrines to the world, and wrought miracles in confirmation of them, were so far from being men of known virtue and good sense, that they were absolute strangers in every country to which they went when they first proposed these doctrines; and in their own country itself they were men of no position, of no learning, of the lowest class, and without any earthly qualification to recommend them.

The deist or atheist, therefore, may allow all that our learned author says, and yet persist in denying the Christian revelation; because the case which he supposes is certainly not applicable either to its doctrines or to the persons who first taught them to the world. In fact, the whole reasoning of our author is a mere fictitious hypothesis expressed in good language, and likely to impose upon the reader's imagination; but in reality more calculated to undermine Christianity than to support it, because absolutely contrary to fact. Can its author produce a single instance in which his hypothesis ever existed? Can he show one example wherein those who were present when miracles were wrought, ever dreamed of the long process of argument which he describes, and at last rested satisfied that the sublime incomprehensible doctrines proposed must be from God, merely because he was an honest man that said so? No; miracles go more directly to work, and make a more immediate and convincing impression upon the heart of man. Those whom Almighty God sends to declare His will to man, and by whom He works miracles to confirm what they declare, appeal to their miracles as to the voice of God Himself, attesting the truth of what they teach. As the voice of God they are received by those who see them, and this gives not a mere probability, as the author of the 'Dissertation' pretends, but an absolute conviction that these doctrines are from God. Consequently, the connection between the miracle and the revelation of the doctrine is not remote, requiring intermediate steps to bring us to the knowledge of it; but it is an immediate connection, like the credentials of an ambassador from his master, both giving him his commission to act, and also authorising him to make those very demands and proposals which he does to those to whom he is sent.

VI. But to return to my own subject. Having shown the authority of miracles in proof of doctrine from the light of reason, I now proceed to show how great is that authority by proof drawn from revelation. Proofs of this kind we find in abundance throughout the whole sacred Scripture, both Old and New Testaments. I shall consider them separately, and begin with those from the old law. First, we see there that Almighty God Himself appeals to miracles as the most undoubted and convincing proofs of the divine revelation of what He wishes to communicate to His creatures. Thus, when He appeared to Moses in the wilderness, and gave him his commission to go to Egypt and deliver His people from their slavery, Moses was unwilling to undertake that charge, and proposed several objections on his own part, which Almighty God answered. At last he proposed one on the part of the people, saying, "They will not believe me, nor hearken to my words; for they will say, The Lord hath not appeared unto thee;" upon which Almighty God immediately has recourse to miracles, performs two before him, gives him the power of performing the same and others before the people as his credentials, and assures him that they will have the desired effect in convincing the people that his commission is divine—which they did accordingly; see Exod. iii. and iv. Now, would a God of infinite wisdom have given Moses the power of miracles as an undoubted means to convince the people of his being sent by Him, if miracles were not a certain and undoubted proof of the doctrine for which they are performed? Let common-sense judge and determine.

Secondly, At the time when the people of Israel were brought out of Egypt, idolatry had made an amazing progress in all the other nations, especially among the Egyptians, and the Israelites in that respect were prone to follow the example of their neighbours. On the other hand, Almighty God desired nothing more than to preserve them from that abomination, and to convince them that He, and He alone, was their sovereign Lord and God, and that besides Him there was no other God. We cannot possibly doubt that His sovereign wisdom would make use of the most proper means for effectually convincing them of this truth; and we find that the means which He employed were the miracles which He performed among them. Thus God Himself declares to Moses, that He had performed so many signs on Pharaoh, " that ye may know how that I am the Lord," Exod. x. 2. And Moses, recounting all the signs and wonders which God had done, says to the people: " Unto thee it was shown, that thou mightest know that the Lord He is God; there is none else besides Him," Deut. iv. 35. We conclude, then, that miracles are a full and certain proof of the revelation of those doctrines for which they are wrought, seeing that God Himself uses them as the means most effectual for that end.

Thirdly, We find that God declares true miracles to be the most undoubted proof that the one who works them is God. Thus, by the mouth of the prophet Isaiah, He challenges all false gods to perform, if they can, a true miracle in proof of their being gods. " Let them show us what shall happen," says He, Isa. xli. 22, 23—" show unto us the things that are to come, that *we may know* that ye are gods." True miracles, then, are not only the work, but they are also the language of God, by which He speaks to men, and discloses to them His will; and as it is impossible for the devil to speak in this language, so it is impossible for Almighty God to use it in attestation of a falsehood. When, therefore, He speaks in this way in attestation of any doctrine proposed, this is a decisive proof that the doctrine is from Him, and consequently true.

Fourthly, Another convincing proof of this we have from the divine justice. It is impossible for the divine justice to find fault where there is none, or to punish where there is no crime. On the other hand, there can be no crime where there is no transgression of the law, nor can there be any transgression where the law is not sufficiently known. Consequently, wherever we find the divine justice rigorous in punishing, there, we may be assured, there has been some great transgression, and the law fully manifested. Now of this we find most severe examples where the manifestation of the law depended solely upon miracles, and where the acting against so strong a proof of the law was alleged by God as a proof of the greatness of the crime. Whence it is manifest that, in the judgment of God Himself, miracles are a most authentic proof of the revelation of the divine will.

Moses appears before Pharaoh in the name of God, with an order to let the people of Israel go into the wilderness, a thing no less contrary to Pharaoh's interest than to his inclination. Certainly Pharaoh was in no way obliged to take Moses' mere word for what he said. It was necessary that he should give some decisive proof that he really was from God, and authorised by Him to make such a demand. Moses has immediately recourse to miracles as his credentials, and as the most convincing proof that what he had said was true. Pharaoh, however, hardens his heart, and pays no regard to the divine command, notwithstanding this proof of its reality. But immediately the divine vengeance pursues him, and one chastisement after another of the severest kind is inflicted on him and on his people, till at last he and all his host, in punishment of their obstinacy, are drowned in the Red Sea.

Now where, I ask, was Pharaoh's crime? Where was his transgression which could deserve so severe a punishment? Doubtless his crime consisted in refusing to obey the express command of God delivered to him by

Moses, and attested by miracles. But if miracles be not an absolute and decisive attestation of the will of God— if they can ever be connected with falsehood, or if they be not at all times an undoubted proof of truth—then Pharaoh had no certainty of the divine will, and could not be justly blamed for not complying with it. But the conduct of God shows the weakness of this pretext. He punished Pharaoh most severely for not complying with His orders; and as it is impossible for the divine justice to punish a sin more than it deserves, exceedingly great must have been the crime of Pharaoh which could deserve from a just God such a punishment. Hence the divine will must have been fully manifested to him; and as this was only by miracles, it follows as a necessary consequence that they constitute a full, perfect, and decisive proof of the divine will, which none can resist without resisting God Himself.

Another but still more express example we have in Numb. xiv., when the people murmured against God upon hearing the report of the spies. Almighty God was so displeased with their infidelity that He complains to Moses, and threatens to destroy them, taking particular notice of their crime, as arising from their disbelief, notwithstanding all the miracles He had wrought among them. "And the Lord said unto Moses, How long will this people provoke me? how long will it be ere they believe me, for *all the signs which I have showed* among them? I will smite them with the pestilence, and disinherit them," Numb. xiv. 11, 12.

It is true that at the interposition of Moses Almighty God was pleased to remit this threat as to the whole nation, sparing the children and those under twenty years of age; but as to all above that age, except Joshua and Caleb, who had not consented to their crime, He was inexorable, and thus pronounces sentence upon them: "All those men who have seen my glory, and my miracles which I did in Egypt and in the wilderness, and have tempted me now these ten times, and have not hearkened to my voice; surely they shall not see the land which I sware unto their fathers.... Say you unto them, Your carcasses shall fall in the wilderness.... Your children shall wander in the wilderness forty years and bear your whoredoms, until your carcasses be wasted in the wilderness," &c.

From these expressions, and from the severity of the punishment, we see that God was exceedingly offended with them, and that the great cause was that they refused to believe and trust in Him, notwithstanding the proofs He had given them of His almighty power and goodness by repeated miracles. These miracles, then, were a decisive proof of the truth for which they were wrought—a full and convincing evidence, which rendered those who refused to believe it inexcusable before God; and we justly conclude that true miracles are in themselves a decisive proof of doctrine, and an authentic testimony of the divine approbation.

VII. In the New Testament also we find the same truth expressed in the most convincing manner. Our Saviour had declared Himself to the Jews to be the Son of God, at which they took offence, and "sought to kill Him," for saying that "God was His Father, making Himself equal with God," John, v. 18. Upon this He explains to them by several arguments His union and equality with the Father, and He concludes thus: "If I bear witness of myself, my witness is not true. There is another that beareth witness of me, and I know that the witness which He witnesseth of me is true. Ye sent unto John, and he bare witness unto the truth; but I receive not testimony from man. But I have a greater witness than that of John; for the works that the Father hath given me to finish, the same works that I do, bear witness of me that the Father hath sent me; and the Father Himself that hath sent me hath borne witness of me."

Here, then, we see our blessed Saviour declaring to the people a most sublime doctrine, far above all human comprehension, at which they were greatly scandalised—viz., that He, Who to all appearance was a mere man, whose parents and kindred they knew, was in reality the eternal Son of God, equal to His Father—had the same power even to raise the dead as the Father hath; to whom all judgment was committed by the Father, and who could not be dishonoured by any man without the Father being dishonoured at the same time. And to remove the scandal they had taken, and convince them that He was really sent by the Father to reveal this very truth to them, what proof does He bring? No other than the miracles which He performs. "The works that I do, bear witness of me that the Father hath sent me." He adduces no other proof. He prefers it to the testimony of St John the Baptist, and looks upon it as fully sufficient to convince them of the reality of His mission, and of the truth of His doctrine, though in itself so sublime.

VIII. Upon another occasion the Jews earnestly pressed Him to tell them in plain terms if He was the Messiah, and again He had recourse to the same proof, declaring it ought thoroughly to convince them. "The Jews came round about Him, and said unto Him, How long dost Thou make us to doubt? if Thou be the Christ, tell us plainly. Jesus answered them, I told you, and ye believed not; the works that I do in my Father's name, they bear witness of me," John x. 24, &c.; and a little after He concludes, "I and my Father are one." Upon this the Jews were so highly scandalised that "they took up stones to stone Him," as guilty of blasphemy; "because," said they, "Thou being a man makest Thyself God," ver. 33. But again He appeals to His miracles as an undoubted proof of the truth of what He had asserted: "If I do not the works of my Father, believe me not; but if I do, though ye believe not me, believe the works, that ye may know and believe that the Father is in me, and I in Him," ver. 37, 38.

Here we find the Son of God appealing to His works alone, which He declares to be the works of His Father, as the most authentic and decisive proof of His own Godhead—that is, of the most important and fundamental article of the Christian religion; and upon this proof He rests entirely. He seeks no other, regarding this as the most satisfactory argument He can use to convince unprejudiced minds of the truth of His doctrine. Shall we then dare to arraign the wisdom of the Son of God? Shall we dare assert that He made use of an insufficient or equivocal proof on so solemn and important an occasion? It would be the height of blasphemy, and we should be more culpable than the Jews themselves, if we did so. We must conclude, therefore, from these appeals of Jesus Christ Himself, that miracles wrought in attestation of the truth are essentially and undoubtedly connected therewith; and consequently, that the authority of miracles, in proof of doctrine, is absolute and conclusive.

IX. The same also beautifully appears from what our Saviour answered to St Philip in presence of the other apostles, when Philip said to Him, "Lord, show us the

Father, and it sufficeth us." Jesus Christ expressed His surprise at this petition, which showed how little St Philip understood what his Master had often already told them of His divinity and union with the Father; and after explaining it to him again, He appeals to His works, which ought fully to satisfy him: "Jesus saith unto him, Have I been so long time with you, and yet hast thou not known me, Philip? He that hath seen me hath seen the Father; and how sayest thou then, Shew us the Father? Believest thou not that I am in the Father, and the Father in me? The words that I speak unto you, I speak not of myself: but the Father that dwelleth in me, He doth the works. Believe me that I am in the Father, and the Father in me: or else believe me for the very works' sake," John, xiv. 8 *et seq.*

In this beautiful passage, where the Son of God condescends with most endearing mildness to the weakness of His disciple, we not only see another proof of the authority of miracles wrought in attestation of doctrines even the most sublime and incomprehensible, but we also find explained, by Jesus Christ Himself, the connection between the miracle wrought and the doctrine attested by it. "The words that I speak unto you," says He, "I speak not of myself:" I do not give you this doctrine as my own, it was revealed to me by God, and it is from Him I declare it to you. But how shall we know that it is so? He immediately adds, "The Father that dwelleth in me, He doth the works." These works done by Him are His own signature, His own declaration that the doctrine I deliver is from Him also. He employs me as His ambassador to declare to you the doctrine, and He performs the works to attest that the doctrine is His; consequently, as it is absolutely impossible that the God of truth should attest a falsehood, miracles must be a full and decisive proof that the doctrines attested by them are the truths of God, and revealed by Him.

This is confirmed still further by the testimony of St John. "Many other signs truly did Jesus in the presence of His disciples, which are not written in this book: but these are written that ye might believe that Jesus is the Christ, the Son of God; and that believing ye might have life through His name," John, xx. 30, 31.

X. But there is no expression of Jesus Christ which shows this truth more strongly, than when He condemns the obstinacy of the Jews as absolutely inexcusable, in not yielding to the light of the truth, which He brought among them by the splendour of His doctrine and miracles. "If I had not come and spoken unto them," says He, "they had not had sin; but now they have no cloak for their sin," John, xv. 22.

In these words the Jews are condemned without excuse for not receiving the doctrine of our Saviour; but surely they could not in justice have been so condemned for this, nor would it have been even any fault, if Christ had not given them convincing proofs of the divinity both of His mission and doctrine. Now we have seen above that the only proofs to which He had recourse for that end were upon all occasions the miracles He wrought among them; and therefore, a little after, He adds, as the cause of this their severe condemnation, that they had refused to yield to this divine light: "If I had not done amongst them the works which none other man did, they had not had sin; but now they have both seen and hated both me and my Father," ver. 24.

Observe here what it was that rendered them without excuse in the sight of God. God the Father had manifested Himself to them in the most sensible manner by the works which Jesus Christ wrought in His name; yet they obstinately shut their eyes against this divine light, hated Jesus Christ who brought it among them, and consequently hated His Father also; therefore they were rejected by Him, and justly condemned as inexcusably guilty.

XI. I shall not here repeat the appeal made by our Saviour to His miracles as a proof of His being the Messiah, when St John's disciples put the question to Him if He was so; nor His curing the man sick of the palsy, in order to convince the Jews that He, as man, had received power from God to forgive sins. Both these examples prove the essential connection between miracles and the doctrine attested by them; but I must not omit what our Saviour expressly declares on another occasion, when His enemies pretended that His casting out devils was by the power of Satan. Upon His performing a miracle of this kind, and restoring the poor person that had been possessed to the use of his speech and sight, of which he had been deprived by the devil, the people were filled with admiration. But His enemies, fearing the consequences of so striking a demonstration of His power and divinity, seemed to make light of it, and pretended to account for it by saying, "He casteth out devils by Beelzebub the chief of the devils." Our Saviour immediately shows the weakness and falsity of this allegation, by observing that Satan could not fight against himself, and that such a miracle could be performed only by the power of God; and concludes thus,—"If I, by the finger of God, cast out devils, *no doubt* the kingdom of God is come upon you," Matt. xii., and Luke, xi.

Observe here the very point, which all along we have had in view, declared in express terms by Jesus Christ Himself. He came among the Jews to establish a kingdom of God among them. The proof He brings of His mission, and the arguments He uses to establish that kingdom, are His miracles, and such miracles as could be performed by none but God, among which this of His casting out the devil held a distinguished place; and He declares that these miracles are proofs so decisive of the truth of His doctrine, that it could admit of no doubt: "If I, by the finger of God, cast out devils, *no doubt* the kingdom of God is come upon you."

XII. The same method that Jesus Christ Himself took to convince the Jews of the truth of His doctrine He was pleased should be followed by His apostles also, whom He sent to preach that doctrine to the whole world. He gave them the power of working miracles— or, to speak more properly, He wrought many miracles by their means—in order thereby to convince the world of the divinity of their mission, and to establish and confirm the doctrine taught by them.

After His ascension, when they had received the Holy Ghost, they immediately began to execute the great work which their Master had given them to do, which St Mark expresses in these words: "And they went forth and preached everywhere; the Lord working with them, and *confirming* the word with signs following," Mark, xvi. 20. In the Acts also we are told that "the apostles with *great power* gave witness of the resurrection of the Lord Jesus," Acts, iv. 33. St Paul, in like manner, when called to the same glorious employment, used the same means in promoting his Master's cause; for thus he tells us in his Epistle to the Romans, that it was by miracles that he planted the Gospel wherever he went: "By mighty signs and wonders, by the power of the Spirit of God; so that from Jerusalem, and round about to Illyrium, I have fully preached the Gospel of Christ," Rom. xv. 19. And again, writing to the Corinthians: "When I came to you, I came not with excellency of speech or of wisdom, declaring to you the testimony of God; for I determined not to know anything among you save Jesus Christ, and Him crucified. And my speech and my preaching was not with enticing words of man's wisdom, but in *demonstration of the Spirit, and of power;* that your faith should not stand in the wisdom of man, but in *the power of God,*" 1 Cor. ii.

Here this great apostle informs us of the means which he used in planting the Gospel: the only doctrine he preached, the only wisdom he pretended to teach, was the great mystery of a crucified God. This, in the preceding chapter, he assures us was a stumbling-block to the Jews, and to the Greeks foolishness. To persuade the Corinthians to receive and embrace this unheard-of doctrine as the truth of God, he laid aside all human means; he used no pomp of eloquence, no enticing words of man's wisdom; he called upon the Spirit of God to attest and demonstrate the truth of the word preached to them by exerting His almighty power in working miracles, as the means best adapted to that end; and by these he converted them to Christianity.

Now, seeing that in all these cases the divine wisdom made use of miracles as the most proper means to convince the world that the truths of the Gospel, so sublime and incomprehensible in themselves, and so foolish in the eyes of worldly wisdom, were nevertheless the truths of God, and revealed by Him, shall we dare to say this means was improper, inadequate, or incapable of procuring the end intended by them? Certainly no one can do so who believes the Scripture to be the word of God. We must therefore again conclude that miracles are decisive proofs of doctrine, and that their authority is incontrovertible.

St Paul was so sensible of this, that he declares there is no salvation for such as refuse to embrace the doctrine of Christ, which is demonstrated to be the truth of God by evidence so convincing. For after beginning his Epistle to the Hebrews by informing us that God, who in former times had spoken to men, and declared His will to them by the ministry of angels, had in these latter days spoken to us by His Son—by whom He also made the world: he then proceeds to show the supereminent excellence of the Son above the angels, from which he draws this obvious consequence, that we ought to pay so much the greater regard to what He has taught us, and be so much the more careful not to lose it. "Therefore we ought to give the more earnest heed to the things which we have heard, lest at any time we should let them slip," Heb. ii. 1. Then alluding to the punishments inflicted on those who transgressed, or disobeyed what had been delivered by angels, he draws as a natural conclusion, that it is impossible we should escape if we refuse what has been delivered by the Lord of angels; especially when so strongly manifested by the many miracles wrought to attest and confirm it: "For if the word spoken by angels," says he, "was steadfast, and every transgression and disobedience received a just recompense of reward; how shall we escape, if we neglect so great salvation; which at the first began to be spoken by the Lord, and was confirmed unto us by them that heard Him; God also bearing them witness, both with signs and wonders, and with divers miracles, and gifts of the Holy Ghost, according to His own will?" ver. 2, 3, 4. From these words it is plain that St Paul, or rather the Holy Ghost who inspired him, regarded miracles wrought by

God in confirmation of doctrine, to be a full, perfect, and decisive proof that the doctrine so confirmed is divine truth; and held all who refuse to believe it on such proof to be inexcusable before God.

XIII. The several passages of Holy Scripture of which I have here made use, have necessarily carried me to a considerable length, and occasioned repetitions in the application of them, which to some may seem superfluous. Yet as the subject is so important, and as each of these passages has some peculiar force in proving the point in question, I was unwilling either to omit any or even to unite them together in one argument; united, they would have lost much of that weight and strength of proof which a separate and distinct view of each will naturally have, and I particularly desired to make the subject intelligible to all capacities.

XIV. It is for the same reason that, though the arguments I have already given, both from reason and revelation, be more than sufficient to prove the authority of miracles wrought by God in proof of doctrine, I shall adduce one or two more, in order to fortify this important subject on all sides, and show how blamable are those who call it in question. The first argument I shall propose is an appeal to experience, and to the common sentiments of mankind. Let us only examine what effect miracles have always had on the heart of man, and this will palpably demonstrate the authority and weight of their evidence.

When Elijah had raised to life the widow's son, and restored him to his mother, she immediately cried out, in raptures of joy and admiration, "Now *by this* I know that thou art a man of God, and that the word of the Lord in thy mouth is truth," 1 Kings, xvii. 24. The moment Naaman was so miraculously cured of the leprosy, he was converted upon the spot from his idolatry, and said to Elisha, "Behold, now I know that there is no God in all the earth but in Israel," 2 Kings, v. 15. In the well-known contest betwixt Elijah and the prophets of Baal, whether the Lord or Baal was the true God, with one consent it was put to the test of a miracle; and when this was performed in favour of Almighty God, all the people yielded to the heavenly light, and with one voice cried out, "The Lord He is God, the Lord He is God," 1 Kings, xviii. 39.

Nebuchadnezzar, a heathen prince, whose haughty spirit could not bow to acknowledge, even in God, a power superior to his own, said to the holy children, "And who is the God that shall deliver you out of my hand?" Dan. iii. 15. Yet so confounded was he when he saw their miraculous deliverance from the fiery furnace, that he instantly acknowledged their God to be the only true God, and made a decree whereby he commanded Him to be reverenced through all his empire, and threatened destruction to any one who should dare to speak anything amiss against Him. The same effect the delivery of Daniel in the den of lions had upon King Darius, who made a decree like the former, wherein, convinced by the brilliant light of Daniel's miraculous preservation, he acknowledges that "his God is the living God, and steadfast for ever, and His kingdom that which shall not be destroyed, and his dominion shall be even unto the end;" that "He delivereth and rescueth, and worketh signs and wonders in the heavens and in the earth, who hath delivered Daniel from the power of the lions," Dan. vi.

XV. Nothing could be more revolting to the common sentiments of mankind than to imagine that man upon earth should have the power of forgiving sins committed against the God of heaven. We see in what an odious light almost all the Reformed Churches look upon a claim of this kind, and the Jews esteemed it downright blasphemy. Yet no sooner did our blessed Saviour work the miracle of curing the sick man of the palsy, to prove that He as man, and whom the Jews then looked upon as a mere man, had this power, than immediately His most inveterate enemies were struck dumb. They had not a word more to say against it; and both they and the whole multitude present were filled with amazement at so luminous a proof, acknowledged that to be a divine truth which before they had esteemed a downright blasphemy, and glorified God who had given such power unto men, Matt. ix. 8.

What was it that convinced Nicodemus of the divine mission of our Saviour but the splendour of His miracles! "Rabbi," said he to Him, "we know that Thou art a teacher come from God; for no man can do these miracles that Thou doest, except God be with him," John, iii. 2. When the man to whom our Saviour restored his sight, though he had been born blind, heard the Pharisees speaking disrespectfully of his benefactor, he immediately undertook His vindication by this natural argument, a consequence of the miraculous cure He had performed: "Now we know that God heareth not sinners; but if any man be a worshipper of God, and doth His will, him He heareth. Since the world began was it not heard that any man opened the eyes of one that was born blind. If this man were not of God, He could do nothing," John, ix. 31, &c.

Observe here with what strength of argument he proves the divine mission of Jesus Christ. First he lays down this principle, that God doth not perform wondrous things at the desire of sinners, but is ready to hear those who are His friends and servants; then he considers the nature of the miracle performed, which shows itself evidently to be the work of God, the like of which had not been heard of from the beginning of the world: and from these two premises he draws this necessary conclusion; since, therefore, God has wrought this miracle at the desire, and by means of Jesus Christ, He must undoubtedly be from God, and God must be with Him: this is the natural language which true miracles speak; this is the impression which they never fail to make on the heart of man.

XVI. It were endless to collect the many instances in the Gospel of this natural yet deep impression which the miracles of Jesus Christ made upon the Jews. The overpowering weight of this proof at once convinced them, and they sought no further evidence of the truth of what He said. But perhaps it will be here objected, that in reality this impression was not general; that many, and those the most learned and of the greatest authority, paid no regard to the miracles of our Saviour, and instead of being persuaded that His doctrine was true, looked upon Him only as an impostor, and condemned Him at last as an impious malefactor.

XVII. This objection, far from weakening the force of our argument, greatly strengthens it; for it is evident, from the whole history of our Saviour's public life, that the continual opposition of the chief priests, scribes, and Pharisees, was entirely owing to the inveterate hatred and envy which they had conceived against Him. They could not bear to see the esteem and credit which His miracles procured Him among the people; and therefore, blinded by their passions, they did violence to themselves in resisting the natural impression which these miracles made upon them.

Let us only consider the conviction produced and

the conflict excited in their hearts by opposing that evidence. Read the account given of their conduct when the blind man's sight was restored. The evidence of this miracle confounded them. They called the man, and interrogated him as to what had been done to him. They would not believe that he had been born blind. They questioned his parents. They asked the man himself what he thought of the matter. They tried by every means to discredit the miracle. But why all this? Doubtless because of the conviction which the miracle carried with it, that the person who wrought it was from God, which their imbittered hearts were determined never to acknowledge. But in spite of this it gained even upon some of them, who said, "How can a man that is a sinner do such miracles? and there was a division among them," John, ix. 16. And again, when some said, "He hath a devil and is mad," others immediately replied, " Can a devil open the eyes of the blind?" John, x. 10, 21.

From this, then, it appears that even His enemies themselves were convinced by His miracles, though their passions so blinded them that they never would allow themselves to yield to conviction, much less to acknowledge it. This appears still further from their conduct when Lazarus was raised from the dead. This stupendous miracle so alarmed them, that they immediately called a council to deliberate what was to be done; and when they were met, they plainly acknowleged both the reality of our Saviour's miracles and the natural effect which they must undoubtedly have among the people. "This man doth many miracles," say they; "if we let Him thus alone, all men will believe on Him." Could there be a greater proof of the impression these miracles made upon themselves? They plainly acknowledge their power to persuade; and if they themselves are not persuaded, it is because the strength of their passions counteracts the evidence of the proof.

Another proof we have of this their unhappy disposition when St Peter and St John cured the lame man at the gate of the temple. This miracle had so surprising an effect, that about five thousand persons were converted. The chief priests and rulers were not a little grieved, and laid hands on them, bringing them before their council, and the man that had been cured along with them. Here St Peter boldly declared that this miraculous cure was performed in the name of Jesus Christ, in attestation of His being risen from the dead, and that there is no salvation but through Him. This proof was so convincing that the Scripture expressly observes "they had nothing to say against it."

This miracle, then, made the proper impression upon the hearts even of the most inveterate enemies of Jesus. They were convinced by it. They could answer nothing to its evidence, but through the malice of their hearts they would not be converted; and putting the apostles aside, they said, "What shall we do to these men? for that indeed a notable miracle has been done by them, is manifest to all them that dwell at Jerusalem, and we cannot deny it." Observe here the impression which the miracle made upon them. But instead of yielding to its light, they added, "But that it spread no further among the people, let us straitly threaten them that they speak henceforth to no man in this name," Acts, iv. Even those whose hearts were so blinded that they were determined not to yield to conviction, could not help giving such plain indications of the deep impression made upon their minds by the miracles of Christ and His apostles, and showed how sensible they were of the effects they must produce in others. This testimony from adversaries is of all the most valuable and the most convincing proof in this matter of the common sentiments of all mankind.

XVIII. As we proceed in our induction, proofs multiply upon us. After our Saviour had ascended to heaven, His apostles entered upon the grand work of reforming the world, overturning all established religions, rooting out the most inveterate opinions, destroying the deepest prejudices, enlightening the most rude nations with the knowledge of the sublime truths of salvation; and, in a word, of subjecting the whole world to the faith and law of Jesus Christ. The undertaking was vast, replete with danger, and the difficulties seemed insurmountable. The apostles themselves were poor illiterate men, without any worldly qualification to recommend them, or any help of man to aid them; yet they boldly entered upon the glorious work; and, carried forward by the ardour of their zeal, they never ceased till they had accomplished it. The means they made use of were not the "enticing words of human wisdom," but the stupendous miracles they everywhere performed. These served them instead of everything else, and produced the most amazing effects in the hearts of the spectators; for being regarded as the voice of heaven, which they really were, they at once overcame their most inveterate prejudices, and captivated their understandings in obedience to Christ, convinced them that the doctrines attested by these miracles were the truths of God, and without other argument converted them to Christianity. When St Peter came to Lydda, "there he found a certain man named Æneas, which had kept his bed eight years, and was sick of a palsy. And Peter said to him, Æneas, Jesus Christ maketh thee whole: arise, and make thy bed. And he arose immediately." This was enough; there was no need of other arguments to convince the people of that place of the truths of the Gospel. This miracle alone was the most decisive proof of their being from God; for immediately " all that dwelt at Lydda turned unto the Lord," Acts, ix. 33 *et seq.*

In like manner, when St Philip went down to Samaria to preach the Gospel, numbers were converted. But by what means was this brought about? By the powerful eloquence of his miracles; for " the people with one accord gave heed unto these things which Philip spake, hearing and seeing the miracles which he did. For unclean spirits, crying with a loud voice, came out of many that were possessed with them; and many taken with palsies, and that were lame, were healed; and there was great joy in that city," Acts, viii. Nay, even Simon the magician, who had bewitched the Samaritans with his sorceries, was so confounded at the miracles wrought by Philip, that, unable to resist such evidence, he yielded, and became a Christian.

When Elymas the sorcerer endeavoured to turn away the proconsul Sergius from hearing the Word of God, St Paul, with one sentence, in the name of the Lord, struck him blind, in punishment of his impiety. The deputy Sergius sought no more: this miraculous punishment convinced him at once that the doctrine in defence of which it was performed must be from God; and therefore, " when he saw what was done he believed, being astonished at the doctrine of the Lord," Acts, xiii. 12. What these three great saints did was done by the other apostles and other apostolic men, whom Almighty God made use of to convert the heathen world to Christianity. They used no human means; their arms, like their doctrine, were altogether divine, the voice of the Almighty attesting what they taught by the amazing miracles which He performed. These had everywhere their desired effect, converted vast numbers to the faith of Christ, and confounded those who, through the violence of their passions and their inveterate prejudices, would not be converted.

XIX. Now what is the natural conclusion to be drawn from these examples? Nothing could more clearly demonstrate the voice of unprejudiced nature, and the common sentiments of mankind, with regard to the supreme authority of miracles wrought by Almighty God in proof of doctrine. The evidence of facts shows the deep and immediate impression which divine miracles have always made on the heart of man, irrespective of all circumstances and without any train of reasoning. Here I may appeal even to the hearts of those who pretend to deny this authority. Suppose you had been present in our Saviour's days, and had been eyewitnesses of all He did; suppose you yourselves had been possessed by the devil, or lame, or blind, or paralytic, or otherwise diseased, and had been miraculously and instantaneously cured by Him,—lay your hand upon your breast, and ask your heart what effect, what deep impression, must not this have made upon you? I seek no other proof, I require no other voucher for the truth of what I here defend, than the unprejudiced answer which your own heart will give.

XX. This observation leads me to another argument in proof of the authority of miracles, with which I shall conclude the subject, and that is, the very testimony of our adversaries themselves. Convinced as they are in their hearts of this truth, it is impossible for them, on certain occasions, not to show it. Some of them, indeed, have acknowledged it in express terms; but all agree in confessing it indirectly, when they take such pains to argue against and ridicule it. What could have induced a David Hume to bewilder himself, and spend so much time and study in inventing, dressing up, and publishing the argument by which he would pretend to demonstrate that it is impossible ever to prove the existence of a miracle? What could move him to this but his internal conviction that if one single true miracle should be allowed in proof of Christianity, that alone would outweigh all his flimsy sophistry in favour of infidelity? What could have induced a Rousseau to use arts so insidious throughout the whole of his 'Emilius' when he speaks of miracles, confounding the true state of the question, making false suppositions, and general appeals to the Scripture for what is not to be found in one single text; and sometimes even plainly contradicting himself and his own principles, in order by these ungenerous means to weaken the force and authority of miracles? What could make him be guilty of such conduct but his internal conviction on the one hand of the greatness of that authority which he desired to destroy, and his resolute determination on the other, like that of the chief priests and rulers of the Jews, never to acknowledge it? What, in a word, can induce a Voltaire, and his brother deists, to take such pains to turn all miracles, even those of the sacred Scripture, into ridicule, and to throw out their impious sneers on all occasions against them, but their conviction of the effect they must have, if received and believed; and that they can find no other solid reason against them?

Dr Conyers Middleton, the most violent enemy that ever Christian miracles had, treats as forgeries and impostures all miracles occurring after the apostolic age. He does so for this plain reason, that if their existence is allowed in one age after the apostles, it cannot reasonably be denied in succeeding ages, seeing that the proofs are absolutely the same in every age; and then, if this be granted, there is no contesting the truth of Popery. The following are his own words: "A clear succession of miracles, deduced through all history, from the apostolic times down to our own, is a proof of all others the most striking to all minds, and the most decisive indeed to all minds, as far as it is believed to be true," Introd. Disc., p. 41. Could anything but the force of truth extort such an acknowledgment from so declared an enemy?

Those learned gentlemen who differ from Dr Middleton about the period of the cessation of miracles agree with him, however, as to their authority in proof of doctrine. It must be granted, says Dr Church in his Vindication, p. 62, 63, that present facts, which are appeals to the senses, are more striking and satisfactory than any long intricate reasonings. And hence miracles may be pronounced to be the shortest and clearest means of conviction of the divine authority of any mission, and consequently of any doctrine, to those who see them. And further, as we may have sufficient certainty of their having been worked in times past, they must, if well attested, be full proofs even to us who do not see them.

This is a just observation, founded on the nature of the thing itself; and it is owing to the full conviction of this truth, that Dr Middleton's adversaries, though disagreeing from him as to the precise period when miracles ceased in the Christian Church, yet all concur in doing their utmost to prove that they have actually long since ceased, and at such periods as they respectively think proper to assign. They suppose that, at these assumed periods, corruptions of Popery began; and to admit true miracles after that, would, according to the above principle, be fairly yielding the day in favour of Popery. For it is worth observing, that what atheists and deists are forced to do against Christian miracles in general, the children of the Reformation are obliged, upon the self-same principle, to do against the miracles wrought in the Catholic Church; each of them feeling the weight of such a proof, are determined never to acknowledge it where their prejudices or passions induce them to reject the doctrine; because such an acknowledgment would be an utter condemnation of themselves. In this they follow the example of the chief priests and rulers of the Jews in their conduct with regard to the miracles of Christ and His apostles.

Having thus established the authority of miracles, I should now proceed to examine the objections brought against it. But as their weakness will be better seen when we have considered the criterion of miracles, I shall delay taking notice of them till we have considered that important subject.

CHAPTER X.

THE CRITERION OF MIRACLES.

I. FROM what we have said above on the authority of miracles, and especially from the explanation there given, it is evident that two things are required to establish this authority: first, that the miraculous facts do actually exist; secondly, that they be performed by Almighty God, either immediately by His own power, or by angels commissioned by Him. If no miracle exist, or be asserted to exist, there is an end of the question. But when we are certain of the fact, we easily see that its whole weight depends on the supposition that Almighty God is its Author; for if we know, or even suspect, that what is done is not the work of God, its authority at once falls to the ground. Hence there arise two other important questions which the enemies of religion have endeavoured to confound and obscure.

The first is, How shall we know that the miraculous facts did ever actually exist? Deism and infidelity reply here, it is impossible ever to know this. "Where," cries Rousseau, "are these miracles to be seen? Are they related only in books? Pray who wrote these books? Men. Who were witnesses to these miracles? Men. Who attest them? What! always human testimonies! Is it always men who tell me what other men have told them? What a number of these are constantly between me and the Deity!" Emil. iii. 108.

At other times he pretends to disprove their existence, as if it were unworthy of the Deity to have recourse to such means of convincing His creatures; and would persuade us that the very number of miracles said to have occurred is a proof that none ever existed. So that, according to him and his brethren—for he only speaks the language common to his party—it is impossible to know with certainty that any miracle ever existed of which we were not ourselves eyewitnesses.

It is also well known how strenuously the celebrated David Hume, another noted champion of infidelity, has attacked the existence of miracles, employing all the power of genius, and every art of sophistry, to persuade the world that a miracle supported by any human testimony is more properly a subject of derision than of argument; and that no testimony for any kind of miracle can ever possibly amount to a probability, much less to a proof, Ess. on Mir., p. 194, 202. How far common-sense approves of this assertion is evident from the contempt with which his famous argument, in which he trusted, is now everywhere treated. But these endeavours show the spirit of the party, their conviction of the invincible force of miracles so fatal to their cause, and their consequent dread of the very thought of their existence.

The second question follows from the former; for on the supposition that a miraculous operation is actually performed, it comes next to be inquired, How shall we know that it is truly the work of God, and not a delusion of Satan? If infidelity labours hard to disprove the existence of miracles, it endeavours with no less ardour to persuade us that, though they should be admitted, we are no nearer our point, because it is impossible to distinguish whether they be from God or from the devil; and consequently, that we can never have any certainty of what is sought to be proved by them. But without repeating here the arguments with which these gentlemen have favoured the world on this subject, and their many arts to obscure the truth, and confound the true state of the question, I shall proceed to remove the rubbish which they have cast upon it, and then to lay down those principles which reason and religion point out as proper to show that both the existence of miracles can be proved beyond contradiction, and that it can be known with equal certainty what miracles are, and what are not, from God.

II. By the criterion of miracles, in its general sense, may be understood the rules by which we form a right judgment of these two questions—that is, of the existence of a miracle, and of its being, or not being, the work of the Deity. But this is not the sense in which it is commonly taken.

The existence of a miracle is a question of fact, to be determined, like other questions of a similar nature, by that kind of evidence which is common to all facts; but whether a miraculous event is, or is not the work of God, is a question of a peculiar kind, which must be determined by certain rules of judging proper to this subject only. And by the term Criterion of Miracles, we more commonly understand the rules laid down for this purpose. It is only in this sense that I at present use it; and to find out this criterion—that is, to investigate and lay down those rules, by which we may be enabled to judge with certainty if a miraculous event be the work of God, or the operation of Satan—is the subject of our present inquiry. To do this, however, with the requisite clearness and precision, a few things must be premised.

III. 1. We must distinguish between these two terms, to tempt, and to induce into error. To tempt is to present, or not to remove such occasions as solicit and entice us to act contrary to duty, but do not force us. This may occur in two ways, either when the act is known to be contrary to duty, as when a person is solicited by others to rob or steal; or when the evil action is proposed to us under the appearance of being good and lawful, or even a duty itself, but the fallacy of which we can discover if we use due care. Thus Eve was tempted to eat the forbidden fruit, under the appearance of improving her condition, in order to become as gods; though, had she reflected, she would easily have seen that even this, though true, could never excuse her transgressing the express command of God. Saul also was tempted to transgress the orders delivered to him by the prophet Samuel, from an appearance of necessity, when he offered up sacrifice before that prophet's arrival, 1 Sam. xv. But he might easily have discovered the delusion.

In temptations of this kind, Satan, as the Scripture expresses it, "transforms himself into an angel of light," the better to compass his ends against us. Now in all these cases we are solicited, we are enticed, to do the evil proposed, but we are not compelled. We have it in our power to withhold our consent, to discover the delusion, and to reject the proposal.

But to "lead into error" is of a very different nature. This is to lay before us an inevitable necessity of falling, to prepare for us a certain and infallible determination to evil, to put a snare in our way, which we are unable to escape. This also may be conceived to be done in two ways: First, when a person sees the evil, and knows it to be evil, if we suppose him to be deprived of interior liberty, and irresistibly determined by some invisible agent to choose that evil. In this case his fall is inevitable. He wills the evil which he knows, and it is impossible for him not to will it, being, as we suppose, antecedently and irresistibly determined by something distinct from himself to will it. Secondly, if we suppose the evil action proposed under the appearance of duty, and that of strict obligation, but in such circumstances that it is impossible for him to discover the fallacy and delusion. Here also that person would necessarily be led into error, which he cannot avoid; because, as we suppose, it is presented to him under appearances so delusive that it is not in his power to penetrate them. Now it is evident that though Almighty God may, for His own just and wise ends, tempt us Himself, or permit us to be tempted by others, yet it is absolutely impossible He should either Himself lead us into error, or permit others to do so; because, by so doing He would manifestly contradict Himself, and act contrary to His own divine attributes, His justice, veracity, and goodness; that is, He would Himself become the author of sin, error, and falsehood..

God permitted Job to be tempted to impatience by his wife, his three friends, and by the devil. But Job knowing that impatience was a sin, and that duty required him to receive with submission whatever the Divine Providence should send or permit to come upon him, resisted the temptation, and preserved his innocence. When Satan tempted our Saviour Himself, he proposed two temptations under the appearance of good,—namely, to prove Himself by an act of omnipotence to be the Son of God, commanding the stones to be made bread; and to show his confidence in the divine protection, by throwing Himself down from the pinnacle of the temple, in hopes of being preserved by angels, according to the text of Scripture cited. In both cases our Saviour well knew the delusion, and rejected the temptation.

As to leading us into evil, the Word of God expressly declares that "God is faithful, who will not suffer you to be tempted above what you are able, but with the temptation will also make a way to escape, that you may be able to bear it," 1 Cor. x. 13. In these words it is declared that Almighty God never will permit us to be led into evil, or to be so tempted that it will not be in our power to escape; nay, that to do so would be inconsistent with His fidelity.

This will appear still more if we consider what is meant when we say that God Himself tempts us, or permits us to be tempted; for we must carefully observe, that Almighty God, neither in the temptations which He sends Himself, nor in those which He permits from others, ever intends that the person so tempted should consent to the temptation and commit sin: far from it; He expressly commands the contrary. The views of Almighty God in tempting man, either by Himself or others, are to prove, to try him; to see if, in fact, he be faithful: to give him an occasion of acquiring greater good by overcoming the temptation, and thereby improving himself in solid virtue; and sometimes also it may be in just punishment of sins committed, and abuse of grace. Thus it is said that "God tempted Abraham," Gen. xxii. 1; and in several other places of Scripture He is said to prove or tempt His people (see Exod. xv. 25, and xvi. 4.) Also, an angel of Satan was permitted to tempt St Paul, for his greater humiliation and exercise in virtue; but God Himself assured him that His grace was sufficient for him. It is true that when the wicked spirits are permitted to tempt man, their desire indeed is to lead us to sin; but in this sense God never tempts: and for this reason the Scripture says of God, "Let no man when he is tempted say, I am tempted of God; for God cannot be tempted with evil, neither tempteth He any man," James, i. 13. Seeing, then, that God cannot tempt any one, or permit him to be tempted, with the direct view and intention that he should fall into sin, much less can He, a God of infinite goodness, holiness, and truth, lead man into error or sin, by putting him under an inevitable necessity of falling into either.

2. We have seen, from the repeated testimony of Scripture, that Almighty God has at all times made use of miracles to attest the revelation of His will to man, or to confirm the truth of His revelation formerly made when called in question; and that He bestows the gift of miracles as His divine credentials on those whom He sends as His messengers. Nay, we have seen that He looks upon this kind of proof as so perfect and sufficient, that He condemns and punishes severely those who refuse to submit to its evidence. From this, then, it follows as a necessary consequence, that it is impossible that Almighty God should ever so abuse this kind of proof as to make it infallibly promote and patronise error, or that He should even permit others so to do; for this would not only be unworthy of Himself, but would invalidate every revelation of His will hitherto made to His creatures, and give them just cause to call it in question, and even to deny it.

3. We have also seen, from examples both of friends and enemies, that a proof from miracles is of all the most convincing and decisive; that it makes the deepest impression on the human heart; that it acts immediately,

and of itself, prior to all reasoning or reflection—our nature being so constituted, that no sooner do we apprehend any miraculous operation as the work of God, than we instantly feel the full weight of its authority in proof of the doctrine attested by it. Now this immediate perception of the necessary connection between miracles wrought in proof of doctrine, and the truth of the doctrine itself, or the universal persuasion which all men have that the doctrine must be from God, when He Himself works miracles in attestation of it—this being a part of our natural constitution by the Deity, it is plainly repugnant to our ideas of God, and of His perfections, to suppose that He should ever abuse this disposition of our nature by making use of it Himself, or permitting others to do so, as an *inevitable* and *infallible* means of leading us into sin or error.

IV. From these three observations, the justice of which cannot be called in question, the following conclusions necessarily result, and may be considered axioms or fundamental principles in the present question.

1. Almighty God cannot possibly work a miracle, in any case or in any circumstance whatever, in order to attest or sanction falsehood. This proposition is evident in its very terms. God is a Being of infinite veracity, who cannot possibly will or intend falsehood, much less set His hand and seal to promote it by a miracle. Neither can He lay His creatures under an inevitable necessity of falling into error, or make use of that supreme influence which He Himself has given to miracles over the hearts of men, as an infallible means to deceive; of all which He would be guilty if He ever worked a miracle in attestation of a falsehood.

2. God can never permit any created agent to work a miracle in order to attest or sanction falsehood, when

it is impossible for mankind to discover that the miracle wrought is only a relative miracle, and within the natural abilities of a creature. There are many kinds of miraculous operations which supernatural created agents can perform; there are others which can be performed only by the almighty power of God: but as we know not the extent of the power of created agents, there are doubtless many miraculous operations within their power, which yet we could not discover to be so, nor distinguish from what is proper to God alone. It is only to these that this present axiom applies; for, if we suppose the miracle performed, though in itself only a relative one, within the natural abilities of the angels, whether good or bad, yet to be of such uncommon greatness that it had all the appearance of a divine miracle—on this supposition it is impossible that Almighty God should permit any created agent to perform such a miracle in attestation or defence of falsehood. The reason is plain; because such a miracle in its effects on man would be entirely the same as if wrought by God Himself; and would necessarily lead His creatures into error.

Dr Clarke justly observes, that " God cannot work miracles to deceive men Himself, nor permit evil spirits to impose upon men when the error would be invincible, which would be the very same thing as if He worked them Himself," Evid. of Nat. and Rev. Rel., p. 228. Hence it follows that our ignorance of the extent of the powers of supernatural beings in performing things miraculous can be no prejudice to us; because God's divine perfections, His veracity, fidelity, sanctity, and goodness, are our certain guarantees that He never will allow them to so exert these powers as invincibly to deceive us and lead us into error.

3. God cannot allow evil spirits to perform any rela-

tive miracle, known to be such, in attestation or defence of falsehood and error, when it would inevitably lead men to believe the falsehood, and consequently lead them into error. This proceeds upon the same grounds as the former axioms; for if mankind would necessarily be led into error, either by the greatness of the thing done or by the circumstances of the miracle; if God should permit such a miracle to be performed by evil spirits in favour of error, He would be equally guilty of acting against His own divine perfections.

We have an example of this in the contest betwixt Elijah and the prophets of Baal. The question was, whether the Lord or Baal was the true God. The people were divided in their hearts and "halted between two opinions." To fix their minds in the truth, Elijah proposed to refer the decision of the question to a miracle; and the miracle was, that he on the part of God, and the prophets of Baal on his part, should each build an altar, and lay on it a victim, and call upon their respective deities, and that the one who should send down fire from heaven to consume the victim should be esteemed the only true God; and Elijah allowed the prophets of Baal to make the first trial. Here we must observe: First, the miracle proposed, of sending down fire to consume the victim, was certainly within the natural power of Satan; for we are assured that he, by God's permission, sent down fire on Job's numerous flocks of sheep, and consumed them and all his servants, except one who escaped to tell him of the disaster. It is true that this servant, in relating what had happened, uses this expression, "the fire of God hath fallen;" but the whole tenor of the narrative shows that Satan was the immediate agent in all that happened; for Almighty God expressly says, when He gave him permission to afflict Job, "Behold, all that he hath is in thy power, only upon himself put not forth thy hand;" and it is a usual expression in Scripture to say, "the mountains of God, the cedars of God," to express the greatness of these objects. Besides, the Scripture only relates here what Job's servant said, who seeing the dreadful fire that fell, and the mischief it did, but not knowing anything of the cause, very naturally used that expression, and called it the fire of God. Secondly, Satan was here exceedingly interested to have the miracle performed; his worship was at stake, his honour engaged, and he must either stand or disgracefully fall, according as he did or did not perform it. We cannot doubt then either of his power, or of his will, if Almighty God had permitted him. Thirdly, if Satan had been permitted to perform this miracle, the people must inevitably have been led to idolatry, and confirmed in it. Their minds were fluctuating; the whole regal power in the hands of an imperious heathen queen was employed in support of idolatry. Every worldly motive conspired to encourage the people to embrace it. All the priests and prophets of God had been destroyed except Elijah, who alone appeared in defence of the true God; but what was he alone against such numbers? He appeals, therefore, to a miracle; he proposes one, and he allows the prophets of Baal to make the first trial. The whole people, anxious to see their doubts solved by so convincing an argument, readily embrace the proposal, determined to stand on that side on which the miracle should be performed.

It is manifest that had the devil been permitted to send down fire at the prayers of Baal's prophets, there could have been no remedy—the whole people must have been inevitably confirmed in their idolatry; the priests of Baal would immediately have triumphed, and probably would have fallen upon Elijah, and destroyed him without a hearing. And even had they been a little more patient, what could he have said? He himself had put this case to the test; and it had declared in favour of his adversaries. He might say, I also will obtain fire on my victim; but even if he had, this would only have placed both sides upon an equal footing. The question would have remained undecided; and the people having no superior conviction in favour of the true God, and influenced by every worldly motive, besides their natural proneness, to idolatry, must have continued in their false worship, and given themselves up more and more to it. In these circumstances, therefore, Almighty God restrained the natural power of Satan, and would not permit him to exert it in performing the miracle proposed, which otherwise he easily could have done; because the consequences would have been fatal to the people, and the permission itself contrary to the divine wisdom, veracity, and goodness. The same arguments equally show, that what Almighty God did here He is no less bound to do in all similar cases; and that He never can permit wicked spirits to perform even such miraculous operations as are within the sphere of their natural powers, in favour of error, when their doing so would necessarily seduce mankind into error.

4. If Almighty God, for His own wise and good ends, whether to try His servants or to punish sinners, should at any time permit evil spirits, by their agents upon earth, to perform miraculous operations in favour of false doctrine, He is obliged by His own divine perfections to give mankind sufficient means to discover the delusion, and prevent their seduction from being inevitable. This is a necessary consequence of the three preceding axioms, grounded upon the same reasons, and is what

God Almighty has actually done in all those cases which are recorded in the Scriptures.

V. Though what I have here said admits of no reply, and is fully sufficient to show the truth of the above axioms; yet, as it is highly important to establish them in the most solid manner, I shall here add one more observation to illustrate the whole, and place it in another point of view.

Created beings having received from God all their powers and faculties, are totally dependent upon Him in the exercise of them. They can never exert them but by His will or permission; for to say that they could act as they pleased, independently of God, would be to withdraw them from being creatures. If, therefore, Almighty God should permit evil spirits to use the freedom of their will without control, and to exert their natural faculties in deceiving mankind, by performing such amazing signs and wonders as could not possibly be distinguished from true miracles, how could men act? what side should or could they take? If they embrace the false doctrine attested by these delusive operations, they immediately become the dupes of the devil's malice, and their fall is inevitable. If they refuse to submit to that light which persuades them, then they resist the highest evidence, they refuse subjection to what they are convinced is the will of their Creator; and consequently, in this case also, their ruin is undoubted. Would God be a God of infinite goodness and love to His creatures, were He to allow poor helpless man to be thus miserably imposed upon, and reduced to such a sad dilemma?

Again, considering the evident and necessary connection which reason clearly perceives between miracles wrought by God to attest any doctrine, and the truth of that doctrine itself, and considering the almost irresistible force that this has over the mind of man to convince, it may be justly said, that there can be no more convincing proof of the truth of any doctrine than a miracle wrought by God for that purpose; and therefore, that miracles are truly the language of God, by which He speaks to man, and the seal of heaven by which divine truths are authenticated and confirmed. If, therefore, we suppose that Almighty God should allow evil spirits to speak in this language, in order to deceive mankind, and to use this seal, thereby to give a sanction to falsehood and error—that is, should He allow them in attestation of false doctrine to work miracles, of such a kind, and in such circumstances, as should give them all the appearance of divine miracles, and leave no means for mankind to discover the delusion—what must be the consequence? It is evident that mankind would of necessity be led into error; falsehood and lies would be propagated and upheld, and the language of God and the seal of heaven would be the means of doing so. Would God be a God of truth, a God of fidelity, a God of holiness, if He permitted this, and allowed His name to give such a sanction to error? We justly conclude, then, that these four axioms cannot be contested without calling in question the goodness, veracity, and sanctity of the Deity; they stand upon the same basis with these divine perfections, and both must stand or fall together.

VI. From these axioms we shall easily see the criterion we are in quest of, or the rules by which we can certainly know what miraculous operations are, and what are not, from God, when wrought in defence of doctrine.

First rule: "When any miracle is performed which evidently implies an act, either of almighty power, or of infinite wisdom, such a miracle carries its own proof that it is the work of God."

This rule requires no explanation—it is evident in its terms; but we may consider a little more minutely the particular kinds of miracles which fall under this head. And first, with regard to omnipotence; a miraculous operation may require the power of God to perform it, either from the thing done, or from the manner of doing it. Of the first class are these following: 1. The real transmutation, or change of one substance into another, —as the change of Moses's rod into a serpent; of the waters of Egypt into blood; and of the water, at the marriage of Cana, into wine. These were real changes of substance, the work of the almighty power of God, Who, having at the beginning created all things out of nothing, can alone, in an instant, change one thing into another. As to the rods which the magicians are said to have changed also into serpents, this was not a real change of substance, but either a substitution of one thing for another, or, at most, an apparent change, the work of enchantment and fascination. 2. The raising a dead man to life; which may be considered a kind of creation, being a production of life where there was none, and which supposes in the agent an absolute dominion over both the soul and body of man, so as to reunite them in one living principle of action and sensation, after they had been, by the dissolution of the body, entirely separated. Now we can scarcely conceive any creature having such absolute dominion over the soul and body of man; but as God alone at the beginning breathed into the human body "the breath of life," so it would seem impossible for any creature to do that again by its own natural strength, when God had been pleased to take that breath away.

3. The restoring lost members, or giving them to those who never had them. 4. Dispossessing the devil; which implies a power superior to that of Satan, as our Saviour justly argues against those who pretended that He cast out devils by the power of the devil. 5. The power of multiplying any material substance, and causing it to be in different places at the same time.

These and other such operations seem clearly to be the proper work of the almighty power of God; and we shall afterwards see that they are declared such by God Himself in His Holy Scriptures. The manner, also, by which a miracle is performed, may show it to be the work of omnipotence, when it is evidently above all created power; and such it is when the effect is produced by a simple act of the will in the agent, and that instantaneously and perfectly. The light of reason clearly shows that no created being can have such power over other creatures as to make them act or produce any physical effect merely by willing it. This is a prerogative which solely belongs to the Creator, who at the beginning said: "Let the light be made; and immediately," obedient to His holy will, "the light was made;" and who, when He cleansed the poor man of the leprosy (Matt. viii.), said,—" I will, be thou cleansed; and immediately," obedient to His almighty will, "his leprosy was cleansed."

When a natural agent wishes to produce a physical effect upon any creature, he must act upon it physically, and use, perhaps, the help of other creatures, as means or instruments. He must also have time before the effect can be produced; it is not enough that he wills it—his willing it alone will never be sufficient. Hence, therefore, to produce any such effect by the sole act of the will, can belong to Him alone, who by His sole will at first created all things out of nothing, and to whose almighty will alone all things are perfectly subjected. Hence, many of those effects which may be brought about, without any miracle, by ordinary means, and by the help of natural causes, do yet become real miracles, and such as are proper only to almighty power, when they are performed without the help of natural causes, and in an instant, at the sole desire, command, or will of the person by whom they are performed. On this account, giving sight to the blind, cleansing the lepers, curing the deaf, healing the sick, and the like, which may be brought about in time by the use of medicines, when performed all at once, as our blessed Saviour performed them, by His touch, or command, or the simple act of His will, and in a perfect and permanent manner, are evidently the work of the divine power, and far superior to the ability of all created agents. But if the thing performed be itself a work proper to omnipotence, as those above mentioned—for example, the raising of a dead man to life—and it be performed in this manner, instantaneously by the sole act of the will,—this will give a double lustre to such miracles, and show them beyond all contradiction to be the work of the Almighty God.

VII. A miracle is also proved to be the work of God alone, when it is evidently an effect of infinite wisdom. Two particulars come under this head; namely, penetrating into the heart of man, so as to discover his most secret thoughts—and knowing future contingent events, which solely depend on the free-will of others. We see no manifest impossibility that a created intelligence should be so extensive as to see and comprehend all those things which at present have an actual existence in nature—of understanding their properties, causes, relations, and effects; as also, those actions of men which are in any way manifested outwardly. But to penetrate into the heart of man, to understand his most secret thoughts, and those simple acts which arise from and solely depend upon his free-will, much more to foretell what will be the acts of his free-will in after-times, and even of those who are yet unborn, and what they will say and do in consequence of their free choice—all this, as is plain from the bare statement, is far beyond the utmost reach of a created intelligence, and is competent to that great Being alone, who, having created the heart of man, perfectly knows all that he is capable of willing and thinking, all that he actually does will or think, and all he afterwards will think or do, to all eternity. Wherefore, the discovering the secret thoughts of the heart of man, and the foretelling with certainty future contingent events many ages before they happen, exceed all created knowledge, and are proper to God alone.

VIII. There remains another rule for knowing what miracles belong to almighty power alone—namely, the sacred Scriptures; for, when these divine oracles ascribe any miraculous operation to God alone, as a thing proper to His almighty power, this must be a most convincing proof to all who believe the Scriptures to be the Word of God. Now from this unerring guide we draw ample confirmation of all we have advanced on this subject, and find that each of the particular miracles which can be attributed to no cause less than infinite power or infinite wisdom, are in these sacred oracles expressly declared to be operations competent to none but the Almighty Creator. Let us examine some of the most remarkable.

1. *Raising the dead to life.*—Of this Almighty God says of Himself: " See now that I, even I am He, and there is

no God with me; I kill and I make alive, I wound and
I heal," Deut. xxxii. 39; where His being the only author
of life is appealed to as a proof of His being the only God.
Hannah, the mother of Samuel, in her hymn of thanksgiving for her son, acknowledges the same truth: "The
Lord killeth and maketh alive, He bringeth down to the
grave and bringeth up," 1 Sam. ii. 6. In the Book of
Wisdom the same truth is beautifully expressed thus:
"For it is thou, O Lord, that hast power of life and
death, and leadest down to the gates of death, and
bringest back again," Wisd. xvi. 13.

In the New Testament the proofs of this are
strong and conclusive. When our Saviour had cured the
sick man upon the Sabbath-day, who had been labour-
ing under his infirmity for thirty-eight years, and upon
that occasion had declared Himself to be the Son of God,
the Jews sought to kill Him, both for breaking the Sabbath by curing upon it, and for making Himself equal to
God. All that He said in His own defence was an appeal
to His works; and He particularly mentions raising the
dead as superior to all the rest, and by which, as being
a work proper to the Father, He proves Himself equal to
the Father; "For," says He, "as the Father raiseth up
the dead and quickeneth them, even so the Son quickeneth whom He will," John, v. 21. A little after He adds:
"The hour is coming, and now is, when the dead shall
hear the voice of the Son of God, and they that hear
shall live; for as the Father hath life in Himself, so hath
He given to the Son to have life in Himself," ver. 25.

In these words we see the power of raising the dead
to life declared to be a power proper to God, and His
great prerogative; and its being given by the Father to
the Son is assigned as the cause why the dead shall be
restored to life at hearing the voice of the Son, and con-

sequently, as a convincing proof that Jesus Christ, at whose voice the dead were actually raised to life, is this very Son of God. Now this reasoning would have been inconclusive had the power of raising the dead been competent to any creature. In like manner, when our Saviour raised Lazarus, He did so to convince those present that He was sent from God, which it could never have done if the raising the dead had not been a miracle proper to the almighty power of God.

Lastly, not only the poor widow of Sarephta was convinced that Elijah "was a man of God, and that the word of the Lord was true in his mouth," when she saw her dead son restored to life by his means; but also when our Saviour raised the widow's son of Naim, the whole people present were persuaded that this was the work of God; for "there came a great fear upon all, and they glorified God saying, a great prophet is risen up amongst us, and God has visited His people," Luke, vii. 16.

2. *Restoring lost members, or giving them to those who never had them.*—This also in Scripture is attributed solely to God as a work proper to Him alone. When the apostles asked our blessed Saviour about the man born blind, whether this was in punishment of his own sins or those of his parents, He answered "Neither, but that the works of God might be made manifest in him," John, ix. 3. Consequently, to give sight to one born blind is properly the work of God, above the power of any creature; and this man was born without his sight, in order to manifest the work of God in him; and, indeed, this miracle was so evident a proof of the finger of God, that the Pharisees were confounded, and knew not what to say against it. Their pride would not allow them to yield to its conviction, and they disputed among them-

selves; whilst the poor man, sensible of the greatness of the miracle, cries out before them all, "Since the world began it was not heard that any man opened the eyes of one born blind; if this man was not of God he could do nothing."

3. Miracles performed "in an instant by the sole act of the will," are not only attributed to the power of God alone in the Holy Scriptures, but to these, in a particular manner, our Saviour appeals as proofs of His being the Messias, in His answer to St John the Baptist; for most of the cures mentioned in that answer were *miraculous* only in the *manner*, and would have been very inconclusive proofs of His being the Messias, if they could be performed in that manner by any creature. Also, Jesus Christ declares that the works which He did "were given Him by His Father to do," and that "they bear witness to Him that the Father had sent Him," John, v. 36. And in another place He says: "If I do not the works of my Father, believe me not: but if I do, though ye believe not me, believe the works, that ye may know and believe that the Father is in me, and I in Him," John, x. 37.

In these texts He expressly affirms His works to be the works of His Father, and incontestable proofs of His mission. Now, generally, the works which He did, and to which He here appeals, were such as might be brought about in time by the help of natural means, but were miraculous, and such as God alone can perform, only on account of their being done without any natural means, in an instant, at His command, and by the sole act of His will.

4. As to the two instances of omniscience, the knowledge of the secrets of the heart of man, and foreseeing things to come, these also in Scripture are attributed to

God alone. With regard to the first, Almighty God expressly claims it as His own proper prerogative: "The heart is deceitful above all things, and desperately wicked, who can know it? I the Lord search the heart and try the reins," Jer. xvii. 9, 10. Solomon also, in the Proverbs, declares the same: "Hell and destruction are before the Lord; how much more then the hearts of the children of men?" Prov. xv. 11. And still more expressly in his prayer at the dedication of the temple, "For Thou, even Thou only, knowest the hearts of all the children of men," 1 Kings, viii. 39.

The knowledge of futurity is so essentially proper to God only, that He himself challenges the gods of the heathens to foretell what is to come, and promises to acknowledge them as gods if they do so: "Produce your cause, saith the Lord; bring forth your strong reasons, saith the King of Jacob. Let them bring them forth, and show us what shall happen; or declare to us the things to come. Show the things that are to come hereafter, that we may know that ye are gods," Isaiah, xli. 21. This needs no application.

IX. From what has been said under this first rule of the criterion, it appears that miracles of this order need no extrinsic proof of being the work of God; they carry conviction with them: wherever they have been performed they have conquered at sight, and convinced the minds of the spectators that they were the work of the Almighty. But to remove every possible pretext of ambiguity, we need only apply to them the other rules of the criterion.

X. Second rule: "When any miraculous operation is performed, which appears to be the work of God, and cannot be known by men to be within the power of created agents, though in itself perhaps it may be; such a miracle is certainly either the work of God, or of good angels commissioned and authorised by Him."

This is a necessary consequence of the second axiom; and, in fact, such miracles as we here speak of are in every respect, with regard to man, the same as those of the former rule; for to man they must appear as much the work of God, and consequently make as deep an impression on his heart, as those which can be done only by God Himself. Now, as it is evidently impossible that God should permit evil spirits to work such miraculous operations in defence of error, as mankind could not possibly distinguish from the works of God, it follows that they are to be esteemed either as the immediate operation of God Himself, or as done by positive commission from Him, and therefore to be considered in the same light as those of the former rule.

XI. Third rule: "When any new doctrine is taught as coming from God, and the teacher works miracles in the name of God, and by invoking Him to perform them in attestation of his commission, and of the doctrine he teaches, such miracles are certainly the work of God, and done by authority from Him."

All the principles and axioms above established conspire to prove the justness of this rule, and plainly show that it is impossible Almighty God should either Himself perform the miracle, or permit any creature, if the teacher of this new doctrine be not commissioned by Him to teach it. The reason is plain; because if He acted otherwise, this would evidently be to allow His name, His language, and His seal to be used in defence of falsehood, and infallibly to lead men into error.

Let us explain the case: I pretend to be sent by God, and I am not; I teach a doctrine which I protest was revealed to me by God, when I know it was not; or, if you please, deluded by the enthusiastic frenzy of a heated imagination, I fancy myself sent by God to teach a doctrine which I erroneously imagine He had revealed to me,—and I call upon God to work a miracle to attest that what I say is true. Is it not repugnant to the very idea we have of God, to suppose that He would grant my petition in either case proposed, and work the miracle I desire?

Let us suppose, again, that I had a compact with the devil to perform the miracle, and that my calling upon God is only a pretence, the more easily to gain credit; but that upon my doing so, Satan engages to do what I ask. Is it not here also evidently impossible that God in these circumstances should allow the devil to do any thing miraculous? Would not such permission be equally concurring to promote error and falsehood, as if He wrought the miracle Himself? We may conclude, then, that any miracle performed in the name of Almighty God, and by calling upon Him, is undoubtedly the work either of God Himself, or of those commissioned and authorised by Him.

When a person openly opposes himself to God, or to His known truth, we easily perceive that God, for His own wise ends, may permit the devil in this case, by means of such a person, to perform signs and wonders; but there is abundant resource against the delusion, which carries on its front its own condemnation. If, however, a person should pretend to be sent from God, and teach false doctrine, and work miracles in proof of what he teaches, in this case it is plain that there is no resource; our ruin and seduction are inevitable, and God Himself becomes the abettor of falsehood, and the cause of our fall. It is impossible, therefore, in such circumstances, that Almighty God should permit anything miraculous; and consequently, a miracle performed in His name, and by calling upon Him, is assuredly the work of His hand.

XII. This is fully confirmed by the example of Jesus Christ, who appeals to this very rule as the criterion to prove that the miracles wrought by Him were the works of His Father: "The works that I do," says he, "IN MY FATHER'S NAME, bear witness of me that the Father hath sent me," John, x. 25. And when He was about to raise Lazarus to life, addressing Himself to His Father, He said: "Father, I thank Thee that Thou hast heard me, and I know that Thou hearest me always; but because of the people that stand by, I said it, that they may believe that Thou hast sent me," John, xi. 41, 42.

In the former of these texts He declares that His doing His works in His Father's name is a full and sufficient testimony of His being sent by Him, and consequently that their being done in His name is a full proof that He is the author of them. In the other text, having prayed to His Father to grant His request in raising up Lazarus, He thanks Him for hearing Him before all present, and expressly declares that He does so, that they, seeing this miracle performed by invoking Almighty God, may thereby be convinced that He was sent by His Father; and consequently, that the miracle He wrought by calling upon God, and acknowledging it to be from Him, was, by that very circumstance, undoubtedly proved to be His work.

After our Saviour's ascension, the apostles, taught by their Master's example, took the same method to convince the world that Jesus Christ was true God, and really risen from the dead, as they preached, by working miracles in His name. Thus, when St Peter restored the poor cripple to the use of his limbs, he said, "In THE NAME of Jesus of Nazareth, arise and walk," Acts, iii. 6.

And when the people ran together marvelling at so extraordinary a miracle, he first took occasion to declare to them that Jesus is the Son of God, and risen from the dead; and then added, in proof of this,—" And His name, through faith in His name, hath made this man strong, whom ye see and know," verse 16. In these words we see that the performance of this miracle is given as the proof that He is the Son of God, and the miracle itself is proved to be His work, because done in His name; nay, Jesus Christ Himself, when He gave His apostles commission to preach His Gospel, and the power of working miracles in its confirmation, declares, at the same time, that these miracles should be done in His name: "In my name they shall cast out devils, they shall speak with new tongues," &c., Mark xvi.; thereby plainly intimating that their being done in His name would be the proof that He was the author of them. From this we justly conclude, that Almighty God never will nor can permit miracles to be performed in His name, but when He Himself is their author.

XIII. Fourth rule: "When any point of doctrine, believed to have been formerly revealed, comes afterwards to be called in question or denied; if any person shall, in the name of God, and by invoking Him, perform a miracle in favour of either side, such miracle is undoubtedly from God."

This rule stands upon the same foundation as the one just mentioned, and, strictly speaking, they may be considered identical. For the same reasons which show that Almighty God will never allow His sacred name to be used by an impostor who falsely pretends to be sent by Him, convince us that He never will allow it to be used in defence of any kind of falsehood; and therefore, where a dispute arises about any point of doctrine, if a miracle should be wrought in the name of God to attest either side of the question, that miracle is undoubtedly from God, and must decide the controversy.

The case of Elijah and the prophets of Baal applies exactly here. The received belief of the people of Israel was, that the Lord was the only true God; but for some time, by the authority and politics of their kings, they had been induced to forsake the service of the Lord, and to worship the idol Baal as the true God. Many, from their natural proneness to idolatry, had gone headlong into this delusion. Some few preserving their integrity had not bowed their knee to Baal; but multitudes fluctuated, and halted between the two opinions. At last the decision of the question is put to the test, and the event shows the truth of the rule—namely, that in such cases God Almighty never will allow any miracle to be performed in the name of the true God, that is not actually from Him, and in defence of His truth.

We must observe, however, that if the former revelation of the received opinion be grounded on sufficient authority, it is not incumbent on Almighty God to work a miracle in its defence when it is called in question; and therefore the absence of a miracle, though demanded in attestation of the received doctrine, is no proof, nor even presumption, against it. In the days of Elijah, the people of Israel were inexcusable in admitting a doubt as to who was the true God, considering the convincing arguments by which the Lord had proved Himself to be so to their fathers; and therefore He was nowise obliged to work another miracle to attest His divinity, though He was obliged not to permit the devil to work one to the contrary. What God did, then, on this occasion, was the effect of His infinite goodness, condescending to the weakness of His people.

The case is very different, however, with those who call in question or deny any article already received as a truth formerly revealed by God. This denial is a new doctrine, tending to overturn a truth believed to be divine; and as nothing less than divine authority can be sufficient to destroy it, whoever attacks any such received doctrine, or its revelation, is bound to prove his commission and authority, especially if he pretends to be sent by God for that end. And as miracles are the proper proofs of such commission, and the usual credentials given by Almighty God to those whom He sends, it is therefore justly demanded of all such innovators to perform miracles in proof of their mission; and their inability to do so is a just presumption against them, if not their entire condemnation.

Upon this ground it was that the Catholic Church challenged Luther and the other Reformers to prove their pretended mission by miracles. Had they been, as they pretended, commissioned and authorised by God to reform the doctrine of the Church, to condemn as falsehoods so many articles of her faith, and to reject as errors many points held from time immemorial as revealed truths, it is clear that in this case Almighty God was obliged to give unquestionable proofs that He had sent and commissioned them. The Church, therefore, with reason demanded from them the proof of miracles; and as they could never give it, she justly rejected them as impostors, and condemned their novelties as heresy and false doctrine.

XIV. Fifth rule: "If the miracles had been foretold by prophecy long before they were performed, and afterwards were performed in the very manner foretold, this is another convincing proof that such miracles are from God."

As this rule contains three distinct points, we must

consider them separately, in order to unfold its full meaning.

The first point regards prophecy itself considered as a miracle, and as an undoubted proof of the finger of God. We have seen above, that to foreknow and predict contingent future events, especially a considerable time before they happen, is the prerogative of God alone, who perfectly knows all things past, present, and to come. But I observed that superior beings, from their more intimate knowledge of the secrets of nature, from their greater power of penetrating the inclinations and dispositions of the human heart, or from what they themselves have resolved to do by God's permission, can on many occasions foreknow and foretell, by their visible agents, not only necessary events, but even things contingent, with a very high degree of probability, which will seldom fail to be accomplished. Suppose, then, that an impostor, assisted and instructed by evil spirits, should endeavour by such prophecies to delude mankind, how should we discover the delusion, and know with certainty when these prophecies are from God or from the devil? The rule given above for other miracles is particularly to be applied here—that is, "If the prophecy be made in the name of God, and is afterwards verified by its accomplishment, that prophecy is doubtless from God."

This is the very rule given by God Himself as the infallible criterion of the divinity of a prophecy: "The prophet who shall presume to speak a word in my name, which I have not commanded him to speak—even that prophet shall die. And if thou say in thine heart, How shall we know the word which the Lord hath not spoken? when a prophet speaketh in the name of the Lord, if the thing follow not, nor come to pass, that is the thing which the Lord hath not spoken," Deut. xviii. 20-

22. Consequently, by a necessary inference, if the thing follow and come to pass, that is the thing which the Lord hath spoken. The reason is plain, from what we have said above, founded on this evident truth, that "Almighty God never will, nor, consistently with His own divine perfections, ever can, permit His sacred name to be used to sanction error or promote falsehood."

The second point refers to all other miraculous facts foretold by prophecy, and may be expressed: "When any miraculous operations which are performed had been predicted long before they happened, and were foretold in the name of the living God, and as miracles to be wrought by persons commissioned and sent by Him; this also is an incontestable proof that they are from God." This was a glorious prerogative of the miracles of Christ, that they had been foretold by the prophets in the name of the Lord some hundreds of years before He came into the world; and from this is drawn a most unanswerable proof that Christ is the true God, which Origen very justly urges against Celsus.

Isaiah, some ages before Christ, had foretold that God Himself would come amongst us to save us, and that He would restore sight to the blind, hearing to the deaf, strength to the weak, and the like: "They shall see the glory of the Lord, and the excellency of our God. Strengthen ye the weak hands, and confirm the feeble knees. Say to them that are of a feeble heart, Be strong, fear not: behold, your God will come with vengeance, even God with a recompense; He will come and save you. Then the eyes of the blind shall be opened, and the ears of the deaf shall be unstopped: then shall the lame man leap as an hart, and the tongue of the dumb shall sing," Isaiah, xxxv. After many years Christ appears in the world; He declares Himself to be the Son of God, and that He is come "to seek and to save those that were lost;" and as a proof that His words are true, He performs all those very miracles predicted of our Saviour by the prophet. As, therefore, none but God could foretell such events so long before, and as this prophecy was made in the name of God, and was literally fulfilled in the person of Jesus Christ, we justly conclude that His miracles are from God, and He Himself is that very God whom the prophet foretold would come to save us, and work these very miracles which He did in proof of His divinity.

"If it should be objected," says St Irenæus, "that the devil had done things (miracles) of this kind by illusions, we carry them back to the prophecies, and will demonstrate from them that all things had been most exactly performed by Jesus Christ as they had been foretold, and that He alone is the Son of God," Iren. lib. 2. contr. Hær. c. 32. And, indeed, it must be owned that this argument is the most convincing refutation of the objections of both Jews and heathens against the miracles of our Saviour, in pretending that they were done by art-magic, and by the help of the devil.

St Augustine very beautifully displays this argument: "The prophetic testimony accompanies the preaching of the apostolic doctrine. To prevent what the apostles announced from being despised, these things were shown to have been foretold by the prophets; for though they appealed to their miracles, there would not have been wanting then, as there are not wanting now, those who would ascribe them all to magical powers, had not such a thought been overpowered by the testimony of the prophets; for none, sure, will say, that they had by art-magic provided prophets beforehand to foretell their miracles, and this long before they themselves were born," lib. xii. contr. Faust.

In his Sermon xxvii., also on the words of the apostle, he inculcates the same argument: "Who of us does not wonder at the saying of an apostle that prophecy is more firm and sure than a voice from heaven? Observe, he said, it was more sure—not better, nor truer; for that word from heaven was as true as the prophetic word, and as good and as profitable. How then more sure, unless more calculated to convince the hearer? and why more calculated? because there are infidels so injurious to Christ as to say, that He wrought His miracles by art-magic—who might also refer the voice from heaven to the same art. But the prophets were not only before this same voice, but before Christ was born in the flesh. Christ sent His prophets before He had assumed our flesh; whoso then says that He was a magician, and as such made Himself to be worshipped even after His death, will he also say that He was a magician before He was born? You see the reason why the apostle says, we have a more sure word of prophecy. The voice from heaven was to admonish the faithful; the prophetic word, to convince the infidel."

The third point regards those miracles which the person himself foretells he is to perform, and even leaves to others to appoint the circumstances of time, place, and manner of working them, or even to ask what miracle they please, and foretells he will do as they shall please to determine. When he does so, this is also an undoubted proof that miracles so wrought are by the power of God, and that he who so performs them is sent by Him.

On this account the miracles of Moses carried with them evidence of their being from God, because he foretold Pharaoh how he was to punish and when to deliver him. He sometimes even left to Pharaoh himself to appoint the very hour of his deliverance. Isaiah also left it to Hezekiah's own choice whether the sun should advance or go back ten degrees upon the dial, as a proof that what the prophet told him of the recovery of his health was true, 2 Kings, xx. 9. Miracles of this kind carry the conviction with them that they are from God, because they show that the power which works them is unlimited, and able to perform whatever is demanded, in whatever manner; which evidently is the prerogative of God alone.

XV. Sixth rule: " When the doctrine attested by miracles is conformable to the known truth—or, if it be new doctrine, not manifestly contrary to the known truth and subversive of it—this affords a good presumption that the miracles are from God; but when the doctrine is contrary to the known truth, this is a certain proof that the miracles are not from God."

This rule brings us to an important point, whether or not, and in what manner, miracles are proved by doctrine? Different authors treat this question differently, according to the point which they wish to prove, or to the light in which they view it. Some argue generally that miracles are a certain proof of doctrine, and that their authority is independent of the doctrine and of the circumstances which accompany it.—See the authors of the Vindication of the Christian Religion against Rousseau, p. 173. Others, again, contend that miracles are not always of themselves infallible proofs of doctrine, but that the miracles and the doctrine mutually support and justify one another.—See Houteville 'Rel. Chret. prouvée par les faits,' liv. 3, 8me difficulté. Both sides reason correctly, according to their own view; but it is necessary to analyse the question, that we may see the precise sense in which the above rule applies.

First, then, if a miracle be performed in attestation of any point of doctrine, and we know certainly by any of the above rules that that miracle is the work of God, then without doubt such a miracle is a full and perfect evidence that the doctrine attested by it is true. This we have seen in the preceding chapter, "On the authority of miracles." In this sense, then, the authors of the Vindication are right in asserting that true miracles are certain proofs of doctrine, and that their authority is quite independent of the doctrine attested by them, or of any circumstance attending it. Nor is it to the point to say, "What if the doctrine so attested be evidently false, and contrary to the known truth?" This is an impossible supposition, for Almighty God never will nor can work a miracle in testimony of false doctrine; if, therefore, we know with certainty that the miracle is the work of God, we must be equally certain that the doctrine attested by it is so also.

Secondly, When we are uncertain whether the miraculous fact performed be from God or from Satan, but find nothing in the doctrine attested by it contrary to the known truth, in this case the doctrine, though true, is not an absolute proof that the miracle is the work of God; because it is possible that Satan, who often transforms himself into an angel of light, the better to deceive, may, by his agents, perform miracles in favour of true doctrine, the better thereby to gain credit and deceive. Still, the soundness of the doctrine is a strong presumption in favour of the miracle, especially if there be no positive reason to suspect it. This, however, is a case the solution of which will be easily obtained from the other attending circumstances, as some one or other of the foregoing rules of the criterion will never be wanting when the miracle is from God.

Thirdly, When the doctrine is evidently false, and contrary to the known truth, then this is an undoubted proof that the miracle is not from God, but, like the false doctrine it attests, is the work of Satan. This is in a manner self-evident, and a necessary consequence of the principles laid down, both in this chapter and before, on the authority of miracles; for God cannot contradict Himself—He cannot use His power to promote falsehood or sanction error. Whenever, then, we see that the doctrine attested by a miracle is certainly false, this is an evident sign that the doubtful miracle is not the work of God. In this sense, then, what Houteville asserts is correct, that the miracle and doctrine mutually support each other; namely, when we are certain that the miracle is from God, but doubt the truth of the doctrine. The miracle in this case undoubtedly proves the truth of the doctrine; and when we are certain that the doctrine is false, and doubt of the miracle, the falsity of the doctrine evidently proves that the miracle is not from God. Upon the whole, then, it appears that this sixth rule of our criterion is, properly speaking, calculated solely to detect false miracles by false doctrine, when we are doubtful of the miracle, and from what source it proceeds; but alone it is not a proper criterion to distinguish with certainty the nature of the miracle.

It was necessary, however, to mention and explain this here, because we find that Almighty God makes particular use of this third part of it for the direction of His people against seduction, both in the Old and New Testaments, which it will be proper to consider a little more particularly.

XVI. When God revealed His law and religion to His people by Moses, He did so in such a manner as to leave no doubt of His being its author. The miracles wrought were so stupendous, so frequently repeated, and in such circumstances, as to give the most complete conviction that they were performed by Him, and consequently, that the doctrine attested by them was certainly the doctrine of God, and therefore true. At the same time He well knew, that whatever attempts the devil would afterwards make to corrupt the minds of His people, and seduce them from His service, he never could work any miracles in proof of his false doctrine, equal, or in any degree comparable, to what He Himself had done in favour of the truth; but that all the attempts of the devil would be only lying signs and false wonders. For this reason, then, He warned His people against them; and the plain rule He gave by which to discover the falsity of such pretended miracles, was the one of which we are here treating, "if they tended to lead them away from His service." The falsity and evil tendency of the doctrine, contrary to the known truth which He had revealed to their fathers, was the infallible touchstone by which to discover the falsity of all such lying signs. "If there arise among you a prophet, or a dreamer of dreams, and giveth thee a sign or a wonder; and the sign or the wonder come to pass whereof he spake unto thee, saying, Let us go after other gods, and let us serve them : thou shalt not hearken unto the words of that prophet, or that dreamer of dreams; for the Lord your God proveth you, to know whether you love the Lord your God with all your heart and with all your soul," Deut. xiii. 1.

In these words we see, first, the case proposed, of a false prophet endeavouring to seduce the people from the service of God. Secondly, the supposition made, that he even works a sign or wonder to persuade them to follow his seduction. Thirdly, the conduct which God demands of them on such an occasion, which is absolutely to reject and not to listen to such a prophet. Fourthly, the view which God has in permitting such attempts to seduce them; which is in order to try, to prove them, and to see if they will be faithful to Him.

From this we may justly conclude, that whatever signs or wonders such false prophets could use to support their doctrine, they will never in any degree be comparable to those by which Almighty God established His truth; and that the doctrine which they proposed being contrary to the known truth, this alone was a just reason for rejecting them. Nay, in the following verse, God commands the seducing prophet to be put to death, notwithstanding all his signs; and gives only this reason, both for rejecting his proposal and punishing himself so severely,—"Because he hath spoken to turn you away from the Lord your God, that brought you out of the land of Egypt, and redeemed you out of the house of bondage," ver. 5; thereby plainly intimating, that their delivery out of Egypt amidst such manifest miracles wrought by the hand of God, ought far to outweigh all the false miracles that might afterwards be brought to seduce them.

XVII. In the new law, our blessed Saviour established His doctrine by miracles far superior to those of Moses, and to which likewise all those of Moses and the prophets concurred; declares therefore, by the mouth of His holy apostle St Paul, that if an angel from heaven should come and teach any other gospel than what he taught, anything contrary to the known truth so revealed by Christ and His apostles, and by them preached to the world; this circumstance alone would warrant us in rejecting him as a false teacher, and as one accursed by God, Gal. i. 8.

Upon these grounds He requires from us the same conduct as God did in the old law, when false teachers arise: "If any man shall say unto you, Lo, here is Christ, or there; believe it not. For there shall arise false Christs and false prophets, and shall show great signs and wonders; insomuch that, if it were possible, they shall deceive the very elect. Behold, I have told you before," Matt. xxiv. 23, &c. Here we see that the infallible rule to discover the delusion of their great signs and wonders is, that they teach falsehood contrary to the known truth revealed by Jesus Christ, and established by such amazing miracles as far outweigh whatever may be afterwards wrought by those seducers in proof of their false Christs and false doctrine. Hence we see that this sixth rule of our criterion, though not directly calculated to discover true miracles, is yet an infallible means to detect such as are false, however great or amazing they may seem; and we see that it is used and recommended by Almighty God in the old law, and by our blessed Saviour in the new, for this very purpose.

XVIII. To these six rules, which compose the criterion by which we may with all security judge when a miraculous operation is from God, I shall here subjoin the general characteristic of divine miracles; which, though not an absolute proof alone, yet, when added to the criterion, confirms its decisions.

It is a just observation, that divine miracles generally tend to the good of mankind, and to promote it, either for soul or body, or for both. They are the effects of goodness as well as of power; but those performed by the devil are either indifferent, or, more commonly, consist in doing evil. They are the effects of power and malice, but never of goodness; nay, the doing good to mankind, the promoting their happiness, seems so exclusively connected with divine miracles, that when the emissaries of Satan or teachers of false doctrine attempt such, even in the name of Christ, they are disappointed and defeated. Thus we are told that when " certain Jews took upon them to call over them who had evil spirits the name of the Lord Jesus, saying, We adjure you by Jesus whom Paul preacheth; the evil spirit answered and said, Jesus I know, and Paul I know, but who are ye? And the man in whom the evil spirit was, leaped upon them, and overcame them, and prevailed against them, so that they fled out of that house naked and wounded," Acts, xix. An accident of the same kind is related of Luther by Staphilus, who was an eyewitness; and the fatal consequence of the attempt made by Calvin to raise a pretended dead man to life, by which the poor man actually died, is well known to all who are acquainted with his history. See his Life by Boscus, who relates it at length.

St Irenæus takes particular notice of this characteristic of divine miracles in opposition to those of Satan. The heretics of this time attempted to gain credit to their false tenets by the effects of magic, of which they boasted as of miracles performed to confirm their doctrines. Of these the saint says: " Moreover, the followers of Simon and Carpocrates, and whoever else are said to work miracles, will be convicted of not performing what they do by the power of God, nor in truth, nor to the advantage of men, but to their ruin, and to deceive them by magical illusions, and rather to hurt them by all kind of impostures, than to benefit those whom they seduce to believe their errors. For they cannot give sight to the blind nor hearing to the deaf, nor put to flight all devils, except those whom they have brought on, if they even do this. And they are so far from raising the dead, as our Lord did, and the apostles by prayer, and as is most frequently done among the brethren, that they even think it impossible," &c. Irenæus, lib. ii. cap. 57.

XIX. Another characteristic of divine miracles is, their being generally performed by men of known piety and virtue. It is true, we have seen above, that God Almighty may make use of wicked men; and the bare possibility of this hinders this characteristic from being entirely decisive; still, the noted sanctity of the person who works miracles is a strong presumption in their favour; and the working of miracles is a favourable testimony of the sanctity of the one who works them.

We have seen above, that one of the great views of Almighty God in miracles is to testify to the sanctity of His servants, and to give them credit and authority with others. We may conclude, therefore, that though on very extraordinary occasions He may make use of bad men, yet this is not the ordinary conduct of His divine providence. Divine miracles, generally speaking, are performed only by truly good men; and when he who works them is known as the reverse, this raises a strong presumption against the miracles which he performs.

XX. It will be necessary, now, before I conclude this subject, to examine some objections which infidelity has raised against the authority of divine miracles; but this will easily be done, as they have already been answered by the principles laid down in this and the preceding chapter.

First, Some writers object to the miracles wrought among the heathens. "There is not a single historian of antiquity," says Dr Middleton, "who has not recorded oracles, prodigies, prophecies, and miracles; many of these are attested in the gravest manner, and by the gravest writers, and were firmly believed at the time by the populace."—*Free Inquiry*, p. 218. Therefore, say they, as Christians themselves admit that no credit ought to be given to these miracles, nor to the doctrines held by those who performed them, so neither ought any credit to be given to others, such as those wrought in favour of Christianity. This is the strength of the objection, if it has any.

In answer to this, I shall not dispute the fact; but, allowing that real prodigies have been performed among the heathens, the question is, Were they performed by Almighty God or by evil spirits? is it possible to distinguish their author? The rules of our criterion will at once answer these questions, and show that these prodigies were the operations of Satan: for, 1. It is plain from their very history that they were not such as exceeded what we know to be within the reach of created power. 2. They were not performed in the name of the true God, but in the names of a multitude of gods, and in the belief of polytheism. 3. The authors of these prodigies and oracles were evidently enemies to mankind, on many occasions demanding to be honoured with human sacrifices, and encouraging impure rites and ceremonies, and approving the most shocking crimes, adulteries, incests, and the like. 4. Such of these wonders as were the effect of art-magic, were professedly done by the help of Satan, in open opposition to the one only living and true God. These reasons evidently show that heathen miracles were not the work of the great God; whereas the contrary reasons as manifestly prove that the miracles wrought in favour of Christianity were undoubtedly wrought by Him; and therefore, that these latter must possess the highest authority, whereas the former can have none.

XXI. Secondly, It is asserted that miracles are uncertain signs of the truth of doctrine; because it appears from the Scriptures themselves, that real miracles have been, and will be, performed in proof of false doctrine. Thus the magicians of Egypt wrought the same miracles in proof of their falsehood as Moses did for the truth. Christ Himself assures us, "that false Christs and false prophets shall arise, and shall show signs and wonders, to seduce, if possible, the very elect," Matt. xiii. Lastly, we are assured from Scripture that even Antichrist himself will perform the most amazing prodigies in support of his impieties. Consequently, miracles, being common to true and false doctrines, can never be an absolute proof of the truth.

In answer to this objection, which infidelity puts forward with great confidence, we must recall some of the principles which we have seen above. The Christian religion readily admits that superior beings can perform many effects in nature, which not only are miraculous with regard to man, but which are so amazingly great that man could not certainly discover from the work itself whether or not it were possible for any created power to perform it. But we have laid down and established as an undoubted axiom, that "if Almighty God, for His own wise ends, should at any time permit evil spirits to perform any such operations in proof of falsehood, He is bound by His own divine perfections to give mankind sufficient means to discover the delusion, and prevent their seduction from being inevitable"—Axiom 4. And we have also seen, in the rules of our criterion, the means which Divine Providence has provided for enabling mankind to distinguish true from false miracles, and the operations of God from those of Satan. We have only to apply those to the cases in the objection, and in an instant its force vanishes.

It will hardly be pretended that the miracles mentioned in the objection—that is to say, those of the Egyptians, of the false Christs, and of Antichrist—were absolute miracles; that is, such as could be performed only by God, and which of course must be performed immediately by Him. It would be ridiculous to suppose this, because it is evidently contrary to our idea of God, and of His divine perfections, to imagine that He can work absolute miracles against Himself, and in attestation of falsehood, as we have proved throughout the whole of this chapter. It is therefore evident from the very objection itself, that the miracles therein referred to are only relative miracles, that they do not exceed the natural abilities of created agents, and that in fact they have the devil for their author. Hence the objection is quite beside the case, and inconclusive.

What the Christian religion contends for, and we have shown it at large, is, that absolute miracles which can have no author but God, and relative miracles known to be wrought by Him, or by commission from Him in attestation of doctrine, are most certain and undoubted proofs that that doctrine is His. If it could be shown that miracles of this kind were wrought also in attestation of false doctrine, then the objection would be unanswerable, and even true miracles would be but equivocal proofs of doctrine. But the very light of reason shows that it is impossible that Almighty God should either perform miracles Himself, or commission others to do so in attestation of falsehood. Besides, we have seen above (Rules of Criterion) that it is impossible He should permit wicked spirits to perform any kind of miracles in proof of falsehood, in such circumstances that mankind could not discover the delusion; hence the total insufficiency of the objection.

The objection, put in its proper form, must run thus:

The Egyptians, the false prophets, and Antichrist, are said in Scripture to work miracles by the help of Satan to attest false doctrine; in such circumstances, however, that human reason can easily discover that they are the work of Satan and not of God; therefore, true miracles, known to be the work of God, cannot be trusted as certain proofs of the doctrine in attestation of which they are performed. Every person of common-sense must see the weakness and total inconsistency of such an argument; and yet this is what impiety and infidelity have boasted of as unanswerable.

Now, that all these miracles mentioned in the objection may be evidently known to be the work of Satan, will easily appear by applying to them the rules of our criterion; for, 1. They are not said to be wrought in the name of the only true living God, but in direct opposition to Him. 2. Those of the Egyptians and of Antichrist are expressly declared to be done by enchantments, and by the operation of Satan. 3. The Egyptians were at last compelled to yield to Moses when he performed miracles which they could not imitate, and to acknowledge that *the finger of God was there;* a clear confession that theirs were not done by the finger of God, but by Satan. 4. Those of the false Christs and false prophets, and of Antichrist, will be performed in defence of a doctrine manifestly opposed to the known truth—the truth which Christ has revealed to the world, and established in the most convincing manner, by the divine miracles which He wrought to attest it. 5. These last have been plainly foretold by Jesus Christ, and we are warned by Him against them; consequently, when false teachers arise, proposing doctrines contrary to the truths of Jesus Christ, endeavouring to seduce men, and performing signs and wonders to persuade men to follow them—these very signs and wonders, instead of serving their cause, are their greatest condemnation, and the most convincing proofs of the truth of the Christian religion; because they show beyond contradiction that Jesus Christ is God, who could foresee so long before what was to happen, foretell it to His followers, and warn them against the danger. When these things come to pass, then God Almighty has provided mankind with a full and ample defence against the seduction. They may easily discover by whose power the signs performed by false prophets and by Antichrist are wrought. To draw an objection from these, therefore, against the authority of true miracles, is altogether frivolous and inconclusive.

XXII. A third objection brought by unbelievers against the authority of miracles, is taken from the incomprehensibility of the doctrines said to be attested by them; for how, say they, can an event, though ever so uncommon and extraordinary, prove a doctrine to be true, which appears to my reason to be contradictory and absurd?

This objection arises from a confusion of ideas, and from not adverting to where the real strength of the proof lies. It has often been satisfactorily answered by those celebrated authors who have written in defence of Christianity; so I shall only lay down briefly a clear explanation of the terms, with a few observations, by which the weakness of the objection will at once be shown.

1. A proposition is absurd, when the two ideas of which it is composed are contradictory, and formally exclude each other; as, a triangle has four angles—or, a part is greater than the whole.

2. In order to know certainly that two ideas are contradictory, we must be fully acquainted with all the

properties of the objects; for if we know them only imperfectly, though in those which are known to us there may be an apparent contradiction, yet in others, of which we are ignorant, there may be the most perfect harmony; and therefore we can never rationally pronounce such a proposition absurd. In the above examples, as we perfectly understand what is meant by a triangle, and what by an angle, we perceive at first sight the contradiction between a *triangle* and *four angles;* and therefore we justly pronounce it an absurd proposition. But this other, " Wheat and oats may grow in the moon," we cannot rationally pronounce contradictory; because, though we know what is meant by wheat and oats, and have a knowledge of their properties, yet we possess but a very imperfect idea of the moon, and little or no knowledge of its nature and properties. Though, therefore, the proposition seems highly improbable, yet we cannot say it is absurd, because of our ignorance of the nature of one of the objects of which it is composed.

3. Propositions, of whose terms we have but an imperfect knowledge, may either be apparently contradictory and absurd, or not. A proposition is apparently contradictory when the properties of its parts which we know appear repugnant to each other—as when we say, there are two lines which, though produced *ad infinitum*, will always approach nearer, but never meet. This, according to our ideas of the terms, seems contradictory, although it be a well-known proposition demonstrated in conic sections. A proposition is apparently not repugnant, when there appears no contradiction between its terms, as far as we know them—as in the above example, wheat may grow in the moon. Whatever contradiction may be in fact between the nature of the moon and the growth of wheat, yet, as far as we know the proper-

ties of wheat and the moon, such contradiction is not evident.

4. Propositions apparently contradictory are either comprehensible to the human understanding or incomprehensible. They are comprehensible, when the mind of man by study can acquire a thorough knowledge of their terms, and see their truth, notwithstanding the contradiction that appeared when they were only known in part. Of this there are various examples, both in mathematics and natural philosophy, where many things when first proposed seem impossible and contradictory, till, by a further and more perfect knowledge of the objects, the contradiction vanishes and truth appears.

Propositions apparently contradictory are incomprehensible, when it is impossible for the human understanding, in its present imperfect state, to acquire a thorough knowledge of the objects of which they are composed, of their properties and different relations. Examples of this are chiefly to be found in supernatural things concerning God and eternity, where the objects are of such a nature that man in his present state cannot acquire a clear and perfect knowledge of them and their properties. Take, for instance, the proposition: God is immense and perfectly present everywhere without extension or parts. According to our ideas of the terms, this seems impossible; nor are we capable in our present state of acquiring such a knowledge of the nature of God, and of place and extension, as to see and comprehend the connection between them in this proposition, which is therefore to us incomprehensible. In like manner, when we say, that in one and the self-same divine nature there are three persons, really distinct among themselves, so that we can say of the one what we cannot affirm of the other; this also, according to our imperfect idea of the terms used—that is, of the divine nature and of the divine persons—seems a contradiction; nor is it possible for us in this life to acquire such a thorough knowledge of these objects as to see and comprehend the perfect union and harmony that exist between them.

5. Propositions apparently contradictory may yet in themselves be perfectly true, whether they be comprehensible to us or not. That a finite space, for example, may be divided into an infinite number of smaller spaces, at first sight appears a manifest contradiction, yet the truth of it is proved by a geometrical demonstration. That the branch of a parabola, and a straight line, produced in their respective directions, will always approach nearer and nearer to one another, but never meet, though in appearance contradictory and impossible, is yet a well-known property of the parabola, and its truth is proved to a demonstration in conic sections.

The same may be shown in many other truths, both in natural philosophy and in mathematics. And though in these examples we are convinced of the truth of the proposition, notwithstanding its apparent contradiction, and yield our assent to the evidence of the demonstration; yet we can neither comprehend how it should be so, nor do we acquire so full and perfect an idea of the objects as to see and comprehend the relation and connection between them. In like manner, in things supernatural, that the superb fabric of the universe should be created out of nothing, without any pre-existent matter, seems, to our imperfect ideas, so contradictory and impossible, that human reason, unassisted by revelation, had laid it down as an incontestable axiom, that "nothing can be produced from nothing," *Ex nihilo nihil fit.* Yet we know with certainty, from the testimony of God Himself, that this was actually the case; that the whole visible creation was created by Him out of nothing, by the sole act of His almighty will; nay, human reason itself, assisted by the light of revelation, can now demonstrate the impossibility of a pre-existent uncreated matter. However incomprehensible, then, the creation of the world may be, however contradictory it may appear to our weak reason, yet it is certainly true, nor can the truth of it be called in question by any Christian.

The following propositions also seem contradictory: There is a first cause of all things, which itself had no cause; there is a Being which neither made itself nor was made by any other; God is immense without extension; God fills every place, yet is confined to no place; the soul of man is in every part of the body, and yet is neither multiplied nor divided among the several parts of the body. These and many more, from our imperfect knowledge of the objects, seem at first sight impossible, and are to us incomprehensible; and yet deists themselves are obliged to acknowledge them to be true and incontestable. It is plain, then, that propositions, apparently contradictory, may yet in themselves be perfectly true; and many such undoubtedly are true, both in natural and supernatural things, as we have seen in the above examples.

6. We acquire an absolute certainty of the truth of many propositions apparently contradictory and impossible, even though we be incapable of comprehending the nature and properties of their objects. We do not see the immediate connection between the objects themselves, because our ideas of them are too imperfect; and therefore it is not properly from intrinsic evidence that we know the truth of the propositions, but either from external demonstration, or from the undoubted testimony of

those who are perfectly acquainted with them. Thus the truth of the proposition, that there are two lines, which being produced *ad infinitum*, will be always approaching, but never meet, a pupil may learn either by studying the known properties of the parabola, and the demonstration thence drawn to prove it, or by believing on the authority and testimony of his teacher.

7. In supernatural things the testimony of God Himself is the most assured means to acquire the knowledge of the truth of such propositions as seem to our weak reason contradictory, and are to us in our present state incomprehensible. Supernatural objects are far above the reach of our natural powers; our ideas of them are exceedingly imperfect, as their properties are of a different kind from anything with which we are acquainted in natural objects; consequently there must be innumerable truths concerning them which at present we can never comprehend—nay, which according to our limited ideas may appear contradictory and absurd. But Almighty God perfectly comprehends the nature of all these things; He knows their properties and relations of whatever kind. On the other hand, He is a being of infinite veracity, and can never deceive His creatures. If, therefore, He reveals to man anything concerning Himself or supernatural objects, which seems contradictory, and which in our present state we cannot comprehend, still this testimony must give us the assured conviction that what He so reveals is true; nay, it is by His testimony alone that we can arrive at any certain knowledge of these matters.

8. By the word "mystery" in the Christian religion is understood "a proposition revealed by God, concerning Himself or supernatural objects, the truth of which we cannot perceive, by reason of our limited and imper-

fect knowledge; which proposition is therefore to us incomprehensible, and may in some cases appear contradictory." The possibility of a mystery as here explained is evident from all the above reasoning. That God may reveal to man truths concerning Himself and supernatural things, is not called in question. That in numberless cases these truths must be above our comprehension is self-evident. That our limited and imperfect ideas of these objects may in some cases appear contradictory, though the objects in themselves are far from being so, is plain from the fact that this is not unfrequently the case in natural things when our knowledge of them is imperfect; but that the testimony of God revealing them is the most convincing proof that they are true, notwithstanding any apparent contradiction, is a necessary consequence of His perfect knowledge and His infinite veracity.

XXIII. If, now, we apply these observations to the objection against the authority of miracles, from the nature of the doctrine attested by them, we shall easily see its fallacy. For if the doctrines proposed by revelation, and attested by miracles, regarded objects of which we had full and adequate information, and between which we evidently saw an absolute contradiction—as, for example, should we suppose a miracle wrought to prove that "a part is greater than the whole"—then it will be acknowledged that no miracle whatever could suffice to render such a doctrine credible; but it is no less evident to common-sense that a true and divine miracle never was, and never will be, performed in attestation of such a doctrine. The truths proposed by revelation as objects of belief are all concerning supernatural things, of whose properties our knowledge is exceedingly limited and imperfect. Though then, according to our ideas, there should be an appearance of contradiction, we cannot assert that there is a contradiction in reality. In the natural world many things are true notwithstanding apparent contradictions, and much more must this be the case in the supernatural world.

The human mind is unable to investigate supernatural objects, or to demonstrate supernatural truths by mere reason, we can arrive at the knowledge of them only by divine revelation. If, then, God reveals them, and attests His revelation by miracles, it is evident that there cannot be a greater or more convincing proof, both that such revelation is from God, and that the doctrine so revealed is certainly true, however contradictory it may seem to us from our imperfect ideas of its objects. Hence, then, it appears that the fallacy of the objection lies in confounding a mystery with an absurdity; which it supposes to be synonymous terms, but which we have seen are widely different; and also in supposing that a miracle can be wrought, or is pretended to be wrought, by God, in attestation of a doctrine evidently contradictory—which supposition is itself a manifest absurdity.

XXIV. Before we conclude this chapter, it will not be amiss to consider the different cases that may be supposed of miracles and the doctrine attested by them, which will put the matter in the clearest light, laying it before the eye in a single point of view.

Case 1. If a miracle, known with certainty to be from God, be wrought in attestation of a doctrine evidently false or impious. In this supposition all authority of miracles would be destroyed; but this is a case which, as we have seen above, is manifestly impossible.

Case 2. If the doctrine be evidently true, but the miracle doubtful. In this case, though the soundness of the doctrine does not absolutely prove the miracle to be from God, yet it is a strong presumption in its favour, and greatly corroborates the other proof that may be brought for its being a divine miracle.

Case 3. If the miracle be evidently from God, but the doctrine itself is doubtful; then the miracle absolutely proves the doctrine to be true, and entirely removes all doubt that might otherwise be entertained concerning it.

Case 4. If the doctrine be undoubtedly bad, and contrary to the known truth; the miracle wrought in its favour is undoubtedly a false miracle, and performed by the operation of Satan.

END OF THE FIRST VOLUME ON MIRACLES.

PRINTED BY WILLIAM BLACKWOOD AND SONS, EDINBURGH.

www.ingramcontent.com/pod-product-compliance
Lightning Source LLC
Chambersburg PA
CBHW030806230426
43667CB00008B/1093